A round the World i ... inus 1

Here are the portraits of most of the friends I met on my journey around the world, Sept 20th 2006 to Jan 26th 2007

Those whom I met abroad

Sadly I have no photos of Sandra McWha, Pat Nelson , Vandana nor Rhiannon

A round the World in 128 days Minus 1

By Chris Phillips

First Published in 2012
By Philcovers (Chris Phillips)

ISBN 978 - 0 - 9574259 - 0 - 3

Whilst the vast majority of this book is the work of Chris Phillips, some maps scanned from the internet are the copyright of Google. These maps have been accredited. I have also used scans of some advertising materials for the railways and other places that I visited. Some details of history & geography of places, countries and regions has also been acquired and reproduced here, which hopefully do not infringe upon anyone's copyright. If any holders of such copyright exist, please accept my apologies, and if you do not wish me to advertise them in any future printings please contact me.

Printed by McRay Press unit 3 64 - 66 Londesborough Rd,
Scarborough, North Yorks, YO12 5AF. 01723 370967
www.mcraypress.co.uk email mike@mcraypress.co.uk
Using Lucida Sans typeface

Contents

A WORD OF WARNING

When arranging to meet up with anyone whom you have never met in person before, it is strongly advised that at least one extra person is present at least at the start, and only meet up with people you have confidence in.

Chris waiting at Scarborough railway station for the train to arrive to take him on his first leg of his 4 month world tour

For
anyone
who Contemplates
Making a
Journey
ROUND THE WORLD

This book is dedicated to all the friends who had the courage to meet me even though they had never met me in person before. Thanks to the WWW, Yahoo & Zorpia for making this method of communication possible, and to my lovely wife for not only putting up with my absence for 4 months, but also for painstakingly reading through my exploits, and daring to change some spellings, grammar, punctuation and meanings!

Chapter 1
In the Beginning was the Plan.

{Geeta & Gordon}

Then there was the planning. Then the story unfolds.

This is the true story of my journey round the world, 20th Sept 2006 to 26th Jan 2007.

Some people thought me mad to attempt such a journey. Others thought I was brave. In fact it was neither. But this is not about why or how, but about what happened.

To say that everything went according to plan would not be admitting the truth! Very little went ex-

actly to plan. And it would have been surprising if it had!

I actually started my journey on Wednesday 20th Sept. 2006. After saying goodbye to Dilys in Scarborough I got on the train to Manchester. My very good friends Geeta and Gordon very kindly agreed to find me a bed space in their very recently moved into flat. It was great to see them again. I had known Geeta since about 2002, when she lived in Mumbai, India, with her mum. After a few years she met and married Gordon, who is English and lived in Nelson, Lancs. That evening Geeta showed me around part of the Manchester Mall, and we talked about old times on the net. So Geeta and Gordon were the first two Internet friends I met on my trip, though both Dilys and I had met them before when they came to stay with us a few days, about a year earlier.

I was up at 5 am for the start of a VERY long day. A day which ended in a way that was not all planned. The BA plane took off about 20 minutes late from Manchester airport, and I was on my way. The flight was uneventful, except that they fed me well with a good

vegan meal and what seemed like a constant supply of drinks. Anyone who likes to be served early should order veggie meals - “specials” get first service! Well, as we landed at JFK Airport, on my way to Halifax (Canada) I could not know what was going to happen later. I knew that I would have a 5 hour wait for my next plane, but I was unprepared for the first shock!

I have always had an aversion to mobile phones! But I was persuaded of the usefulness of having one for this trip of a lifetime, to keep in touch in emergencies. Now I had planned to set up and store all my friends' phone numbers on my mobile phone that I had bought, with its SIM card which could be used anywhere in the world, and to text Jonathan to let Dilys know that I had arrived in New York. After all, I had 5 hours of nothing much to do. As it turned out it was 5 hours with nothing to do! The mobile phone refused to connect with anyone, because it could not make a connection with any server! I kept trying but could not make it work at all. Yet I knew it worked in England. Being frustrated, I finally gave up, and eventually boarded a small plane to Halifax, flying back over the route I had already passed over (well, almost)!. Halifax felt my footsteps on its soil about 45 minutes later. My first ever venture to Canada.

My mobile still refused to work. So I phoned from a call box to Kim to let her know I had arrived in Halifax. I just had time in my minute (for $3.50) to explain I had arrived and would hopefully be at her house in about two & a half to three hours ! It was now 9 pm and dark! I went to the car hire firm with whom I had booked in advance a car for the long weekend. I was given the keys, and expected to be shown to the car and how it worked! After all, I was from UK with different driving conditions etc. But no! No one asked me if I was use to automatic cars. No one wanted to know if I had driven on the RIGHT hand side of the road, and the fact that I had never driven a left hand drive car was of no interest to them . One thing that I forgot, because I had not driven an automatic for MANY years, was that such cars are totally suitable for one legged people, so long as it was the right leg that was not missing! Well, at first I forgot that my left leg was redundant, and it was determined to push the left pedal, in unison with the accelerator. A number of bump starts and stops resulted, before I told my left leg it was to hide! Then I mastered the long forgotten art of driving a non clutch car. Well this was just the first of a clutch of problems. The night was still young!

The car and I gradually became friends and worked well together, arriving in Truro in good time. (For what reason Truro was in Nova Scotia I have no idea!) In

Truro I could not find any signs to Antigonish, or any places for that matter! So after a while I found some students and asked then the way to Antigonish. I tried my best to remember their instructions, and drove along, not happy, but cautiously looking for signs. I was passing a cyclist so I stopped and asked him if I was on the right road, he said I was. So I carried on a little more confidently and after about 4 or 5 Km a white truck overtook me on double white lines, and indicated for me to stop! To say that I was a little concerned was a bit mild! I pulled up anyway, and asked him what the matter was. He responded with a question! "Are you Lost?" I thought! And said, "Am I on the right road to Antigonish?" He looked unsurprised, well as much as one can in the dark, and said "OH! NO! Look turn your car round and I will too, then follow me." Curiouser and curiouser.

So I did as asked and followed him back to Truro, and out again on another road. After about 5 miles, he pulled up and said if you continue on this road, you will get to Antigonish. This just goes to show that there are kind human beings in this world. I was indeed MOST grateful to this man. He told me that If I had continued on the other road that I would have ended up on a dirt track on top of a mountain !

And I still had a mountain to climb!

It was still a long way till I saw any signs that said Antigonish, and after a couple of backtracking errors I eventually did make it to Antigonish town centre, and turned left, something I had remembered from the map I had got from Yahoo. I have not explained that I had been unable to see the maps in the car, because I could not find the switch for the interior light. So I had to open the door or read it in the headlights! Anyway it was now 12.30 am, and I saw a small group of what looked like 12 year old girls coming out of a party, and asked them where Kim's road was; none of them knew, but I showed them the map, and they told me I was on the road leading to it! *SMILES*. Now I was nearly there! And I found the road, went to number 4, but could not find 4b. So I looked at the map and decided that the street sign had misled me, and it had. I went to the street off the one I was in and again found number 4 and a 4b. I knocked on 4b, the house was in darkness. No one answered, and as I saw a man walking down the street I asked him if I was in the correct street, He said no I wasn't! But he didn't know where it was either! But I then drove further up the other road and found the real road I wanted. The house Number 4 had a 4 on one side & 4B on the other! "HURRAY" I thought, I am there! I went to the door near the 4B and rang the bell, Once then a second time.....

It was now about 1 am! What to do? Here I am at the right house, no one answers, I am in a car in a country that I have never been to before, where the drivers sit and drive on opposite sides to us, my mobile phone refuses to work, and I have arrived so late that my friends must have gone to bed. I did notice a light on in the basement, but no other sign of life. I decided that I had best sleep in the car. But not in this built up area. Someone might be worrying if they saw a stranger sleeping in a car outside their house at night, so I found a place just out of the built up area, near a field. By golly I needed that field! What a relief! I then unpacked my dressing gown and covered myself and now having found out how to have the inside light on I read my book, and when I was drowsy put out the light and slept for about an hour, waking up and being tired I wanted sleep so I read again (reading is my way of getting to sleep!) This happened several times. By 6 am I was feeling cold, by 6.30 I was too cold! So I got the car started again, remembered where I was in a LHD car for RHD road! I found a shop open near where Kim lived, bought a bottle of water and asked if there was a toilet I could use. They very kindly allowed me to use the staff toilet. Thank goodness, I really could not have waited much longer! But when I flushed the toilet, the floor flooded! (Just water, thank goodness) URGH. So with several paper towels I dried the floor as best I could, and left, thanking the shop keeper very much.

I then drove into town and back again to Kim's house, and pulled up outside and decided to wait till I saw signs of life. This was about 7 am. 15 minutes later I noticed a car in their drive backing out. I got up from my reading, and the driver got out, it was a young man, it was JAMES! Kim's boy friend! He was just going out to try and find me!

Having got over this shock, I was led round the back to their entrance. Kim had forgotten to tell me their entrance was round the back and down the stairs—and had not heard the door bell because it wasn't their bell! The 4B on the front was for the letter box, not their part of the house!

Poor Kim & James had sat up till 3.30 am for me! Kim was so sorry about not having told me where their entrance was! Had I known I would have had a bed, and they would have had a longer sleep!
BUT it was so lovely to see Kim after all these years (6) of knowing her only on line.

Chapter 2

Introduction - The Age of REASON

Why go round the world ?

There were several places I wanted to see in the world, places far too far away for me to just go on a few days away trip and come back and forth say once a year. The main problem was cost, but also time, and in these days awareness of the damage to the Earth's atmosphere by flying. So I worked out that by going on a single trip taking several months I could save at least half of the air travel and costs to me and the environment. I was also planning on using train as much as possible, particularly in Canada, USA and Australia. The cost was partially overcome by being given shares in the Halifax Building Society when they became a bank. These shares paid for the majority of the cost. As it turned out, I chose the right time to sell those shares, almost at their peak value. Later their value was about a tenth of what they were then!

I "discovered" the world of the internet through the medium of some Yahoo groups in the previous Millennium (JUST - in 1999!) In some of these I started making friends around the world, in Veggie groups, cat groups, astronomy lovers, weather fanatics, gardening for food, philately, theatre, Quaker, nature, birds, Beatles and photographic. Quite a few of these friends I started getting to know very well. They were of all ages, from 16 to 50's; I rarely found people above 50. Most were in their teens, twenties or thirties. Gradually I started meeting a few of them, mainly in the UK. Most of the friends were from the UK, Canada, USA and Australia. But a few I found in Argentina, New Zealand, Hong Kong and Philippines.

My main hobbies at home were Philately, Drama, gardening and photography, all of which I had had interests in from a young age.

Before the internet, I thought it would be nice to visit the countries that I collected stamps of: Burma (now Myanmar), Nepal, Bolivia, New Zealand, Malaysia and Australia. My Father was actually born in Burma (in early 1900's). I also had this idea of seeing the Pyramids in Egypt, and places in India. After Internet, I thought how nice it would be to visit some of my best internet friends, so Canada, USA, Argentina, New Zealand, Philippines and Hong Kong were added to my areas of intended visitation.

My earliest Yahoo friend lived in Arizona. She was 18 when I first got to know her. She was like a number of other friends, who seemed to find it easy to talk about personal things, like fears, worries, dreams and their lives. I never made any pretence about my age and that I had a loving and loved wife. At the time I was working part time, having semi-retired, as an educational publisher's sales rep. (Franklin Watts), selling their books to schools in North Yorkshire and Humberside.

When I first started talking to people on the net I never expected to make "close" friends. I have never really found it easy to "talk" to people anyway. But on the net it seemed safe, and anyway young people (in particular) seemed to trust me with their quite intimate feelings, about their lives, their boy/girl friends, parents, their interests, etc. Something that in "real" life had only happened to me with my first wife (Christine) and Dilys my present (2nd) wife. As a school teacher (1964~1985) I had had a few children tell me a few small personal things, but never quite like this; but on the internet these were teenagers (16 upwards) and adults. This was a whole new world opening up for me. I found it easier to talk about my own personal inner feelings, partially in return for their trust in telling me theirs.

Anyway my first friend I met in a cat lovers' group

in Yahoo. Her ID name was Pluto, and she had this picture of her cat Pluto with a bandage on. I surmised that she was interested in astronomy as well. (My second choice was Disney's creation, but I was right, she was not giving her cat a dog-like name, as I had for one of our cats, Bach!) My assumption was correct and that got us talking about planets, stars, astronomy and weather, and the Meteor crater in Arizona, near where she lived. We also talked about the famous Grand Canyon, and how she went there with her boyfriend (from whom she subsequently parted) and gave him the screaming jeebies when she stood on the edge of a mile drop!

After about 6 months, when in Yahoo Messenger chat one morning (for me and late night for her), she suddenly announced that she wanted me to come to her wedding, when she had a boyfriend again and married him. She added that if I did she would take me around Arizona for a week and show me the places we had talked about. About a year later in early 2002, she DID invite me, and in November 2002 I visited Arizona in their cool season, and attended their public wedding blessing; they had married a few months earlier. I was taken to the Meteor crater, the Grand Canyon, Sedona and the Astronomical Guest House in Southern Arizona to see the night sky in a cool clear atmosphere on the top of a small hill. Also this was where many of the famous "western" films were shot. This was a wonderful experience for me, and I am MOST grateful to Jess for being such a wonderful friend.

On my way home I stopped off at Cleveland (I had to change planes in Chicago anyway), to visit briefly another Friend (Stamp Collector, Stamp Addicts, Yahoo group). This was Philly and her family. She had two little children. Back in the UK I met up with a few other internet friends from USA and UK. I was now wanting to meet a whole lot of other "special" friends too.

Thus the world tour idea was born.

PLANS

Well, first of all I asked a few of those I considered best friends if they would like me to meet them if I went on a trip round the world to meet up with many friends. I did a rough plan one morning when I awoke early when on holiday in Skye (August 2004), and didn't want to disturb Dilys. I worked out how long it would take to do such a trip, staying in places near my friends for a few days each. I then asked Dilys what she thought of such a trip? The idea was at first that we would both go. I think she wanted to go, but there were two things that put doubts in her mind. 1)The flying. She was not happy at all about this, apart from the scariness of flights, it was the environmental damage that this kind of travelling did to the atmosphere! It is far worse than any other normal form of transport. 2) The length of time needed to be away from home - she was a self-employed tutor and would have lost most of her clients.

She said she wanted time to consider it. Eventually, reluctantly, she said I would have to travel on my own.

I decided that where possible I would travel by train in Canada, the USA and Australia. I found that travel agents were hopeless for arranging such a trip. For a start, they didn't have rail travel on their itineraries. But one local firm told me about "One World" air travel. This was a group of about 6 international airlines who worked together, covering flights to most places in the world, where you paid one fixed fee for visiting a number of continents. My trip meant travelling to 4 and the fee was in the order of £1,700 for my air flights round the world (plus airport taxes). I found out on the internet that I could go to all the places I wanted except Egypt and Burma by this method. So that cut out these two countries. To get to Bolivia it meant going to Argentina first and then back again. As I didn't know anyone there, I cut that out. So I found reasonable flights to get from UK to Canada, USA to Argentina, Argentina to New Zealand, New Zealand to Australia, Australia to Philippines (via Hong Kong), back to Hong Kong, then via Thailand to India, and finally India to Home.

I then found that I could get Rail passes in Canada, USA & Australia. These gave me more or less unlimited free rail journeys in those countries for a one off fee. I did need to book in advance all the long journeys. Then I had to decide whether or not to book sleeper service on overnight trips. I decided that as the seats were reclinable ones, for a single overnight journey I would just sleep in the seat, but for two or more nights in a row I would take a sleeper service. Thus from Toronto to Vancouver, Seattle to Chicago, and Sydney to Perth I booked a sleeper service. The supplement for these was nearly as much again as the rail pass fees! But it was worth it; in Canada and the USA that fee included meals, and I could order vegan ones!

Now that I was armed with greater knowledge of travelling and its costs, I had to check with all my friends who originally said they would like to meet me. I found some could let me stay with them for a few nights, but with others I needed to find my own accommodation near them and they would meet me.

Because Dilys was no longer able to come with me, I decided it best to go when I had fully retired from work, and Dilys was still working. As it happened, the time chosen was the best for both of us anyway, from other factors that we hadn't considered. One was that Dilys finally won a seat on the Scarborough Borough Council, for the Green Party, not long after my return, and the other was the credit crunch of 2008/12.

So I finally got the go ahead from the 20 or so friends that I knew from the Yahoo Groups, and then I asked other friends if they too would like to meet me whilst I was in or passing their vicinity. Meanwhile I had joined www.Zorpia.com in November 2005, and had started making new friends there. And about 10 of these wanted to meet me in USA, New Zealand, Australia, Philippines, Hong Kong and Singapore. So Singapore was added to the list, and slightly longer stays were organised in the other places.

So finally I booked the flights, and they took so long actually sending me the tickets, that it held up my train and hotel bookings. Eventually the tickets arrived, and I booked the trains (via the internet and phone). I had renewed my passport and organised a decent credit card (Nationwide) that charged no currency fees for using abroad. I bought a mobile phone to be able to stay in contact on my trip around the world. Also because I was planning a trip to the Central Yukon with my Native American friend in Vancouver, I also needed to book a flight to and from Whitehorse, and later a car to drive to central Yukon. I also found I needed to hire a car to get from the airport, Halifax, to Antigonish. My flight from Manchester was too early to catch in time from Scarborough, so I stayed a night with my Yahoovian friend in Manchester. I found two veggie guest houses in Canada (Montreal and Toronto) and one ordinary guest house near the Niagara Falls. And due to lack of time I decided to book the other hotels whilst on the journeys.

I was ready! Well, as near as I could be. The basic planning was over and I was ready to go.

So back to the story.

Chapter 3
Antigonish, Nova Scotia Sept 22nd to 25th.

{Kim, James, Erica & Pat}

James led me down the stairs to the basement and I saw Kim for the first time. I had known Kim for about 5 years or more. We had met in a Yahoo Group for Animal Welfare; at the time Kim was not veggie, but a few months later she decided to become vegetarian, and she joined a number of veggie Yahoo groups and one that Danielle from Australia started called Mystical Dreamland (here a group of us had got to know each other well, and I was to meet up with more from this group later).

After a friendly hug I was offered some breakfast and James had to go off to work for the day. Kim had kept herself free from work & study for the duration of my stay. We talked a lot and caught up on things from the past. Kim was very interested in animal welfare and world affairs and green issues. She is a thinker, and it was her intelligent and understanding way of talking that I liked very much about her. We had arranged to meet up with James for his lunch break in the town centre, so we walked into town, and had a look around the shops etc, making our way to the Tall & Small Cafe, which served good quality food, and understood Vegan food!

After James had returned to work, (and he was working till late,11pm), we did a bit of shopping. I had found out that my electric razor didn't fit my universal socket/plug adaptor, so I had to purchase a new one! Then we went for walk in the country on the edge of the town. Here I noticed the early signs of Autumn on some of the trees as they had changed to beautiful shades of brown, and I took my first "fall" pictures. We then returned to Kim's flat. We talked some more and watched a Video "7 Years in Tibet". I know that I, and probably Kim too, fell asleep during part of it. Whilst Kim got us a meal I was able to check on my emails on her computer. Then we talked some more till James returned and we flopped into bed! I slept quite well on their settee and we awoke to another pleasant day.

One of the things about going on a trip like mine was that one did not go just to all the "touristy" areas. The next day was one such adventure! After breakfast we drove out of town to a woodland area, and after a longish walk, and meeting a tame toad, we "found" a lovely secluded waterfall in its own little valley. Cutie's Hollow or the James River Falls. I think we saw three or four other people only on this outing. It was so lovely and peaceful, we stayed there for about an hour and James showed his climbing skills by climbing up the rocky wall next the where the falls were, not named after him! Proof of this climb was captured on camera. We got back in time for lunch, which was my first experience of cooking in Canada. I did one of my stir fries, which has about 20 to 30 vegetable ingredients. Even using cooking utensils I had not used before I managed to rustle up a meal that was all eaten up. (In my case and Kim's we saved a bit for later!) After eating, James went off to work again. (3 pm to 11.30 pm)

Kim and I had a long discussion on philosophy, politics, religion etc. Kim is a thinker, and realises that things change all the time. I really loved this deep and friendly discussion. It confirmed what I had thought all along about Kim that she is intelligent and able to express her thoughts well. I was also intro-

Early fall colours in Antigonish

Cape Breton, Isle St Pierre

duced to Kim's two beautiful pets, a pair of rabbits.

I was able to phone Pat Nelson and arranged to meet her in Truro on the Monday for lunch. My mobile still would not work! I also caught up on emails.

For my last full day with Kim & James I took them to Cape Breton Highlands National Park, in my rented car. Our first port of call was to go on a nature trail which included a bog with fly eating plants, called Pitcher Plants, and Benjies lake. We also picked up Erica, one of Kim's friends whom I had talked to quite a bit on MSN. We then went on to Isle St Pierre, and saw the rocky coastline and seals. Kim knew of a restaurant there that served veggie food, called Wabo's. (This was where Kim use to live and went to school.) Kim was now living in Antigonish because she was at university there. We had a fun time on the rocks; James liked to show off and I took a few photos of him apparently in perilous positions! On our way back we called at Kim's parent's house, but they had not yet returned home. After dropping off Erica our next port of call was James' parents home, where we had tea with them. They were very friendly and were interested in my trip round the world and photography, if I remember correctly. It was later that day that we found out that I needed a tri or quad mobile phone when in the whole of the Americas, and it had to be unlocked. I found this out from help with Sims 4 Travel. We retired to bed as it was late. It had been a LOVELY day.

Pitcher plant seen in Benjie's lake , Nova Scotia

Cutie's Hollow or the James River Falls

Next morning was my last in Antigonish, and I had to say goodbye reluctantly to Kim and James. Before I finally departed Kim took me to a phone shop, and it was then that I found out that in Canada it was "illegal" to unlock phones. So as I could not buy one in Canada, I rang Dilys and asked her to buy me a new one and post it to my next permanent (for a few days!) address in Vancouver. So till then I could communicate only by computer (or expensive phone calls). With big hugs with Kim and a handshake with James, I said final farewells. I do so hope that I will meet up with Kim again some time in the future.

I now had to drive the car back to Truro and return it to the hire company before meeting My VeggieSpot (Yahoo Group) friend Pat Nelson. She is a teacher of pupils with learning difficulties, and was able to spend only her lunch hour with me. This was unfortunate as I was really getting to like Pat in this short space of time. But at least we did meet, and had a lovely salad sandwich in a restaurant where you can choose the ingredients. Pat very kindly gave me a large bag of vegan health foods to help me on my way. She took me to the railway station and the next part of my big adventure started at 2 pm: the first of many days spent on a train.

It was a big long train, for a long journey to Montreal arriving at 8.15 am the next morning. These trains seemed made for comfort, only three seats wide, with an aisle between two on one side and one on the other. They were easily reclinable for overnight journeys, more like the business class on an aeroplane. We travelled through some beautiful countryside in the beginning stages of the "fall". We passed through New Brunswick before travelling in a more southerly direction again into Quebec. Passing through Amherst, Moncton, Bathurst, Campbellton, then through what seemed like France, Matapedia,

Mont-Joli, Rimouski, Rivière-du-Loup, Charny and finally Montreal. All this following the famous St Lawrence river. I found that Montreal is really an island between the banks of the St Lawrence river! And so began the next part of my adventure. It was now Tuesday 26th September, Dilys' birthday.

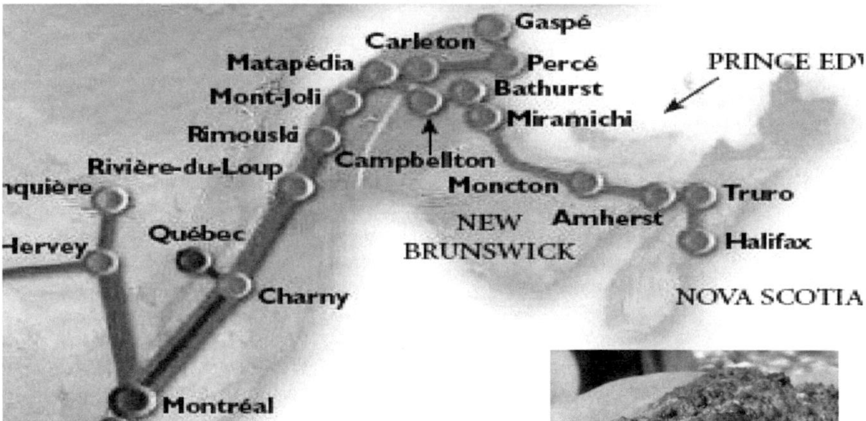

The tame toad

Chapter 4

Montreal Maude

{Maude}

The train pulled in at Montreal about on time, 8.15 am. There was no straightforward bus or metro journey to my Guesthouse, so I took a taxi. Philippe the owner was there to greet me and showed me around. Surprisingly, he was French Canadian, running an exclusively vegan guesthouse in the French part of Canada. In France it is rare to find a Vegetarian Guesthouse, let alone Vegan, and most are run by English people! Philippe was a very friendly and helpful person, and he allowed me to phone Maude who was on her bus to meet me at the railway station. By using the underground train I arrived just before she did, and we met up for the first time.

ChuChai (Chu Chai) , Montreal Thai Veggie Restaurant

Now Maude was one of the few people I was meeting whom I didn't know very well, but we had a mutual friend, Lisa (Melisa) from Argentina, and both of us knew Lisa VERY well. Maude had been to stay with Lisa before and I had talked a lot to Lisa

in one of The Beatles groups. Lisa is a 'lone' veggie in Argentina and I was going to stay with her at her parent's home later. Maude was not veggie, but she knew a good veggie restaurant in Montreal where she often ate. Anyway we recognised each other from photos and so began an interesting day.

Maude gave me a lovely conducted tour of part of Montreal including a long climb up MANY steps to the HUGE church on the top of a hill, Oratoire St-Joseph, from where we had magnificent views of parts of Montreal. We had an interesting salad in a vegetarian Thai restaurant (Chu Chai) A lot of the food was called by fish or meat names, but in fact was soya protein based made to look and taste like what they were called. Not my "normal" type of vegan food, as I am not interested in eating mock meats, but it was good

and tasty, and I suppose good for people who used to be meat eaters.

During that day I got to know Maude much better than before and am now pleased to include her as one of my friends. One of the reasons why she wanted to meet me was to get ideas for her future trip round

Europe the following year, which she did complete and came to stay a night with us in the following September. We said our goodbyes later in the afternoon after much walking.

Back at the guest house I was able to send Dilys a birthday email, and the request to get me a phone that will work in the Americas and send it to Sharon's address in Vancouver. I could also catch up on emails. Philippe was a friendly young man, who was vegan, and I met Merlin, his cat.

I was able to use the house phone to try to ring the other friends I was to have met in Montreal, Pru and Brian (the Admiral) from the Yahoo Beatles group. But I discovered afterwards that I had an old phone number, so I got no answer, and thus missed seeing two more friends, who I discovered later had waited at the restaurant for me in case I turned up. So sad, that.

Next morning before I left I had a lovely all fruit breakfast, nicely laid out. Philippe also explained about Phone cards that can be used in Canada and the USA. I was able to buy one from the shop next door. By using a certain prefixed code on any landline or mobile, I could

phone almost anywhere in the world VERY cheaply. Anyway I didn't have time to experiment straightaway, as I had to catch my next train to Toronto. So after taking a few photos of Philippe (who had become Vegan about three years ago) and Merlin his cat and the breakfast, I taxied to the station in time to leave promptly at 9.40am and passed through Dorval, Brockville, Kingston and Belleville and arrived on time in Toronto at 15.20. So the next part of my journey began.
Sadly Chez Philippe is no longer in the guest house business as I would gladly recommend him.

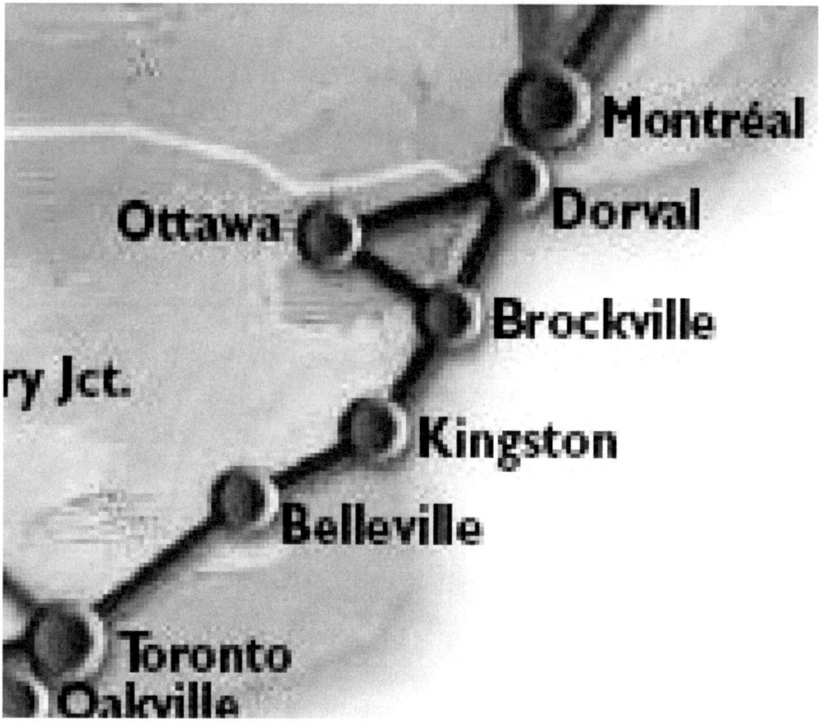

Chapter 5

Time in Toronto

{Chris and Carrie}

Toronto was LARGE! In fact it's the largest city in Canada. On arrival I studied the map of the city and decided I could walk from the station to Les Amis. It was a bit longer than expected, and it renewed the slight heel blister from yesterday's walking. But eventually I made it, and found I needed a code to enter the Guest House. I couldn't find it - it was somewhere in my luggage. So I decided to wait, and in that waiting time I noticed an all black squirrel, just like our UK grey ones! I had never seen a black one before, so I spent a bit of time taking pictures of it. I also saw a grey one scrummaging around for food in a plastic bag, and took a movie. Then a man came along who seemed to know the house entrance system and the guest house. He phoned them for me and eventually got the code number and I was in. My room was on the third floor right at the top! The window was in the ceiling, and through it one could see the towering buildings all around. The guest house was on the side of the road not yet built tall; it was an old terrace of what must have been three storey family homes, now let into flats and guest houses. There was one other guest room on my floor and, oh joy, a phone which guests could use. It was permissible to use it for local calls, and other calls on my special card. This worked out to be a very cheap system. I made arrangements to meet Dave (The Stamp Dad, a friend from Stamp Addicts in Yahoo) the next day, and nearly fixed up to meet Karen Thompson the next day, and with a long call to

Les Amis - Vegetarian Guest House

Vegetarian Haven - Vegan Restaurant

Dilys in England, costing only $1.04, managed to catch up live with what was happening. She had by then bought me a phone that would work, and had posted it to Sharon in Vancouver. From the Internet, before leaving the UK, I had printed pages from "Happy Cow" giving me details of all the Veggie places in Toronto. I found that two were within easy walking distance. The Guest House was a Bed & Breakfast only, and the only Vegetarian one that I stayed in on my whole trip, just as Chez Philippe was the only Vegan one . I never managed to find any others on my whole trip round the world where I could stay when I needed hotels instead of staying with friends. But I did find plenty of restaurants in many cities.

I decided to try Vegetarian Haven, and to my pleasant surprise I found, on asking which meals were vegan, that all food was vegan there! It was a lovely place, quite large inside and very busy with mainly young people. I highly recommend this place to anyone. Later I was able to phone Vandana, Geet's sister. She had very kindly agreed to put me up for the night before my first ever three day rail trip, when I needed to be up early. Things were gradually falling into place, well at least for Canada!

Though I rarely have a cooked breakfast, the guest house proprietor had obviously gone to some trouble to make me some vegan crêpes, spread with maple syrup they were Deeeeeeeeeeeelicious. I also had some very nice fruit and bread. My next disappointment then came by unexpected phone call: Dave had to go to work after all, so he was the next person not to meet up with! So I rang Chris O'Driscol, from the Nature with Digital Photography Yahoo group. I had seen some marvellous photos from him in the group, and now I was to meet him for real with his wife Colleen. They would meet me at the guest house at 3pm.

I now had the morning free and explored on foot

Kim's Bunnies

Giant Chocolate - Toronto

Maid of The Mist
- Niagara Falls

Vancouver

the city centre. I desperately need some blister plasters and eventually found what I needed in a chemist's in a huge mall (Sears Tower). Whilst wandering round I discovered that many places on the street and in shops had large notices "We Unlock Phones." So it was obviously a "trade" lie that it was illegal to unlock phones. But I still needed a Quad phone! And mine wasn't one! I spent an hour on the internet at a Internet café ($3) and caught up with emails etc. I also wandered around the city taking interesting photos of buildings, pavement water fountains and a huge advert of Cadbury's Chocolate bar high up on a building!

Chris & Colleen found my guest house, and there was parking there, so we walked into the city centre and found a nice café in Yonge street, and had a interesting talk. Chris was from Ireland originally and had met Colleen on the internet. Colleen was a "local" and was the one who could drive in Canada! On return to Chris' car he showed me that the back seat and the boot was FULL of cameras! He use to work in journalism back in Ireland.

After saying goodbye to my 6th Internet friend, I tried a different veggie restaurant, which was not so far away as the Vegetarian Haven I had so liked the night before. It was called Le Commensal Vegetarian restaurant. (Commensal 655 Bay St. Toronto, ON M5G K4) This was my first experience of a restaurant where you paid by weight of food. It was all laid out in a buffet style and one just helped oneself. Everything was clearly laid out marked vegan or vegetarian, and some ingredients that people might be allergic to were clearly listed. I chose mainly salad (very light) and avocado. And for "afters" I had a small piece of vegan chocolate cake and a vegan ice cream!

Breakfast next day was porridge with fresh fruit, made especially vegan for me!

Commensal Veggie Restaurant

Pavement fountains, Toronto

Scarborough

A suburb of Toronto is called Scarborough! So I just had to visit it. I was kind of warned off going there, as it wasn't supposed to be a very nice place. Anyway I did make my way there and went by Metro. The Scarborough station was near the newish Mall and borough buildings. I spent most of my time wandering round the Mall, and took many photos to prove I had been to "Scarborough", including ones of the rising and falling hot-air balloons that made an interesting display. I found a place that had some delicious fruit ices.

In the afternoon I tried again to arrange to meet Karen, and found that she may be free on the Monday after 12.30 (She is a student at the Kitchener University).

I did a little shopping and rested my weary blister, hoping it would heal! I also booked my trains from Toronto to Aldershot for next day and the return on the Monday. I tried playing my favourite Freecell card game with real cards instead of on the computer! But of course they did not automatically take their own places as they did on the computer!

My last breakfast at Les Amis Vegetarian Guest House was another of those wonderful wholemeal vegan waffles. What an excellent place to stay! Another perfect example of French speaking Canadians who are Vegetarian, and know about Veganism.

Having a few hours to "kill" (what an expression for a pacifist!) I spent 3 hours catching up online and booked hotels in Flint, Fort Worth, Oklahoma and Los Angeles. I was now organised for the rest of my stays in the USA. But as usual there were a few changes later. As I was beginning to learn, on such a long trip not everything goes to plan!

I found a decent camera shop and bought two filters for my camera, a Polaroid and Ultraviolet. I also bought a plastic bag that would cover the camera for taking pictures in Niagara Falls mist. I had to make a hole in the bag the size of the filter attachment and use a filter to hold the bag to the camera and keep out

any water from it. The man in the shop had explained it to me. I also bought a few small presents for friends. I was able to give a very small present to every one whom I stayed with. After Lunch at Le Commensal Vegetarian Restaurant I caught the planned train to Aldershot. Sounds so odd finding these English places in a far off land !

Niagara Falls

Carrie & Jim were at Aldershot to meet me and took me to my guest house where I was staying a couple of nights, "Sunrise" B&B in Burlington. It was arranged for them to pick me up next morning at around 10 am. This was an exciting prospect! To actually see the great falls! The Guest House was run by a friendly woman, Enid Thomas, and the house was a

splendid one. She even allowed me to use the Guest House computer to catch up with emails etc. I had with me some fruit to eat for the evening meal.

After a pleasant night, I was generously provided with an all fruit breakfast, and as arranged Carrie and Jim arrived, with Jim's daughter Jade, to take me to those legendary falls.

I had met Carrie on the net in the Yahoo Group Veggispot, and she was also in the VeggieBrits group as well. On arrival at the Falls and having parked, eventually, a short walking distance away, I noticed the area was almost totally built up, with hotels and homes etc. in the area overlooking the great falls, in some ways almost dwarfing them, built up the sides of the hills around. Obviously not as it was when Europeans first saw the falls and were amazed by their size and beauty! We were able to walk fairly close to the actual edge, close enough with the camera's zoom to make it feel right on the very edge. There is so much water falling all the time that the edge is gradually

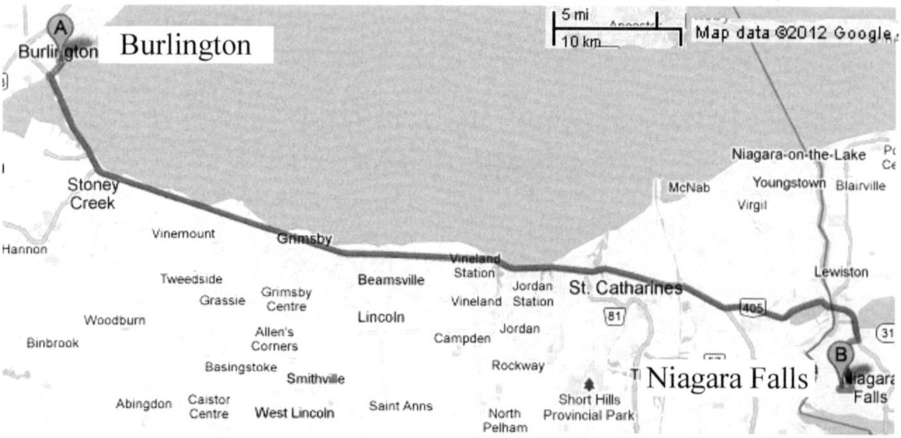

wearing backwards. There are in fact two main parts. The most beautiful part is the long curved edge on the Canadian side. The smaller straight edge is on the USA side. These are separated by an "Island". If seen on their own the USA falls were spectacular enough, but the tremendous volume of water falling and the continuously rising whirling mist of the Canadian horseshoe falls was breathtaking. I was shortly to experience a journey close to where the water fell, in a little but crowded boat called the Maid of the Mist. So, with my camera sealed in the plastic bag and large blue plastic raincoats, supplied by the boat company for all their passengers, we stepped on to the boat for the trip which could be taken no where else on Earth.

There was a sea of blue everywhere; everyone was wearing these long blue plastic overcoats. I was ready armed with my plastic bag covered camera, eager to shoot the falls! We first went past the USA falls. They were certainly impressive, and we could see a few climbers up the cliff. Down in this deep valley we were surrounded by almost vertical rock walls or water tumbling down with deafening roaring. The little boat "The Maid Of The Mist" then headed, bouncing on the waves, towards the falling torrent, often hidden from view by the rising and falling mist. This mist was caused mainly by the huge volume of water striking deep water at the foot of the falls and bouncing back up before finally falling back to water and racing down the Niagara river. I took quite a lot of photos both before and during the period in the mist. This was a sight certainly not to be missed! Near the actual falls the sound of falling water was even louder, and talking to friends was well nigh impossible. The boat held its position being buffeted for a fair while to let the passengers fill their camera cards with pictures. But I noticed few had plastic bags or any kind of protectors. I am so glad I had that advice given to me at the cam-

Niagara Falls
Upper picture—Canada,
Lower picture USA
Middle is my blue “coat”

era shop in Toronto, for I am sure some cameras may well have become useless for being so wet; it was almost like being underwater for a time. Eventually the little boat allowed itself to drift back to port at the cliff foot and we returned to dry land. The plastic coats were collected for disposal, but I decided to keep mine as a souvenir. We then returned to the cliff top that surrounded this most beautiful of sites. My only wish was that I could have seen it all in its true, unadulterated raw state before human beings made this a showcase, but then I would never have been able to enjoy that boat ride! What happened the rest of the day was a bit of a blur! But I know we searched for a suitable restaurant to eat in, and eventually found an Indian restaurant in Burlington (there was not much open, as it was Sunday) and had a late lunch at 5pm!

Carrie and Jim then returned me to my Guesthouse, and we said our final farewells. Jade, Jim's 16 year old daughter, was hoping to train as a Kindergarten teacher some time in the future.

So ended one spectacular day. THANKS Carrie and Jim for such a wonderful day.

Back to Toronto

I tried several times to phone Karen, but not getting any answer, I decided that she still might meet me in her university town of Kitchener, and took a bus to there instead of returning by train to Toronto. I decided that if I did this we might meet up, but if I didn't I would have no chance. Anyway, the bus dropped me off near the railway station, and I tried phoning a few times hoping to meet for lunch, but after eating some packed food I had brought I gave up at 2.15 and caught the bus to Toronto. I had a little walk to find the flat where Vandana and her family lived in University Avenue. This was very convenient for the main railway station, being 5 minutes' walk away. Vandana is Geet's sister, and they live on the 6th floor of a 25 floor building. Here I learnt that Vandana's husband has a form of Parkinson's disease, but was still active in his mind. I talked a lot to Vandana and her daughter, who had just left her IT job and was looking for a new one. The firm she was working for had shifted its work to India, which was rather ironic as they are Indians. I had a lovely fruit dinner. Next morning I was to embark on the most spectacular train journey that I had ever had.

Chapter 6
CANADA'S CLASSIC TRAIN JOURNEY
Toronto to Vancouver via great plains, lakes and the Rockies

I had heard about great train journeys; I had seen videos of great train journeys. Now I was to be part of one of those. This was one of THE great train journeys in the world. And I was going on the first of four such journeys.

Before I left the UK, I had booked country passes for rail travel in Canada, the USA and Australia. In Canada I had 12 days unlimited out of 20 days. This was just about right for me and fitted my arrangements well. It in fact took me right across Canada. The pass price did not include sleeper service - I had to pay extra for that when I used it, as I did for this great rail journey. Never having done anything like this before, I was very excited, and yet had no idea what it would be like. I knew there were observation lounges with 360 degree views, and sleeping in bunk beds, and all meals provided. Obviously I had booked vegan meals, and I was informed that there would be no problems with that.

The first part of my day was getting up and having some fruit for breakfast. Vandana's husband was going to accompany me to the station, but upon emerging from the block of flats we discovered the rain was bucketing down in a terrific thunderstorm! So I persuaded him I would find my own way OK. I had studied the map and had my trusty umbrella with me. It was, after all, only 5 minutes' walk! So with rucksack, large suitcase, camera and shoulder bag I made my way to the huge station, and was there in good time to get checked in. These rail journeys are much more like an aeroplane journey; one books in etc and needs to be there an hour before departure time. Those with sleeper services were called first, and thus my journey of a lifetime began.

I found that in the sleeper carriages there were cabins with seats for four people (two pairs facing each other) on either side of an open passageway. I was on my own; luckily I did not have to share my cabin with anyone. The cabin opposite was occupied by a couple from New Zealand, and they too were going all the way to Vancouver.

Up to now my only real experience of a train journey had been to get from one town to another, in relative comfort and speed. On my first Canadian train I had experienced my first overnight journey, but sleeping in my tip up seat. This time it was not *one* overnight, but three, with a bed and all meals provided as on a hotel with full board! So we had our private seats, there was a 360 degree lounge coach, a lounge coach and a restaurant coach, as well as an all day bar. One of the first things I did was check out the restaurant to see that they were expecting one Vegan for all meals. Indeed they were. Then I investigated the 360 degree lounge, where it was rather like a bus with no roof, but there was a glass roof, so one could see all directions except below one! Here we could see the full length of the train stretched out in front and behind, with three other observation towers spread evenly down the train. I stayed up here for a while,

and got talking to a friendly couple who were from the USA. I think he was a doctor or something. They loved my cats' names. I also told them the joke I had heard on Classic FM Radio that had given me the idea of calling one of our cats Bach! Anyway we were talking a fair amount about names. It turned out to be one of the great coincidences of my journey that the first couple I really had chatted to turned out to be "Phillips".

Later we were called for lunch. There were three or four sittings for each meal, and we were asked which one we preferred at the beginning of the day. I usually chose the first sitting. Non sleeper service passengers could also join in the meals, if there was room. When we arrived we were shown to our seats. I waited in anticipation of what I might get. They prepared for me a Greek Salad (minus the olives and onion) tomato juice and banana. Actually very nice and filling. We were also treated to a glass of champagne. Then I went for my usual midday nap back in my cabin, and woke up to a 25 minute stop at Capreol.

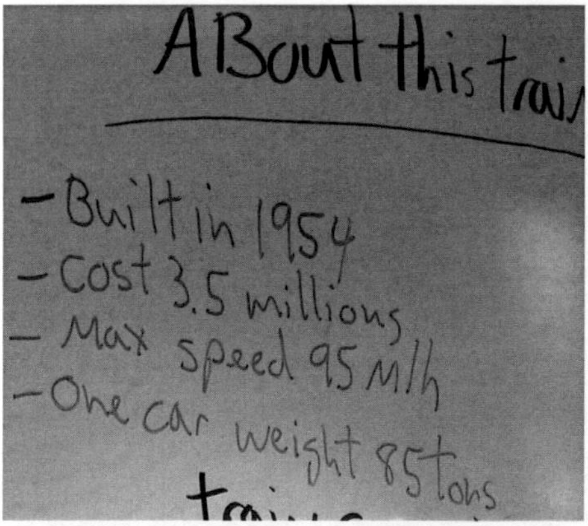

I spent more time in the observation tower and then explored the lounge, where people could play games and watch videos and just talk. Later I chose the early evening sitting for dinner. Before we were served the chief

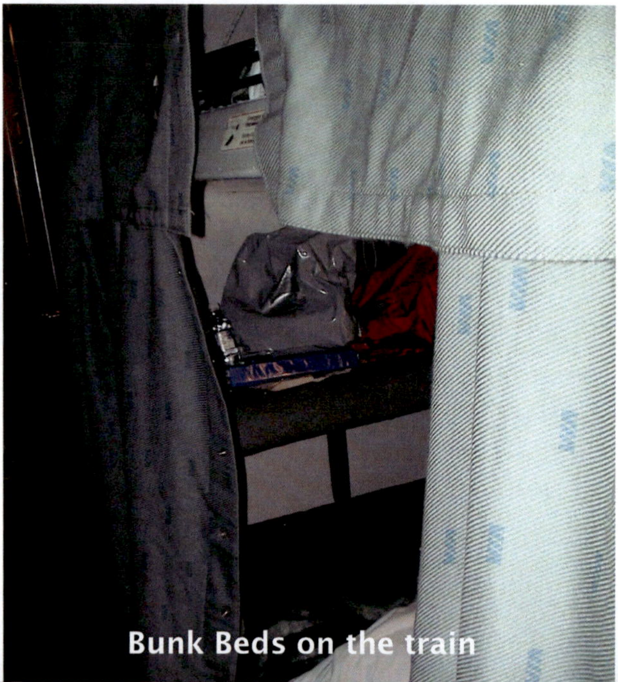

Bunk Beds on the train

Restaurant carriage

Travel certificate >

CANADA'S CLASSIC TRAIN JOURNEY

SILVER & BLUE

To commemorate your journey aboard the Western transcontinental train, the *Canadian*®.

We hope you will fondly remember many special moments from your journey along with the pleasures of travelling in VIA Rail's world-renowned, premier service, *Silver & Blue*™ class.

October 2006	Reg Muir
Date	Service Manager The *Canadian*

VIA™

VIA Rail Canada

® Registered trademark owned by VIA Rail Canada Inc. ™ Trademark owned by VIA Rail Canada Inc.

The other Phillips

New Zealand couple in the opposite bunk

waiter announced that one person's menu had a deliberate mistake in it. The one who had that menu was to be given a bottle of champagne to share with their table (of 4). Some attempted to claim the prize, so I stopped looking, but that was not the error they meant, so we all looked again, and GUESS WHAT? I was the lucky one! So I and the other three all had champers instead of wine served with their meal. This for me was lovely. The caterers seemed very good at adapting a vegetarian meal to being vegan; I think I was the only vegan, but I know there were two or three vegetarians. The main dish was rice with a mixture of wild mushrooms and with the other vegetables was delicious.

Whilst we were eating, the service staff had been converting our cabins to bunk beds and curtains were now drawn right across so my cabin and the New Zealand couple's became two separate rooms. Before retiring I went to the lounge and watched the evening video. It was about a court case where a woman had been sexually harassed at work by the men, and she eventually won her case after much trial and tribulation, as of course the men lied and now ostracised her.

So ended my first day on a train. The bed was comfortable but I didn't sleep too well, as there had been some onion in the meal.

The clocks went back an hour every day on this journey, so we got used to it! I decided to rise at dawn and dress to try to take the sunrise over the end of the train, but unfortunately the lines were not quite in line with the sunrise and the trees at either side got in the way! I did get a few pictures, but not what I really wanted. I later went for breakfast, which was good, and after that the train stopped for a while at Sioux Lookout. We were still in Ontario after a whole day's travelling! At these stopping places we were always allowed to get out and walk about. It was cold here and there was frost on the ground.

Later it was our last lunch with the original restaurant crew, as at the next stop, Winnipeg, the crew had a break and they had an all change. The chief Steward then made a speech thanking all his staff, and us the passengers for being such good people, so at the end I got up and said a few words saying that there was one person he had not thanked! That was himself! We had all been well entertained by himself and his crew and I made it clear that we had enjoyed our trip and thanked him for taking care of us so well.

By now we had entered the start of the prairie-lands. These lands brought back memories of my geography lessons at Skinners' School with Mr A J Clark. And now here I was passing over those exotic places: Manitoba, Saskatchewan (I never could spell that) and Alberta. These states were the vast wheat and cereal crop lands, the bread bin not only of Canada but the world. And the lakes! Everywhere there seemed to be large lakes. We saw many lakes on the maps, and here were lakes that in the UK would have each been marked on our maps, but clearly in Canada many were not! We had an hour's stop at Winnipeg. Yes, we even got to stop in each state, and Dilys would have liked the Environmental Library/exhibition in Winnipeg station. It was very interesting.

Back on board, and later I sampled the new catering team's vegan meal for me. Later that evening I watched the coach's video, "The March the Penguins". This reminded me of a David Attenborough BBC Series film about those intriguing King Penguins who march hundreds of miles inland to the cold and dark snowy wastelands to lay their eggs, well away from their predators on the coast of Antarctica. The females lay their eggs balanced on their feet and transfer them to the male to his feet. The egg must not touch the snow, or it would be frozen solid in minutes. The females go

Rockies

Totem at Jasper

off back to the coast to fish and eat, leaving thousands of males huddled together constantly changing places so that the same ones are not always on the perimeter. Weeks later the warmth of their bodies allows the eggs to hatch and the penguins then march back to the coast with their babies. If my memory serves me well, the babies were fed some substance from a special gland, that only these penguins have by the dads, just in time for the females return to feed them fresh, regurgitated, food. The males then leave and go back to the coast to catch food for the first time for weeks, Later the males return just in time as the females feeds have run out. They then all march back to the sea The timing seems so exact, and the story was amazing! If anyone has not seen this film, SEE IT!

I have said little about what I did in my spare time on this journey. I was rarely bored! In the quieter times I read or played Sudoku, at other times we passengers just chatted. I slept better the second night. The clocks went back an hour again. So each day was like 25 hours long! It was now Thursday Oct 5th   - Kim's Birthday! (Kim from Nova Scotia!)

I tried again to snap the sunrise at the end of the train; the chances of capturing it were easier as there were fewer trees, but it just never really happened the way I wanted it! I still got some interesting pictures though. Breakfast was earlier, at 7.30 am, and was the same as yesterday. The reason for the early meal was the stop at Edmonton. We were now in the Alberta Capital, and we were able to walk around at the station area. The next stop was for even longer, for at Jasper about half the passengers left the train and went on another journey by coach to see the Rockies at close at hand. As a consequence, the train stopped for a longer time, as so many rooms had to be cleaned to make them ready for new passengers, though fewer than before. But it gave me time to give Dilys a sur-

Sunrise over the back of the train

The waterfall in the Rockies

prise phone call from Jasper. It was here that we saw the Totem pole at the station, reminding us that Canada was indeed first populated by first nation people before the Europeans took over. Jasper was also the gateway to the famous Rockies. We were about to see a dramatic change in landscape, from flat country to mountain peaks and shapes unseen for a long time. The train went especially slowly through the mountain ranges, often stopping for people to get good views of the waterfalls and snowy mountains. The clicking of cameras reach a crescendo, and a number of people forgot to turn off their flashes. I did explain to a few that they were likely to get their own reflections in the glass windows, unless they turned off the flash!

The meals were again very good, and well served, but the spirit given us by the previous crew was not quite there. But no complaints. By nightfall we had passed through the best of the Rockies. The timetable of the trains was obviously timed to see them at their best. At no time had the trains seemed in a hurry, unlike our UK intercity trains, as we seemed to cruise between 60 and 80 mph. These journeys were more for their enjoyment than getting there as fast as possible. So nightfall, and a final reminder that clocks go back another hour, and that breakfast was served early again for our arrival at the end of the line in Vancouver.

And then it was the next stage of my travel, meeting up with a young lady who has been through many trials and tribulations, and spent so much time talking to me on Yahoo or MSN. Sharon is a full blooded First Nation national from the Yukon; she is one of the Kaska people .

Chapter 7

Meeting the "Ice Maiden".

{Sharon & Wendy}

The great train journey ended as the 23 items of railway stock pulled gently to a halt in Vancouver station. After a three day journey, only a few minutes late was not bad. One thing that I particularly noticed with these Canadian trains was that one hardly ever noticed when the train started or stopped. The acceleration was so smooth we hardly noticed the change. The control the Engineers had (in Canada the train drivers are called Engineers) was superb. These trains were nearly twice as long as anything I had ridden on in the UK. The were 4 engines, and 22 coaches. This train was built in 1954 and cost $3.5 MILLION. It was 2442 feet long and weighed 2090 Tons, all for 165 passengers! Its maximum speed was 95 mph, but it rarely exceeded 80, though I think it went fastest at night. One of the engine units was there purely to supply heat and light for the train, as all four were working only when on the steeper inclines.

So after almost exactly three days, Vancouver station was entered only a few minutes late; this was in spite of having to stop several times to allow the freight trains to pass from the other direction. Most of the track was single, with a few passing places, and at the stations.

My "Ice Maiden" was waiting for me at the station (arranged by phone previously) but for some reason I missed her, even though she was holding up a board. But eventually we did meet, and I was surprised by her height; I had never met her before, only talked (for hours) on the internet, and a few times on the phone.

I must explain how her nick-name of Ice Maiden arose! It was due to the land she lived in, especially in the winter months. One of the things I always remember was one January morning Sharon telling me that the temperature had risen an amazing 30C during the day! No, she was not basking in the sun, for the outside temperature was now at MINUS TEN degrees C! At night it had been MINUS 40C! But she was just as warm blooded as us! I was never going to experience such temperatures, even when we went to her home town, Ross River, a few days later.

Sharon suffered from a bad knee so she was not able to walk quickly, but I was slow with such heavy luggage. We walked to the sky train and went a few stops to Surrey (what is Surrey doing in the far side of Canada? Surrey in the UK is a county near London) a district of Vancouver. I noticed how much more like England everything was here. In the rest of Canada I noticed nearly everything was labelled in English and French, but here it was mainly English. In Quebec it was the opposite - nearly everything was in French!

After a while we arrived at Sharon's apartment, and met her friend Sharleen, who was just off to work. My new Mobile phone had arrived from Dilys, one of the latest Motorola with camera and video!

We spent the day at the local shops getting food and cash. How useful that I could put my bank card in 'holes in the wall' and out came the local currency! We actually called briefly at Sharleen's work place, but she was too busy to talk. Back at the apartment we chatted and I tried to make friends with the three cats, but only Chuser (Big Bear) allowed me to touch him!

That evening the three of us made our way by sky train and bus to an Indian/Chinese restaurant, where you picked your own ingredients and they cooked it for you as a kind of stir fry, so it was easy to make sure it was all vegan (for me). After a long walk trying to find a certain chocolate shop, eventually we found it CLOSED! We returned home cold and exhausted! So ended my first day in British Columbia, having met the famous Sharon.

Saturday 7th October was Pat Nelson's birthday, whom I met in Truro.

Sharleen drove us to White Rock beach and I got my fingers wetted by the Pacific Ocean. It was my first ever view of this great ocean, and the bit I saw today *was* pacific. We walked out along the pier over the sea, and found a VEGAN ice cream to eat! Later we ate at the Indian/ Chinese restaurant, and later back at the flat I caught up with emails and made friends with Chuser's brother Chani, called "CiCi" for short. It means Cute Cat! This was a quiet day, for tomorrow Sharon & I were going to visit Whitehorse and Ross River, Sharon's home village, in central Yukon

Next morning Sharleen very kindly drove us to the airport to catch the plane. Flying over the snow-capped mountains and glaciers, we eventually landed at Whitehorse, the capital of Yukon. Whitehorse has a large scattered community, and though the population is small, it covers one of the largest areas of all Cana-

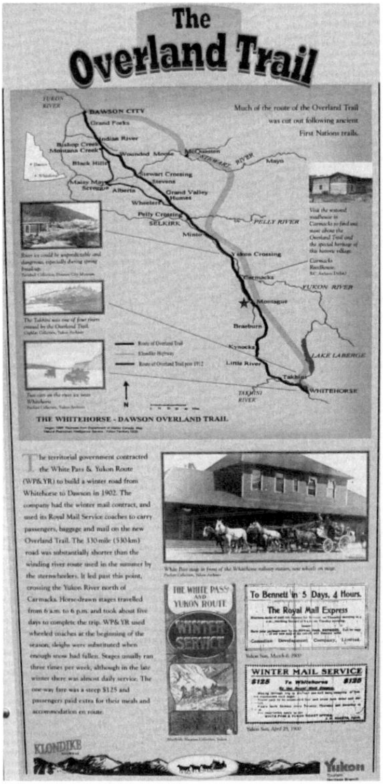

dian Cities, with very few tall buildings. The reason for the low height is because it is in an earthquake area, and no buildings are allowed to be more than 3 stories high.

We hired a car for the next three days, booked in at the Yukon Inn, and then walked into Whitehorse "Downtown". At 5 pm we drove to Wendy and Dan's new home to spend Thanksgiving with them and have dinner. Wendy very kindly had gone to some trouble to make me a vegan version. In the past Wendy had helped Sharon a lot when she was having problems. Wendy is a very kindly and caring person, who has a published book on what happened to her years ago when she was incorrectly diagnosed as depressive, was hospitalized and given ECT treatment, which resulted in her complete loss of memory and a damaged knee cap. With Dan's help she has rebuilt her life, but all past memories are gone. Compensation was paid, but the doctor concerned was not prosecuted, I believe. Wendy only knew what happened by what Dan told her, and from the diary she secretly kept whilst hospitalized. I noticed that Sharon became more animated and was smiling more on meeting Wendy again. I had the great pleasure of meeting Wendy's 13 year old son Conrad, who is very bright and full of initiative. He was soon to be taking his pilot's licence. The aim was to be the youngest ever to do so.

After the lovely evening, Sharon and I returned to

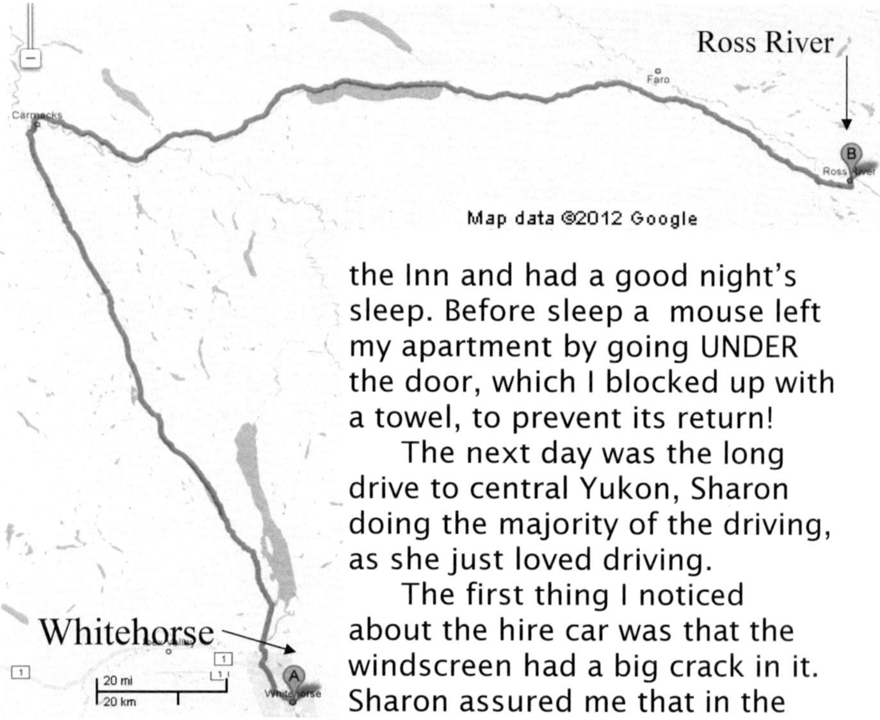

the Inn and had a good night's sleep. Before sleep a mouse left my apartment by going UNDER the door, which I blocked up with a towel, to prevent its return!

The next day was the long drive to central Yukon, Sharon doing the majority of the driving, as she just loved driving.

The first thing I noticed about the hire car was that the windscreen had a big crack in it. Sharon assured me that in the Yukon hardly any cars didn't! Anyway we drove north for a long time, stopping at a historical place on the way, and when we reached a gas station, we stopped to fill up. They are few and far between in this part of the world, and it was a general store as well. We turned right at the next turning, and joined the Campbell Highway. Route 4

The official story of this road:

"Yukon Highway 4 is 362 miles (583 km) long and runs from Watson Lake, Yukon to Carmack, Yukon.
The first portion of Yukon Highway 4, the Robert Campbell Highway, between Watson Lake and Miner Junction, was built in the early 1960s as part of the project to complete road access to Tungsten, Northwest Territories. The portion east and north of Miner Junction is now known as the Nahanni Range Road, and is presently Yukon Territorial Highway #10.

During the late 1960s and continuing to 1971, highways were built to connect Carmacks with Ross River, with a spur road to Faro to serve the new lead-zinc mine that opened in 1969. Additional road work was also completed between Ross River and Miner Junction. The completed road complements the Canol Road, providing two loops and bringing year-round access to Ross River.

The Campbell Highway is mostly gravel, and the most improved section is between Carmacks and Faro, where it has taken the most abuse from trucks hauling ore to Whitehorse and beyond."

Most of the Yukon roads were of the gravel type once out of the towns, hence the cracked windscreens! In spite of this they were relatively smooth, and mainly straight, though not dead straight. By the time we reached Ross River, in five hours we had probably passed about 40 cars! I was allowed to have a short spell of driving! We left the Robert Campbell Highway at the junction to Ross River, and eventually arrived at Sharon's cousin Elizabeth's home. I was also taken to meet Gwendy (the missionary's wife) and her three girls, and then to see the river Pelly, into which the Ross River flows.

After that we drove about ten miles out back on to the Robert Campbell Highway to Brian's Jackfish Lake Guest House. Brian was a local JP, till he found that he was expected to go to "important" meetings the other side of Canada! But he still was on the look out to help people in trouble in this outback of Canada. He also ran a couple of businesses in Ross River, a general store and Post Office and a garage/petrol station.

Jack Fish Lake Bed & Breakfast

A lake near Ross River

Later, Elizabeth came and took us to see a few of their family and friends. One of them was Denis who was a first class carver of moose antlers; these carvings were really excellent. I believe one of his carvings was to be used for the next Winter Olympic games to be held in Canada. Later we went back to Ross River to Gwendy's and met her husband. They were from New York and had now settled in here well. Then it was back to the Guest House for a good night's sleep. I found Brian to be a most interesting person who has been on the look out for Sharon, helping her over a number of years, as has her cousin Elizabeth and Gwendy.

I had been warned that in this area the temperature can fall to minus 10, even in October, but it turned out that the Yukon was having a mini heat wave, and only in the night did the temperature fall below freezing to about -2C! After a good breakfast, I had a little wander around the Guest House grounds with the camera. After we were all up and ready to go, we drove back into Ross River, and visited the Post Office, Brian's store, where I checked my bank account on the net. Then I was given a grand tour of Sharon's town. There was the school, where she proudly showed me some of her own artwork, and family photos; the college she had attended, where she had later been a teacher herself; and then the house she used to live in. This was all a very nostalgic trip for Sharon.

Afterwards we had lunch at Elizabeth's. Then came the trip of a lifetime that few Europeans would ever experience! Denis had an Argo (a forest crashing vehicle on eight wheels), which just had room for the three of us. Denis's dog led the way! And we literally crashed through the undergrowth till we arrived at a lake. We had bumped, crushed small bushes and swayed our way, and apart from our route it seemed so peaceful and unspoilt. Later we returned to Denis's house and I took a few pictures of his carvings. And later we returned to Brian's guest house and I had quite a long chat to him. Incidentally it happened to be election day in the Yukon. Sharon, having had a sleep, got up as I went to bed! Brian was last seen doing something to Sharon's hair.

In the morning we had the long drive back to Whitehorse, and there was a new Sharon, with pink hair! Brian was also a hairdresser ! We drove back to Brian's garage in Ross River to fill up with fuel and said our final farewells to this community of first nation people. An experience I will never forget. It was raining as we left at 9 am but the weather was clear blue sky by the time we arrived back in Whitehorse. Sharon was soon to go on a trip out of Canada with Sharleen, and needed a passport photo. This was arranged and completed, and Wendy's Dan was a suitable signatory. Then at 5.30 we met Wendy, Dan, Conrad and a friend for a meal at the Local Chinese restaurant. After that Sharon SLEPT! We made arrangements to be up early enough to catch the 8 am flight back to Vancouver. Anyone watching me at this point might have wondered if I was OK in the head, because before parting with the hired car I noticed a few gravel dents in the windscreen, which sparkled in the sun, and took a few close up pictures. It is surprising where beauty can be found! At the Whitehorse airport we had time to look around, and Sharon was keen for me to see the very interesting displays, which were about the native, First Nation people.

We arrived back in Vancouver to a summer-like mini heat wave! So much for coming prepared for minus 10C. I had come with winter clothing, which I was to parcel up and post back home, as I was not going to encounter any more really cold places. We then tried to catch the sky train back to Sharon's flat, but discovered chaos. No trains were running. We were di-

Wendy
Me
Sharon

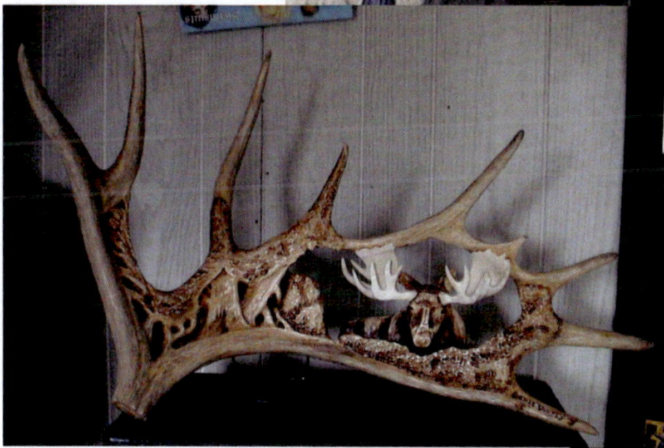

Carvings using Deer Antlers, by Sharon's friend Dennis Shorty, from Ross River.

Beauty as in chipped glass

Carving by Ray Ladue, Sharon's cousin.
"Big people learning"
Hangs in Dena Cho Kanadi, Yukon College

rected to a nearby bus stop and taken by bus part of the way. When we got back Sharon needed to have a good sleep, so as I needed to get my ticket to Seattle for the 14th October, two days hence, I went back into Vancouver to the main railway station. I found the sky trains were still not running from this station, and there was now a regular bus service to replace part of the journey. I took the opportunity to ask one of the train officials what had happened, and was told that a man had committed suicide, at this very station, not long before Sharon and I had returned. On the sky train part of the journey I noticed behind me a couple who were having a kind of riddle game. The young man was asking his lady friend improbable type questions. I felt I knew the answers so I turned round and asked it if was OK to try and answer, as she seemed unable to do so. He was kind of surprised that I was able to more or less answer his riddle. We got talking then, and he explained, as I had remarked that he seemed very knowledgeable, that he was in fact a schizophrenic, and she then explained that she had been in deep depression till they had met at a Help session. They were more or less homeless, and were travelling into Vancouver to try and get more help. I offered them some chocolate when we got off the train, which at first they refused, but I insisted and they were obviously very hungry, so I gave them the rest of the bar; it was definitely obvious that they were VERY hungry. So I offered to buy them a milk shake, and took them to the café in the station and as my time was short I had to leave them, but they were obviously pleased. I never saw them again, and what was good was that they never once asked for anything.

I bought my train ticket for Saturday, which turned out to be a COACH ticket run by Amtrak, railway of the USA. For some reason the morning journey was by coach and the evening by train! I then had a little time to walk around a bit of Vancouver, and found the Science "Bell", a science museum, and took a few pictures. I returned to Surrey, by the now fully operational sky train, and found Sharon had caught up on her sleep, and a little later Sharleen returned from work and was rather "surprised" by Sharon's pink hair! I caught up with emails and later we all went out to eat at a Greek restaurant.

The next day was my last full day in Canada. Using Sharon's computer, I managed to catch up on emails, and messages in Zorpia & Yahoo groups, and booked the rest of the hotels that I needed in the USA: Oklahoma City, Fort Worth, Los Angeles and San Francisco. Also I finished uploading pictures I had taken on the camera to sites on the net. Later I went out and did a little shopping for food to make my stir fry for the evening meal. Both Sharon & Sharleen survived it , and after a good night's sleep they both

were still alive !

The final farewells were said. Sharon very kindly took the parcel of now no longer needed clothes to the post office to post back home. With hugs and farewells, and good wishes for their holiday later in the year, and hugs for the cats, I went to Vancouver railway station and caught the Amtrak coach to take me to Seattle.

The Yukon Hotel we stayed at in Whitehorse

Chapter 8
Cross the Border to Seattle

*"The bluest skies you've ever seen are in Seattle
And the hills the greenest green, in Seattle
Like a beautiful child, growing up, free an' wild
Full of hopes an' full of fears, full of laughter, full of tears
Full of dreams to last the years, in Seattle
. . . in Seattle! ..."* - Perry Como

(Maggie, Teri and Sandra)

Several hours later the coach arrived at the border and we all had to go through Customs and pay visa fees, but with little fuss, not nearly as difficult as by air! Eventually we pulled up at Seattle railway station, and I used my mobile to let Maggie know I had arrived. She was unable to get there for an hour or so, so I used the time to organise my Amtrak bookings for the whole month. There was a lot of confusion at first as they had never had anyone from the UK arrive before in Seattle with already booked tickets! At first they wanted me to pay again. But after an hour of trial and errors we finally got it all sorted! Yes, I had paid! I had one journey still to organise, LA to San Francisco, the final leg. The poor man at the booking office was so pleased that he had got it all sorted.

Not long after 5pm Maggie arrived, as arranged, in her vanilla cream Ford Escort Reg number "LIONESS". It wasn't long before we roared away and arrived at her home and had left-over dinner and salad. Then we went for a walk to the sea, and for the second time I saw the Pacific, but now from the USA! Maggie's friend Joy arrived later and after a lot of chatting we all retired to bed. I had known Maggie in a Beatles Yahoo group and also Mystical Dreamland, and had had a lot of interesting conversations. We had a few more and caught up on a few things. Maggie was having trouble in getting enough work driving school buses, a job she loved.

Next morning after breakfast I was able to phone Dilys, and I texted Tim, as it was his birthday. Joy drove us into a Seattle car park, and we wandered in the rain and mist to the Maritime Museum which was on piers over the sea at Puget Sound. This was all very interesting to see this part of North America. The rain got us all umbrellered when outside all morning, although it did brighten up in the afternoon. My main wheeled suitcase had finally given out, its wheels jammed, and I needed a new one, so Maggie spent the early evening taking me round a number of shops in a big mall to buy a new one. The biggest problem was that they were mostly sold in twos, threes or fours! It was ages before I found a single suitable one, strong enough to take the ravages of a round the world trip, but eventually we did. I then phoned up Teri, who lived in Shelton not very far away, and Maggie arranged to take me there in her car to arrive early the following afternoon. That evening we had a long philosophical discussion.

Next morning Maggie's friend Joy obviously wanted to come with us, so she drove us and we arrived on a pleasant sunny afternoon at Teri's house in Shelton. Here we took photos of me with Maggie and Teri, as I was building up a collection of photos of me meeting all my friends. I said my final farewells to Maggie and Joy, and was now on the next stage of my journey. Teri's house was in a lovely woodland area; her back garden backed on to natural woodland. The only real noise was birds, so lovely and peaceful after my last few days of travelling and being in city areas. I took many photos of the birds visiting Teri's house much

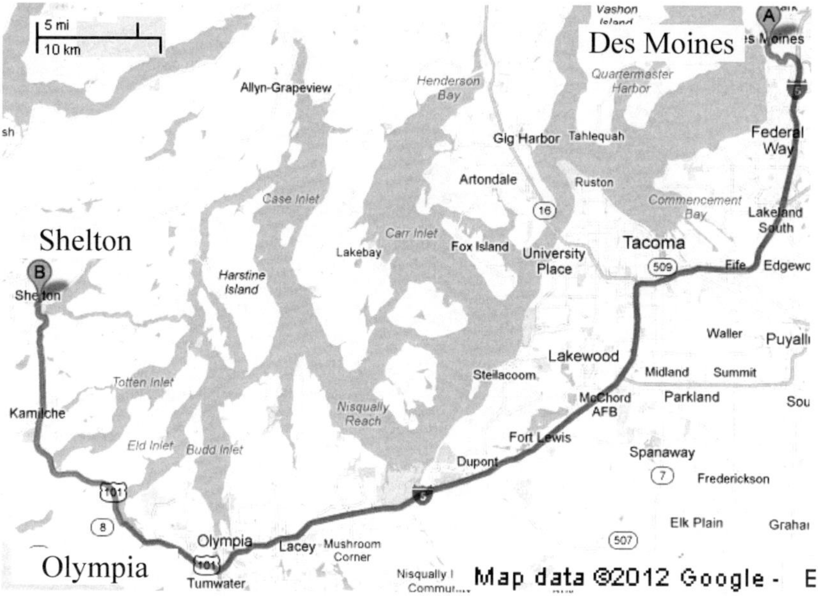

filled bird tables. Most people have ONE table, but not Teri. She was one who loved her wildlife, and had several tables and hanging feeders.

Teri had survived a rather nasty motorcycle accident a few years previously, and had been off work since. She was now in a position to be able to work, at least part-time, and was job hunting, but was finding that difficult.

Next morning after breakfast, the bird tables were quickly being emptied by some very flightless four legged creatures, too large to climb trees, but just large enough to stand and eat at head height. It was amazing! A mother deer and her two children, both girls, arrived and had a lovely time in the garden. No wonder Teri bought so much bird food! These were wild deer, and yet here they were calmly walking around the garden. "Oh! Don't eat *that* plant!" I heard several times from Teri, who obviously wanted the deer there but not to eat her plants, but was so happy she fed them bird food! We photographed them, first

Deer visiting Teri's garden, eating bird food!

Teri's Car Registration

Shaggy Ink Cap

of all through the window, but later, we very quietly open the back door and slowly crept out, and even more amazingly they stayed; they obviously had their eyes on us, but otherwise they carried on eating and I got several close up pictures. Being so close to wild deer was a beautiful experience; we could get to about three yards, before they became uncomfortable and backed away.

Later in the morning we went out shopping for food in Wembley and saw a field of bison. Teri obviously loved animals. We purchased some food for me to make a stir-fry that evening. After lunch we went for a walk in the warm sunshine in the lovely area in woodland and near a lake. It was so peaceful. Teri was so lucky have such a wonderful place to live. During the walk I noticed some Shaggy Ink Caps (wild fungi) and picked them to add them to the stir-fry! Teri was a little concerned about picking wild fungi, but I knew this variety well, having had them many times.

What I must mention is that it was after meeting Teri in the Yahoo Group "VeggieSpot" that she had introduced me to raw food eating, back in 2002. This was one of the most significant changes in my diet and was the most helpful in bringing me into good health. After a trial for three weeks of eating nothing but un-cooked fruit and vegetables, my whole life seemed to change. I lost a little weight, I felt healthier, my eyes seemed clearer, and all my aches and pains in joints, back and bowels almost disappeared overnight. I found I could dig the garden easily again!..... So for me Teri was a great help. She herself had been raw for a long time, but had not only given up being raw but also being totally vegetarian; but she was still mainly so and had a good proportion of raw food in her diet. I had of course stayed totally vegan, but was eating then about 10% food not raw. And stir-fries were the one meal I cooked, about once every 7 to 10 days. The

Teri with her visitors

Lake near Teri's house]

Maggie

Teri's rat

Teri

preparation of this meal was interrupted by a second set of deer; this time a mother and a boy and girl visited us, and I took more pictures, of course.

So for the third time on my world tour I cooked a meal for my kind host. Teri survived the Shaggy Ink Caps! Teri is a lovely woman. One of the things she needs is a steady man in her life. One day I feel sure that one will see what a treasure she is.

That night we watched a TV channel that is not the normal run of USA TV: it was a “telling the TRUTH” kind of news channel. Link TV It puts out the REAL news, not how the right wing want it to be seen. (USA TV, and other media, are mostly controlled by a few organisations that have an “agenda” to follow.) The following morning, before Teri kindly took me to Olympia station, I had to have photos of her pet rat. Sadly I had to say goodbye to Teri. I was so pleased to have met her, especially as it was her who had persuaded me to try the raw food diet.

We had arranged to be at the station about an hour before the train was due, so as to meet a friend from the Stamp Addicts Yahoo Group, Sandra McWha. Teri departed but not before a good hug, and I wished her all the best in her court case, re the nasty accident she had had, and her search for a decent job, and a boy friend!

Sandra arrived in her blue Toyota, and now I was meeting quite a different person. I didn’t know her very well, but I am so glad to have had the chance to meet and talk to her. Originally from Northern Ireland and England, she is retired and divorced, and collects Mint USA and used stamps from other countries. What a pity we had only that hour - she really was interesting. Another “green” and anti-Bush person!

I now had to leave Olympia and return to Seattle for my long two full days on the train to Chicago. So the next stage of my journey was under way.

Chapter 9

Seattle to Chicago via the USA Rockies. TWO day rail journey.

"Chicago, Chicago--that toddlin' town.
Chicago, Chicago--I will show you around. I love it.
Bet your bottom dollar you'll lose the blues in Chicago, Chicago.
The town that Billy Sunday couldn't shut down." -
Frank Sinatra

{Jela (Jeanne)}

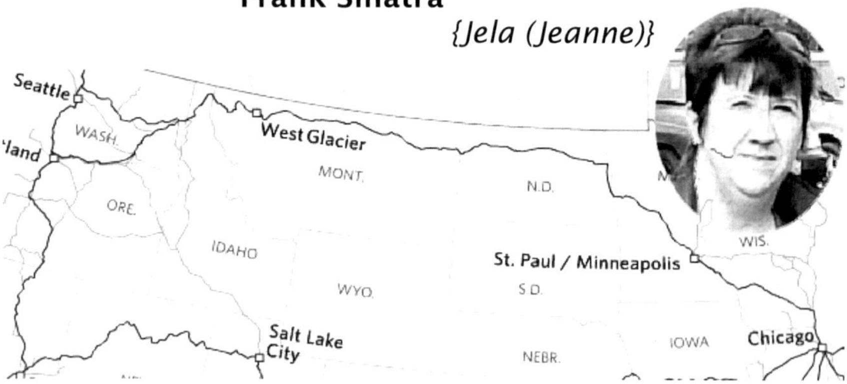

Amtrak left Seattle on time, for a 1,700 mile journey! I was lucky enough to have a cabin room to myself. Here the cabins were with doors, not curtains, to separate us. They even had shower rooms, and wash basins in the bedrooms! Most of the rooms had a pair of bunk beds, but there were a few family rooms for up to 6. The other main difference was the restaurant meals: though primarily for those with cabins, the seated passengers could join the various sittings for meals, and only 30 minutes was allowed per sitting instead of 45. As we started late, the first meal was soon after the train drew out of Seattle. They had been prepared for feeding a vegan, but again things were different in that meals were pre-prepared before departing; they were only heated up for the eating time.

All the carriages in Amtrak trains were double deck-

USA ROCKIES

Sunrise on Seattle to Chicago journey

ers. The sleeping compartments were downstairs and the lounges upstairs. The roof was half glass, so one could see the scenery well, but not as well as in the towers of the Via Rail in Canada.

Although these trains were noisier than the Via Rail, I did get a fairly good night's sleep, but there having been onion in the meal I did suffer a bit from wind during the night. Unlike in Canada, the journey was timed wrongly for seeing the Rockies, as it was a night-time journey through the mountains. Also during the night, at Spokane, the train was joined to a second train from a different starting point (Portland). As daylight dawned we were on the Eastern side of the Rockies; then it soon flattened out, but became less boring later. What was interesting was that we went through Essex, Havre, Malta, Glasgow & Rugby, like being home from home, though like a dream where places are not in the right order and place. For lunch I was given a nice salad, with fruit salad to follow.

For the afternoon entertainment there was a wine tasting session, and we had to say which of 4 we liked best (2 red & 2 white). They were all Washington Wines. We could keep the unused wines for the dinner, which again was nice: though the pre-packed type again, it was different, but it still had some onion in! Whilst on this journey we were fortunate to see some deer.

We had been warned that there was going to be a delay in arrival the next day due to engineering works on a bridge, so I phoned Jela to let her know. Again there was more train noise that night, worse than before. I think my cabin must have been close to the wheels. There seemed less to do on the Amtrak trains than on Via Rail too. As the cost was under half, I suppose that was not too surprising. I spent a lot of time doing Sudoku puzzles in a book I had bought for the purpose of time filling, and I was reading a Dan Brown

Snow on Rockies

Rockies flattening out

book. Some time in that evening I passed through the place where I had hoped to meet up with a Zorpian friend, Ivy, and would have broken the journey had the arrangements to meet been finalised. Anyway I managed to get some sleep, and awoke for breakfast and my last day on this train, passing through famous places such as St Paul, Minneapolis, Wisconsin and Milwaukee. We never seemed to stop for very long, though we did get a chance to stretch our legs on the station from time to time.

Breakfast was cooked oats, fruit, a roll and cranberry juice. The day was misty with no real chance for photos, though later it brightened up. In spite of the warnings of being late, we were in fact only 30 minutes late. I phoned Jela to let her know what time I

Elmhurst

would arrive at Elmhurst. This was by a local train. All trains here seemed to be double deckers, even the local ones!

What a surprise I got on first meeting Jeanne (Jela, as I had known her in her Poetry Yahoo Group and Danielle's Mystical Dreamland group)! She so resembled an Italian friend of my family (Anna), back in the days of my boyhood! And I was right - Jela had Italian connections. Anyway it was lovely to meet her for the

Cantigny House

Cantigny Gardens

first time. She and her husband Fred first of all took me to my hotel (Quality Inn in Elmhurst) and after signing in and depositing nearly all my luggage they took me to their home and we had a wonderful all vegan meal with no onions! Jela had been in contact, via Internet, with Dilys, to find out what to give me. It was the best meal I had had for a while. Thanks so much Jela for going to all that trouble. I met her cat and two dogs and, very briefly, her youngest daughter. Then I was whisked off to the local Artists' Fine Art Guild exhibition, where Jela had three exhibits up on display. The theme was "beauty". Jela is definitely an artist, both in photography and painting. Then they took me back to my hotel and gave me a wonderful welcome bag of goodies, including one of her own pictures transferred to a canvas to resemble a painting. That is now up in our sitting room back home!

I slept well and had a nice breakfast at the hotel, and Jela and Fred came to collect me and took me to a historic house, originally built for the founder and owner of the Chicago Tribune,Joseph Medhill in 1896. Robert Sanderson McCormack married Medhill's daughter Katherine. They then passed the house on to their son Robert Rutherford McCormick and they named the house Cantigny Farm. The son was editor and publisher for 44 years. It was a fascinating place steeped in newspaper history from the 1880's. Those were the days when the Newspapers were ruled by their owners (now they are big corporate owners!). The gardens were lovely and well kept, the house was now a museum steeped in history.

I spent the rest of the day catching up with emails, and later returned to my hotel, where I booked an early morning taxi to take me to the Chicago station for my next destination in Bay City. It was Fred's birthday today. So I wished him a happy birthday and said my grateful farewells.

Cantigny House & Gardens

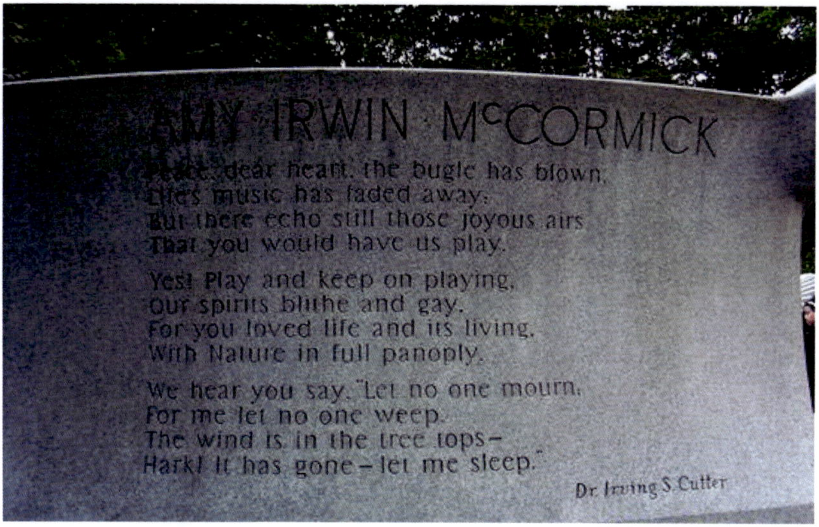

Chapter 10
To BAY CITY (No Rollers!) **and BACK**

{Mary}

The Bay City Rollers do not come from Bay City; in fact they had never heard of the place till they chose their name allegedly by throwing a dart at a map of the United States. The dart landed on the map in the state of Arkansas, but since "Arkansas Rollers" did not sound quite right, and might also lead to problems with pronunciation, they tried again, and this time the dart landed near the community of Bay City, Michigan. Apparently the Rollers have once visited Bay City to give a concert there. Bay City's most famous daughter, though, is "Madonna".

On Sunday October 22nd, I was up at 5 am, signed out at 5.50 am and had a quick breakfast at 6 am, because the taxi arrived at 6.15 to get me to Chicago station in time for the 7.50 am train to Flint. Actually, though there is a rail all the way, at Battle Creek, (where we arrived 30 minutes late) we had to get off and wait 3 hours for our connection, by COACH! For some reason there seem to be several places where Amtrak use coaches on a regular timetable instead of trains. I walked into Battle Creek downtown, but nothing was open. But the exercise was good! I took all my luggage with me. It was a cold day, brrrrr!

There was some good news, as I had to get to Bay City, from Flint by coach (No rail to there!). I found out that this coach was the one that went to Bay City, from Flint, so I didn't have to change, nor worry if it were late into Flint! All I had to do was pay a bit extra for the Flint to Bay City journey. It arrived on time at Flint, but was delayed 30 minutes by a road accident ahead. Anyway Mary was at the bus station to meet me, and we arrived at her house by 8 pm. I had to put my watch forward an hour!

We had an interesting talk, and Mary was my first meeting with a member of the Admiral's Beatle Yahoo Group. Tomorrow was to be my first experience of any school outside the UK. I used to be a maths teacher for 21 years, trying to teach maths to various pupils in a variety of schools in the UK. Those pupils were 11 to 18 years old. One of the reasons for my visit to meet Mary was for me to talk to Mary's pupils (7 to 8 year olds) about the UK. So this was to be a quite new experience.

I was kind of let off for the first day, as on the Monday all the schools in the area were having a joint

staff meeting to discuss a new reading scheme. It was an early start, so we got up at 6 am. I went with Mary and sat in with the first session. My goodness, it was like being back at work again ! It seemed that school teachers in the USA were very similar to UK ones! They had a break at 9 am and I decided it would be nice to get out and explore Bay City. I had a street map and walked into the city centre on a cold clear morning with frost around. It seemed that not only were schools closed today (for pupils at least) but so were shops: the place seemed deserted! There were a few cafes open, and antique type shops. Anyway downtown Bay City seemed quite dead. But I found a lovely café which offered a choice of teas, using REAL tea leaves (not a teabag in sight!) They offered salad snacks too, and they catered for vegetarians and vegans. I had a long chat with the owner, and decided that this was a 'must' place to visit.

I returned to the school after spending time in the library and museum; I was able to spend time on the library computer. Back at Mary's we prepared my talk to the children next morning.

Next day, Tuesday 24th October, was my initiation into USA schooling for 7 year olds! The night before we had prepared a list of English words that have different meanings in the USA & UK. Mary had very kindly written them in large size on sheets of paper

Lollypop	Car boot	Torch	Tap
Pants	Car bonnet	Full stop	Lift
Biscuit	Petrol	Queue	Drawing Pin
Nappy	Post	Mobile	Lorry
Sweets	Naught	Dummy	Petrol
Pavement	Jumper	Shop	Ladybird

for me which we could pin up on the classroom board.

I had prepared 5 things to do with Mary's class over the next two days. The first was to talk to them, with a globe, about my trip round the world. The day started with a maths lesson (I think!) after registration and school assembly. So like a UK school. Anyway after their first lesson, (and I did help one or two pupils who were struggling), I was properly introduced and I first of all told them about my tour of the world, to meet friends from the internet and see places that I would only have this one chance of doing. The children seemed to be quite interested. Then I put up the sheets of words for the class to see and one by one we went through them asking them what they meant.

Most of these have quite different meanings in the USA. The children loved it! Anyway Mary had told some of the other class teachers about me coming and she asked if I would mind talking to a few others as well. That day I also visited a grade 4 class and a "special" class. With the two years older class I found that they were a little bit more aware of these words, but they still enjoyed them. I also read to them my poem "Eventually It Dawned Upon Him", which went down quite well, in spite of its using UK English words ! Even the "special" class seemed to eventually enjoy what I was telling them!

That evening I made my stir-fry for Mary, which I gather she enjoyed; she said afterwards that it encouraged her to try more cooking for herself!

The next day was my final day in Bay City, but it was even busier as word had got round that I was there and several more classes wanted me to talk to them. I gave my talk about my trip round the world and the UK/USA English words to a 2nd, 3rd & 5th grade class. All seemed to enjoy it. One of the girls in the top grade had been to England, and was giggling before some of the rest of the class, as she had been to the UK a year or two ago, and knew some of the answers!

I had two more sessions with Mary's class. In the morning I played them some Beatles music, and the Peter Sellers version of A Hard Day's Night; the children seem to enjoy it all. In the afternoon session I read them one of my children's books that I had written for my son Tim when he was about 4 years old, called "Miss Chief". I was able to show them the illustrations, as I read the book, because the school had a projector. It was for this session that the Headmistress came in as well to hear what I had to say. She seemed impressed as much as the pupils.

I heard from Mary, some time after my visit, that the children had obviously remembered my story, because every time something went missing in the classroom, "Miss Chief" was blamed!

So my two days in a school in the USA had been a success! Some of Mary's class came up to me at the end of the day and gave me little hugs as they went home. After class finished Mary took me to that special **Espresso café** in Bay City, and I had a lovely vegan salad tea, and Mary had a snack as she wasn't yet hungry. I believed she liked it there too. Then she kindly drove me to my hotel in Flint, and I said my goodbyes there, and thanked her for her great hospitality for three days. What an experience. Thank you Mary for giving me that opportunity.

The night before, I had fixed up a hotel to stay at in Flint, as my train the next morning (yes, I went by a real train, not a coach, on my next journey) was too early for Mary or a coach to get me there in time.

So began another chapter in my journey.

Photos of the actual sheets of words

Chapter 11
The Best Vegan Restaurant in the World, in Fort Worth, Texas!

"They sing songs about Chicago all the time
San Francisco and New York, they're all fine!
But there's a song that's written on this heart of mine
About a town, the best around! Let me tell ya!

Fort Worth, No words could tell its worth
Fort Worth, Texas, Best town on earth.
It's Up Town and it's Down Town and it's Cowtown too.
And there's no where like people there say,
Howdy Doo, Glad to see you ....."
by Sanger D. Shafer, Darlene Shafer

{Suzanne}

There are few true all vegan restaurants anywhere in the world, so it was even more surprising that, in the state in the USA which is renowned for its cattle ranching, one can find such a rare phenomenon. Not only that, but since I visited there they have opened up a second one in Dallas!

Anyway on my 37th day, October 26th, my taxi arrived 15 minutes early to catch a 6.41am train from Flint to Chicago. Due to various hold-ups, mainly the frequency of goods trains going in the opposite direction, we eventually arrived in Chicago 2 hours late. It is well known in the USA that goods trains have priority over passenger trains, and not many long distance tracks are dual tracks, so the poor passengers often have to wait in sidings to let the commercial powerhouse trains, who own the rail tracks, and can be up to a mile long, to pass. But even though I was 2 hours late, luckily I had a long wait for the train to take me to

Fort Worth, and managed to catch that train as it left at 4.30 pm on time. We now travelled almost due south, and overnight we eventually reached warmer climes. Although there was much stopping overnight and we were 90 minutes late at one time, we eventually arrived in Fort Worth, after passing through Dallas, only 40 minutes late. We had passed through Missouri and Arkansas, places like St Louis, Pontiac, and the famous Little Rock, and surprisingly, a place called Malvern!

Fort Worth station was a model for all towns and cities everywhere, because it had an excellent travel interchange. One large mall-like pace where one could book travel on trains, buses, coaches and taxis, with good clear indicators for each service and a central waiting area. Each service had its own booking areas, and there was a central information office, as well as a few shops and cafes. Other places could well do with visiting Fort Worth travel centre and trying to copy its approach to integrated travel. I was able to catch a bus to my hotel, which was on the outskirts of Fort Worth, the Regency Inn. I actually had to change buses getting there, but discovered that the second bus only took me two stops, which only really crossed the South Freeway! It was walking distance, even with my heavy luggage. I found there was a hotel restaurant and they made up a vegan version of a Mexican salad for me for the evening meal. That evening, using my phone card, I was able to phone Sharon, Jess, and Suzanne. I also tried to phone Kami, Brooke and Karen.

I arranged to meet Suzanne on the Monday, her only day off. She had wanted to take me to Spiral Diner, the vegan restaurant, but unfortunately it was closed on Mondays. It was with this phone call that I found out about it. I now had three full days in Fort Worth, and only one person to meet, as I never man-

Fort Worth Buses have cycle racks on the front.

SPIRAL DINER - Best Vegan Restaurant in the world

Sunset near Fort Worth

aged to make contact with Brooke, the seventh person I failed to meet up with! So I had Saturday and Sunday to amuse myself in Texas!

I spent most of Saturday 28th October in Fort Worth. I walked across the main highway's bridge to a large out of town shopping centre, explored a few of the shops, found one where I could buy fruit etc, and then caught a bus to the centre, and that went past the Spiral Diner. Suzanne, the one friend I did meet, was a vegetarian, and she had told me about this wonderful place where she often ate, which was all vegan. As we couldn't go there together, I had decided to hunt it out and give it a try. I had one of my favourite drinks there, fresh pressed carrot juice. I then caught another bus to take me into the city centre, and wandered round. I found that the Library service allowed visitors to the USA to use their Internet Service free for an hour a day! So I spent an hour and a half. There was no one waiting to use the computer so I was allowed more time. The other place I spent time in was the large bookshop, where I bought two books. I think they were the two Dan Brown books I had not yet read! I was reading more than usual on this trip, on trains and at night and early mornings.

I also found a Smoothie shop, and discovered that they had some described as vegan, so had my first taste of a smoothie, called Jumba juice! From memory I believe it was based on carrot and beetroot, with a soya base. It really was good. On my bus back I decided to go and eat at Spiral Diner, and asked the rather over-large and friendly bus driver to drop me off; he was not a person, to look at, whom I would have expected to be a patron of such a place, but he spoke enthusiastically about it, and dropped me off at the stop nearest it. Anyway I got a large fresh salad, probably one of the best value salads I have had anywhere in a restaurant. Then I spoilt myself and had some vegan chocolate cake, which was orange in colour! Apparently orange was the Halloween colour, and it was made that way especially for this up and coming "festival".

That evening I ate my fruit dinner, read and had a little wander round near the Motel and took a few sunset pictures. Next morning I stocked up with fruit from the local store; the free breakfast was not much more than a cup of tea and a roll, so I needed more nourishment. There was still no more news from Brooke, so I decided to go and visit the Fort Worth Zoo. I had not been to a zoo for years, and was interested to see if they had improved from the days I remember seeing animals in small cages. Being able to get bus rides for only $1 a day (being over 63!) I took advantage of this. It was a lovely day. The weather was just like the far off days of a hot English summer, and it was almost November! The Zoo was definitely better than the old fashioned types, but still some of the enclosures were far too small. At least the animals did have some space to move and play, and many had acceptable sized enclosures. The main thing in their favour, though, was their work in trying to conserve rare species. Gosh, it was a hot day!

On my way back to my motel I dropped off at Spiral Diner and had another lovely salad, and carrot juice. I took an extra one away with me for my morning drink. Yummy, what a way to start a day! That evening Suzanne rang to check about our meeting the next day. Also Kami rang re my visit there in two weeks near San Francisco.

The next day Suzanne arrived in her Mother's car and took me into Arlington, and we had lunch at an Asian restaurant where she often ate because they knew about Vegetarians and Vegans. She was obviously a regular customer there, because the manager/owner gave us a FREE meal! Suzanne worked at a

Suzanne and the largest sticker ball in the world!

Two of the five history murals at Fort Worth Multi-transport Interchange

store nearby, as did her boyfriend, Eric. Eric, by the way, had phoned her mobile a couple of times to check that she was OK, before I met him later at the store. He seemed a nice guy, of Mexican origin with USA citizenship. We talked a lot in his place of work, a CD/DVD Music shop; Eric was not over rushed with customers. Then Suzanne returned me to my motel, as she had to go and pick up her younger brother from school, the reason why she was able to borrow her mum's car! So it was a short but interesting meeting with a young friend (I think she was in fact the youngest friend whom I met on my trip) whom I had only previously met in a Veggie Yahoo Group. She told me how, not long after we first talked in the group, she had suffered a serious illness whilst on a school trip to Italy, when her appendix burst - thus explaining her long absence. It took a long time to get over that. Anyway she is now in good health. She also very kindly gave a me gift of a book about how vegetarianism is growing in the States. It's a pity we could not have spent more time together, and with Eric too. I really liked her and her boy friend. It was a real pleasure meeting her, and I am still in touch via Facebook.

I phoned the three previous hosts (Maggie, Teri & Mary) mainly to thank them for their hospitality, and also I spoke to Domi for the first time on the phone to set up our meeting in LA.

Day 42 was the last day of October. Today, besides being All Saints Day and Halloween, was my last visit to Spiral Diner and I had another beautiful salad. And another take away carrot juice. Really, anyone who enjoys food, whether or not they are Vegan, and is in this area, should pay them a visit. I found time to spend another hour on the library's free Internet service before catching my train to Oklahoma. The name of this city (or state) always brings back memories of the film "Oklahoma", and here was I actually going there, to stay! And later, not very far away, to stay in another placed famed in song, Tulsa (24 hours from Tulsa, by Gene Pitney). Most of the places I visited in the USA seem to have musical connections!

The day was still hot. My train left on time at 5.25 pm, but as seems to happen on most Amtrak trains, it was nearly an hour late into Oklahoma City. This train ran only twice each way every day, morning and evening, and was subsidised to keep the service, so that Oklahoma was connected to the rail network. The lateness was for the usual reason, that goods trains have priority! Here at the station I met my first Zorpian, ... but that is the Next Chapter.

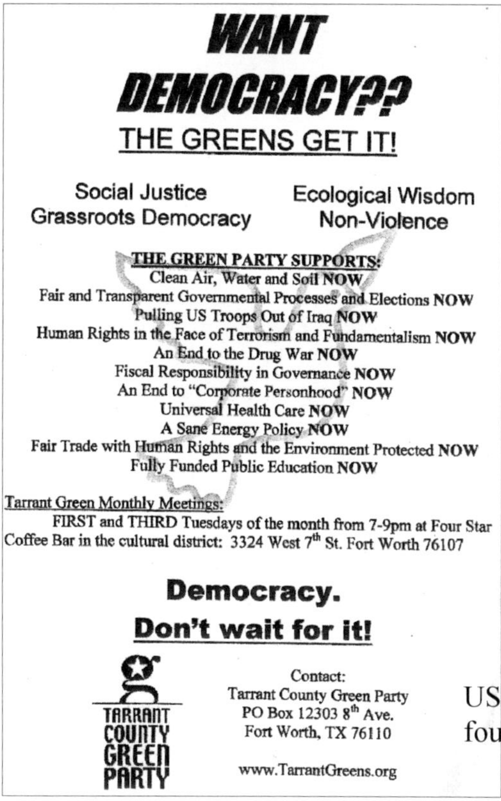

WANT DEMOCRACY??

THE GREENS GET IT!

Social Justice — Ecological Wisdom
Grassroots Democracy — Non-Violence

THE GREEN PARTY SUPPORTS:
Clean Air, Water and Soil **NOW**
Fair and Transparent Governmental Processes and Elections **NOW**
Pulling US Troops Out of Iraq **NOW**
Human Rights in the Face of Terrorism and Fundamentalism **NOW**
An End to the Drug War **NOW**
Fiscal Responsibility in Governance **NOW**
An End to "Corporate Personhood" **NOW**
Universal Health Care **NOW**
A Sane Energy Policy **NOW**
Fair Trade with Human Rights and the Environment Protected **NOW**
Fully Funded Public Education **NOW**

Tarrant Green Monthly Meetings:
FIRST and THIRD Tuesdays of the month from 7-9pm at Four Star Coffee Bar in the cultural district: 3324 West 7th St. Fort Worth 76107

Democracy.
Don't wait for it!

TARRANT COUNTY GREEN PARTY

Contact:
Tarrant County Green Party
PO Box 12303 8th Ave.
Fort Worth, TX 76110

www.TarrantGreens.org

USA Green Party Leaflet found at the "Spiral Diner"

Chapter 12
OKLAHOMA

"We know we belong to the land
And the land we belong to is grand!
And when we say - Yeeow! A-yip-i-o-ee ay!
We're only sayin' You're doin' fine, Oklahoma! Oklahoma - OK"
(Richard Rodgers & Oscar Hammerstein)
{Reggie}

Here at the station, on October 31st, the 42nd day of my journey, I met my first Zorpian, Reggie and her, now, fiancé. They had only JUST that weekend announced their engagement, so I was one of the first to know! They kindly took me to my hotel and arranged to pick me up at 10 am the next day. I was staying at the Econo Lodge.(1750 East Reno Avenue). And here began another chapter in my tour.

Reggie and Joey turned up on time at 10 am and first of all took me to see the sombre memorial for the 1995 Oklahoma massacre.

(The Oklahoma City bombing was a domestic terrorist attack on April 19, 1995 aimed at the U.S. government in which the Alfred P. Murrah Federal Building, an office complex in downtown Oklahoma City, Oklahoma, was bombed. The attack claimed 168 lives and left over 800 people injured. Until the September 11, 2001 attacks, it was the deadliest act of terrorism on U.S. soil. Shortly after the explosion, Oklahoma State Trooper Charlie Hanger stopped 26-year-old Timothy McVeigh for driving without a license plate and arrested him for that offence and for unlawfully carrying a weapon. Within days af-

ter the bombing, Timothy McVeigh and Terry Nichols were both arrested for their roles in the bombing. Investigators determined that they were sympathizers of a militia movement and that their motive was to retaliate against the government's handling of the Waco and Ruby Ridge incidents}

Then they took me to a happier part of Oklahoma, the botanical gardens, including a tropical house. There were many interesting plants here, but my many photos I took were sadly lost, as were most of my photos for the rest of my USA journey (the story about that loss will be told in a later chapter). Afterwards we ate at a Chinese style buffet restaurant, and then Reggie had some university work that needed finishing and I spent a little time catching up on the net and had my mid day nap, back at their flat.

In the evening they took me to their church Meeting for young people, mainly singing, followed by readings and, more interesting to me, discussions. I had thought provoking chats with a few, including one student from Hawaii. Then I was returned to my hotel to rest well for November 2nd, my 44th day, which proved to be very interesting.

When I planned this trip, I never thought that in the USA or anywhere, would I be teaching in primary schools, and even less be a student in universities and even for a few minutes a lecturer in a University, all in the space of three weeks! Well, Oklahoma gave me that chance at the top end. Reggie was a student at Oklahoma University, studying English and literature. She had a few classes to attend whilst I was staying there, and she had asked her lecturers if it would be alright for me to join a couple of lessons, and they said it would be fine. So my first lecture in University since I attended a week's computer course in Cardiff in the early 1980's was in Oklahoma University. They were studying the historical novel by Toni Morrison, a

Reggie & Joey

Reggie & her cat

Marbellous Books
Tulsa Library

renowned coloured writer, about the life and tribulations of a runaway slave girl in the USA in the 1870s, called "Beloved". I found this so interesting that I just had to get a copy and read it, which I did on my return to the UK. For lunch we returned to Reggie's flat and I cooked my stir-fry for Reggie and Joey, which they seemed to enjoy. Then it was back to University where I joined Reggie's class in "Changing English". I can't quite remember how it happened, but I had with me the list of words on a rolled up sheet of paper that I had used at Mary's school in Bay City, and for a short while I took the class, showing how English word usage had changed in the USA. The students were more aware of these words than the 7 year olds, and the Lecturer more aware than the school teachers. But even he was pleased to learn a little!

After that I was returned to Reggie's flat, and whilst Reggie was busy I napped and caught up on emails etc. I also finished off my Stir-fry of which I had had too much to eat in one go at lunch, and the box of Vegan Ice Cream I had discovered when buying food for the stir-fry! Then we spent the evening at Reggie's Church of Christ Bible Meeting and social afterwards.

Afterwards I was returned to my Econo lodge and I prepared for my next journey. Reggie had offered to take me to Tulsa, (which I was now 24 hours away from!) to drop me off to meet my next "daughter". (Well, she called me Papa Bear as did Reggie!) In the early morning I used the internet free in the adjoining hotel, before Reggie and Joey arrived at 10.20 am to transport me to Tulsa Library. I did pay their fuel costs! I had booked one more night in Oklahoma for the night before I was to go on my next great journey, after my meeting with Ruthie (Piglet!) and her husband on my 45th day, Friday November 3rd.

Thanks, Reggie and Joey, for such a wonderful warm few days. HUGS .

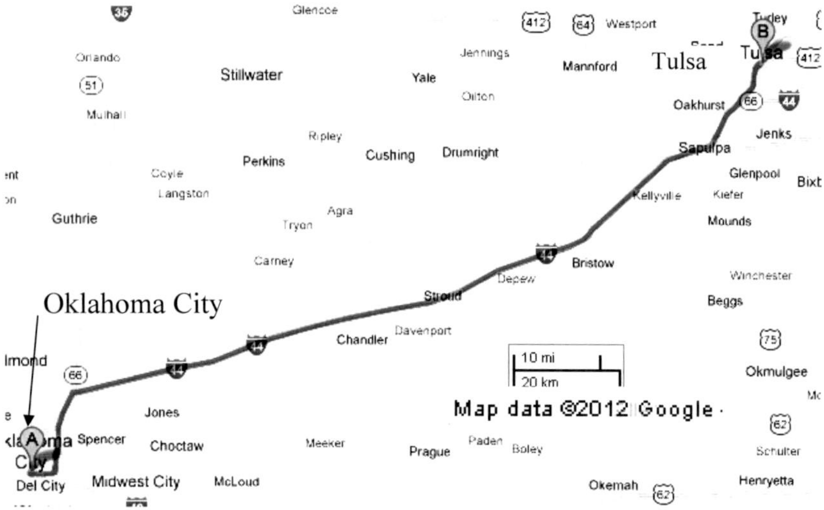
Oklahoma City
Tulsa
Glencoe
Westport
Orlando
Stillwater
Yale
Jennings
Mannford
Oilton
Oakhurst
Mulhall
Ripley
Jenks
Perkins
Cushing
Drumright
Sapulpa
Coyle
Glenpool
Langston
Kellyville
Kiefer
Guthrie
Agra
Tryon
Mounds
Carney
Bristow
Depew
Winchester
Stroud
Beggs
Chandler
Davenport
10 mi
20 km
Okmulgee
Jones
Map data ©2012 Google
Spencer
Choctaw
Meeker
Prague
Paden
Boley
Schulter
Del City
Midwest City
McLoud
Okemah
Henryetta

Chapter 13
TULSA

GENE PITNEY - 24 HOURS FROM TULSA *(H. David; B. Bacharach)*
"Oh I was only 24 hours from Tulsa
Ah only one day away from your arms

{Ruthie}

The words have no bearing on my meeting Ruth, but I just remember that song from the 1960s. Now I was going to another place famous in song, and a chance yet again to get to meet a great Internet friend. We had nick names for each other: she called me Papa Bear, and because she had Pooh Bear with her in one of the first pictures I saw of her I called her Piglet!

So on my 45th day, November 3rd....

Reggie & Joey very kindly left me at the Library, having got a bit lost finding it, and as I had over an hour to wait for Ruth to finish work, I spent an hour on the internet in the Library, free, as it appears to be all over the States. There were some interesting marble statues of books and a man reading a book outside, which I saw rather a lot of, and had to take their pictures! Eventually Ruthie arrived, having had trouble finding me, and at 6 20pm I was whisked away and met for the first time this lovely person, and her husband Denis. I had got to know Ruth in various Yahoo Groups. We had a good chat that evening, well past normal bed time. And yes, Ruth was just like the Ruth I expected from our internet chats and messages in Yahoo groups, only a little older.

After breakfast Ruth and Denis kindly took me to the next state, Kansas, to Coffeyville, to see a historical mansion, The Brown Mansion. Coffeyville's Brown

Mansion makes quite an impression. The three storey 16 room Mansion was completed in 1904. It was far ahead of its time and had features such as an alarm

system, elevator, and a walk-in ice box.

The home was built by W.P. Brown, a businessman who moved to Coffeyville from Ohio in 1890. He first started a lumber company, but discovered one of the largest natural gas wells in the country. He then

founded the Coffeyville Mining and Gas Company and owned several other businesses including a 40 acre amusement park and a Natatorium (spa).

The mansion was designed by Edward Wilder and Thomas Wight, who studied with Stanford White, and the house shares features with several of the famous homes that White designed. Some features of the home (such as the height of the steps) were designed to accommodate Brown's petite wife, Nancy, who was only 4'11".

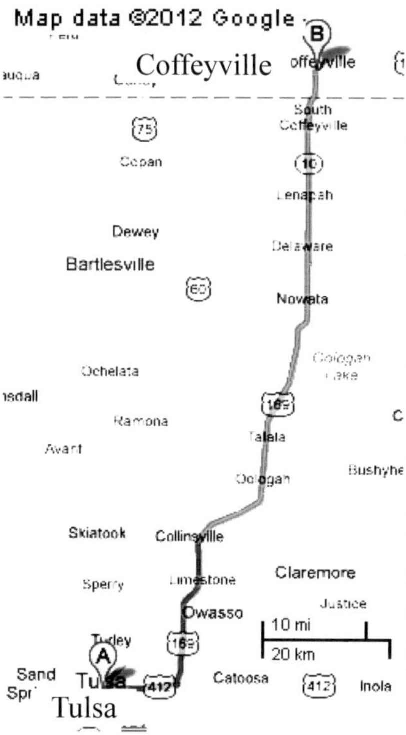

After this interesting visit we found a restaurant and I had a nice salad lunch and returned to their home and had a very interesting evening talking about many things. On the phone I was able to talk to Ruth's mother, and very briefly Sarah, her twin sister, and sister Naomi, and also Dopey, (real name Annie, who for some perverse reason of hers called me "Snow White". Just had to put this in!)

Another late night, after talking and laughing and reminiscing, and a few revelations!

After breakfast the local ducks were swarming (yes, it was swarming and not swimming!) outside their door, and we just had to feed and photograph them! Eventually we dragged ourselves away and met some of Ruthie's friends and ate at a lovely salad bar.

Famous Bank in Coffeyville, Kansas

Me feeding the ducks, outside Ruth's flat

Before returning to their flat, we took the now customary group photos. Then Ruth and I had a another long chat, and Denis slept soundly on the floor with the dog (see picture!)

Eventually we had to say our final goodbyes after Ruth and Denis took me to the bus station to catch the bus back to Oklahoma. Time was only too short, as with my meetings with all my internet friends. The bus was an hour late leaving, and eventually, after a taxi ride from Oklahoma bus station, I arrived back at the Econo Lodge for my last night in this wonderful Oklahoma state, immortalised by Rogers and Hammerstein.

Chapter 14
Oklahoma to Tombstone in Two Days

"Mama's in the fact'ry
She ain't got no shoes
Daddy's in the alley
He's lookin' for the fuse
I'm in the streets
With the Tombstone blues" (Bob Dylan)

Days 48 & 49 (Nov 6th & 7th)

You may have heard of mile long trains in the USA. After breakfasting at the hotel and a taxi ride to Oklahoma in the early morning, I had the experience of seeing such a freight train. Standing on the station looking north one could see a dead straight track to the horizon. After a while one could see a train approaching, apparently very slowly. It seemed just a speck, then gradually it got larger, and eventually one could make out that it was a train. The station tannoy system announced that this was not the passenger train to Fort Worth, and it was not stopping and to stand well back. Eventually its approaching form was close enough for us to see that it was a freight train. It was trundling along at about 50 mph and it looked BIG; engines (I can't remember how many but at least three) were hauling truckloads of huge containers, stacked in twos, and for what seemed ages, containers went by two by two, like animals in Noah's Ark. We could not see the end of the train, and later we could not see either end, but it still passed us by, rattling as freight trains do, for ages. Eventually we saw the end, and that took ages to reach the platform. Gradually silence was restored, and the giant snake was past us and on its way to goodness knows where!

Not long afterwards our passenger train arrived. There were two trains per day, just Oklahoma to Forth Worth and back. This was subsidised by the state to keep the passenger link alive. No other passenger service came this way, though much freight was using the lines that crisscrossed this state of great plains.

On the train I was sitting opposite a lady travelling with two delightful little Native American girls, ages 4 and 6. She was caring for them whilst their parents were serving a term in jail, and was taking them to stay somewhere in Texas for a week or so. The elder one was learning to write, and was keen to show off her new skills, and after showing me she could write her name and a few other words, she wanted to write mine by copying it after I wrote it. She was so proud of her achievement that she copied it several times. She liked drawing too, and made a lovely picture for me, which I have kept with some of her writing. Luckily I used my small camera to take pictures of our meeting on the train. At Fort Worth we all alighted, about an hour late, and, sadly, never saw each other again.

It was kind of weird being back in Fort Worth. After a few hours of waiting, the train from Chicago arrived and we dragged ourselves to the allotted coach and up to the upper floor to our allotted seats.

The two Native American girls

The elder girl drew this picture for me :)

The Texan Bush, low & prickly

The train left a little late; this seemed to be the weakest point in USA trains, lateness. I was seated next to a 70 year old lady from Montreal, Marylyn, who was travelling to Phoenix to stay with her 97 year old mum for the winter. We had a lot of interesting chats. The train got later and later, mainly due to freight trains passing in the opposite way. Out of the windows we saw the Texan desert Bush which was small, low and prickly! And lots of it!

Eventually, after passing through such places as Cleburne, MacGregor, Temple, Taylor and Austin (sounds more like a list of schoolboys than towns), we arrived at San Antonio, where we had a 5 hour wait overnight. Whilst waiting was part of the experience, we spent a great deal the time in movement, being shunted backwards and forwards, for what seemed hours. The point of this was that at San Antonio another train also arrived, but from the East Coast. Both trains were split in two; one half of each was to return to their starting points, Chicago and New York (I think), but then the other two halves had to be joined up - a simple job, one would have thought! But oh no! The various types of coaches had to be in the correct order, keeping the sleeping compartments, and the First Class and second class coaches in the right order throughout the combined train. Although rather tired I was not sleepy, and was watching what was happening all the time. It took ages! I just wonder how most people slept through these seemingly constant backwards and forwards jolting movements. They were in general quite careful in making these movements and re connections, so there were few jerks and crunches. Eventually it was all done and after a long time we left, nearly on time.

While we passed close to the Mexican border during the day, we could actually see Mexico from the train. This was the nearest I got to visiting yet another country! Del Rio and El Paso were particularly close to the border. After leaving the huge state of Texas, we passed through Deming and Lordsburg in the southern state of New Mexico. During the day Marilyn and I continued our interesting chat. Having run out of food, I did sample a lunch-time salad in the train's restaurant, and they were able to rustle up a nice vegan one for me. The train was due to arrive at Benson at 10.45 pm, but we were told it would be an hour late. So I rang Jess to let her know the 'bad' news!

Benson was another "experience"! Till now all stations had been typical USA stations with low platforms and needing portable steps for passengers to get on and off. But arriving at Benson in the middle of the night was like being dropped off at NOWHERE! There was a small hut and no platform of any kind. The train stopped here only if someone was due to get on or off. This great big long train used up loads of energy for stopping and starting for just me to get off, in the dead of night! What a privilege! No lights on the station, but I noticed one person got on! But here I was met by my longest known Internet friend, Jess. I was greeted with a big hug and also met her then partner, Carmen.

Mexico as seen from the train

Chapter 15
"Forward To The Past" or R.I.P. Tombstone!

{Jess}

Tombstone was built up on its silver mines in south Arizona; its main "industry" now is tourism.

Jess and Carmen whisked me off to the hotel where they had booked rooms for us for a couple of days, and we went more or less straight to bed. I was talking to Dilys on the phone at 7am, but her 3pm! After breakfasting we drove to Biosphere 2, just outside Tucson.

Imagine an oversized greenhouse that is completely self-sustained. Here you'll find a controlled environment and a variety of habitats such as desert,

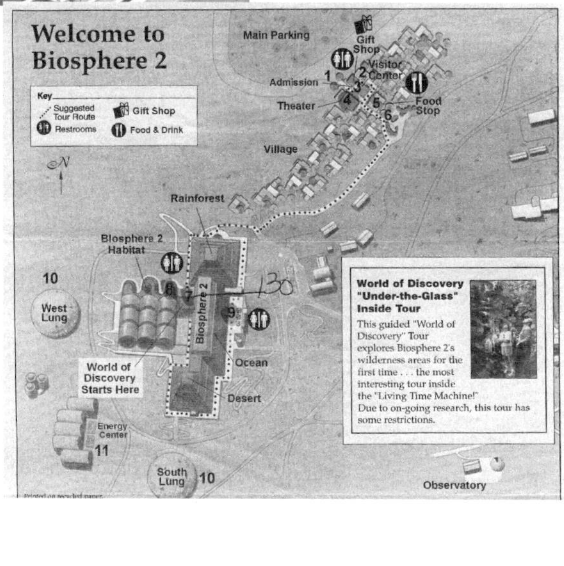

rainforest, ocean and mangroves.

The Biosphere 2 project was built in the 1980's to simulate the environment of Earth, dubbed as Biosphere . This airtight replica of the earth's environment was funded by multi-millionaire Edward Bass. Visions of colonizing the moon and Mars were the inspiration behind this $150 million experiment. By creating an airtight structure and sealing people inside it, the designers hoped to discover the problems that could occur when living in such an enclosed environment.

Two teams of Biospherians lived in the Biosphere. The first team spent two years sealed into this 7.2 million cubic square foot glass structure. They encountered various problems, including limited agricultural productivity and air leaks. The second team of Biospherians suffered socially and was pulled from Biosphere 2 before the 2-year term was up. The Biosphere 2 Project became the subject of much ridicule and lost a great deal of credibility over this. There are no future plans for human habitation in the Biosphere 2.

Since the experiments were suspended, Biosphere 2 opened for tours in November of 1996 and is now a tourist attraction complete with hands-on science activities. The Biosphere 2 has been upgraded with a conference centre, parking, visitor's centre, theatre, and gift shop.

A guided tour "under the glass" will take your breath away as you look down into the rain forest pyramid before seeing the self contained mini world spread out before you. You'll be taken into this incredible world where you'll stand on a cliff above the saltwater ocean. You'll wind your way through the savannahs, tropical thorn scrub, the desert and the techno-sphere where all the controls are located. You'll go into the south lung complex and learn about the "lungs" which prevent the Biosphere 2 from imploding. You'll also go to an underwater viewing exhibit.

Curious how the Biospherians lived and worked? You'll see their living quarters, their farm and their kitchen. A $200,000 trail system throughout the Biosphere lets you get up close and personal to the various parts of this world.

This really was a interesting experiment, and I enjoyed seeing it. It reminded me of the Eden Project back in Cornwall, UK, which I had yet to visit (and did in 2009). After our guided tour, we had time to wander round parts on our own. Later we found a nice salad bar to have lunch.

Now one of the first things I remember Jess talking to me about was ghosts, so when we discovered a Ghost trail in Tombstone for that night, we just had to go. We learnt a bit about the past history of Tombstone and some of the anguish from days gone by and how some spirits were still haunting the town. It had been hot all day, but on the tour, being so late, (10.30 pm to 1.30 am) it got rather cold. The woman who led the tour was obviously an expert in her field, and it was very interesting. But for my part I am sorry to say I never glimpsed a ghost. Though several in the group did believe they saw spirits in the shadows. Certainly a tour not to be missed.

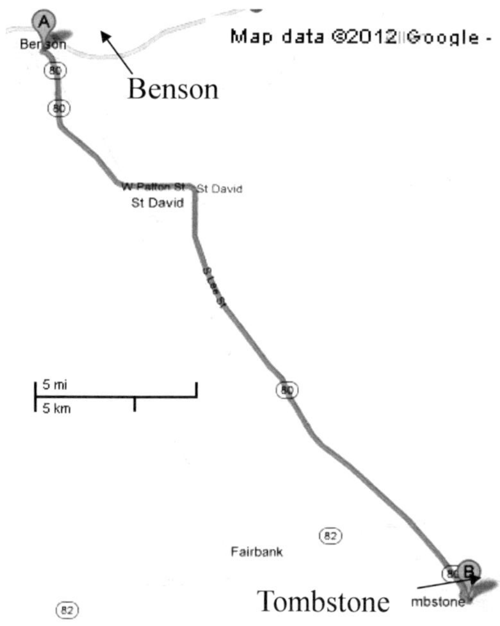

Next morning I woke up and had about 90 minutes on the internet at the hotel, and after a late breakfast we walked around the amazing Tombstone in the day light. Amazing in that the majority of Tombstone had been kept as it was

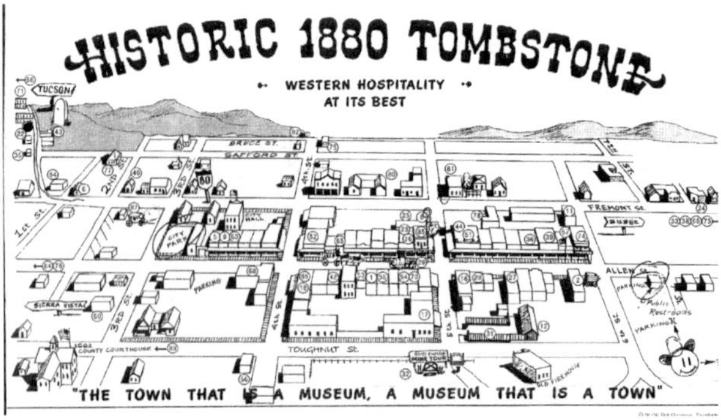

in the 1880's when the famous Wyatt Earp was in charge.

The sidewalks were all of wooden construction, just as they were 125 years ago when the famous street battles took place. The shop fronts were mainly of the same period, and many had actual artefacts from the period or reconstructed stuff to resemble that time zone. Many shop keepers were dressed in the period, and in the street a few people were dressed as though they were people of the period too. NO MOTOR vehicles were allowed after 9 am in the main streets, and only horse drawn vehicles were plying the roads, giving rides to the visitors in stage coaches and carts!

The bars and restaurants were probably the best examples of being "kept" in the past. The whole atmosphere inside was 1880s. The appearance of the people serving, the serving of the food and the entertainment were all very good. Having seen films of this period in the Wild West, one really could feel the atmosphere here. I managed to get a nice salad with French fries (in vegetable oil!) After lunch we found several shops that offered to take photos of people dressed up in costume in singles or groups. Jess, Carmen and I of

Jess

Most of this group of photos are by Jess

High Street, Tombstone

Carmen Jess Me

Stage coach rides in Tombstone

course had to have ours taken too. The costumes were in fact fake, made to easily fit over our normal clothes and fixed up at the back by ties!

After this we went to see the daily re-enactment of the famous Wyatt Earp Gun fight in Tombstone in 1886. This told the story of how and why it happened. We heard what caused the 30-second showdown that left three cowboys dead, Virgil and Morgan Earp wounded. It was presented in an open air theatre. We saw Wyatt Earp, Doc Holliday, Virgil and Morgan Earp fight the McLaurys and Clantons in the daily re-enactment inside the O.K. Corral at 2 p.m. This is repeated every day!

We were afterwards able to stand beside life-size replicas of the nine gunfighters poised on the very spot where the 1881 shoot-out began.

After that we toured C.S. Fly's Photo Gallery and saw his world-famous 1886 photos of the Apache Chief Geronimo, and his historic photos of 1880s Tombstone life; and walked through the O.K. Corral as it appeared in the 1880s.

We were even able to purchase copies of the newspaper of that historic day, including the description of the court case.

After this great historical tour we went back to the future and Jess and Carmen booked in at their hotel, a few minutes away from the "station" of Benson. We then found a restaurant where I was able top get a delicious fruit dinner, and then went to their hotel, in Benson, to await my train at 10.45 pm.

Little did we expect to now be leading actors in our own "drama".

Jess was able to ring Amtrak to check the trains. Remember the Benson station (wooden shed!) was unmanned. Remember also that my train had arrived an hour late! Well, the shock report was that the train was reported to be 4 HOURS behind time, so it was not expected to arrived before 2.30 am! So we had time to kill. We stayed in their hotel room, talking and dozing and reminiscing. After 3 hours we decide to ring Amtrak again (1.30 am) and the lady who answered said the train was at Benson Now!

PANIC! Never in the field of hotels have a group of three people left a room so fast and pulled away at

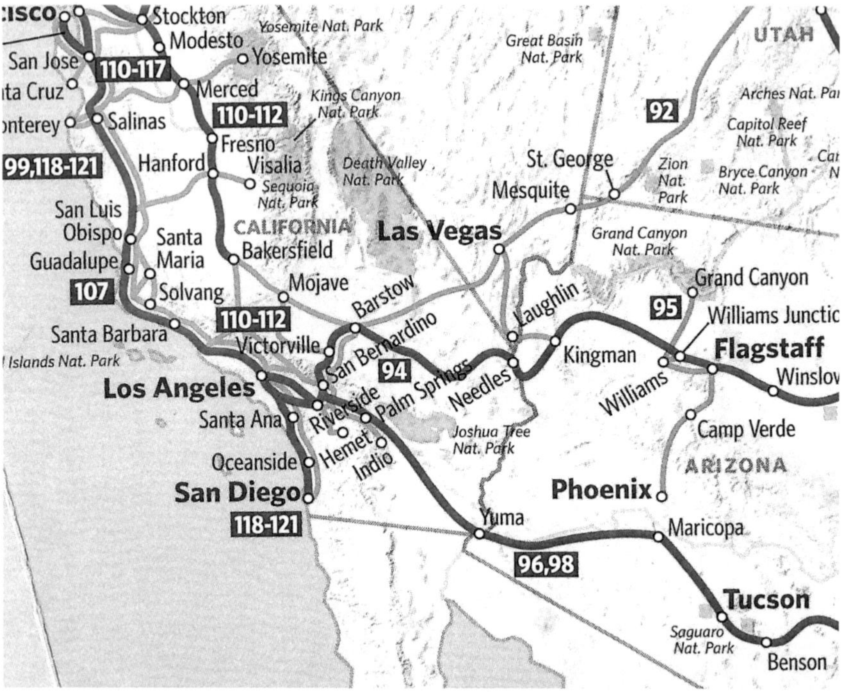

rocket speed for the 5 minute journey to a empty wooden box beside a deserted railway track. The car park was empty, there was no one there, just silence of the pitch-black night. At first we thought the train had gone. Not long after our arrival, a car drew up and parked. The occupants were hoping to pick up a friend off this train. We saw a train coming a long way in the distance; the light was all we could see, and it wound round the track slowly, ever so slowly approaching us. We assumed it was my train and got ready to board, but the engine showed no signs of slowing, and as it passed we knew why... it was one of the infamous freight trains. Eventually it passed and silence returned, and we returned to Jess's car and re contacted Amtrak, to find out that the recent call had been in error, the train was still on track at 4 hours late. Twice more we had false alarms of freight trundling through the dark of the night, and eventually, just after a third person arrived, to catch this train, the train did arrive. The train staff brought out the ubiquitous steps and allowed us two to get on and one get off, not before I said my fond farewells to Jess and Carmen, with big hugs and grateful thanks for such a wonderful two days, with an interesting closing episode!

WHAT a two days that had been. So great to have met you again, Jess. Jess was one of the few internet friends whom I was meeting for a second time. In November 2002 I was invited to her wedding blessing, and went and spent a week in Phoenix with her and her then husband, and had the most wonderful 7 days being shown round Arizona. I do hope that she will have the chance to visit the UK one day, and Dilys and I can show her round, in particular Scarborough.

Chapter 16

California here I come

- Jess to Kami on train **(10th Nov 52nd day)**

*"If you're going to San Francisco
Be sure to wear some flowers in your hair
If you're going to San Francisco
You're gonna meet some gentle people there.*

I was shown to my seat, and checking my diary I find I slept for 5 hours! With dawn hurrying to overtake me, I woke up and had an interesting chat with a man in the lounge, but what about I have no recollection.

I do remember, though, finding out why the train was so delayed! Now, one would have thought that the passengers who were already on board would have known, but surprisingly enough none of those I asked really knew, so I took the obvious liberty of asking the train staff! Apparently the train from the East coast that joins half the Chicago train had had an accident with a car crossing a level crossing before San Antonio, and although the train had stayed on the track, it had had to stop whilst investigations were held, before it could resume its journey. I was worried about the train arriving in LA in time to catch the connection from LA to Bakersfield, and expressed my concern about this to the staff. Anyway, about an hour or two later, as we trundled along, making up NO lost time, near the Mexican border, passing through Tucson, Maricopa, and Yuma, we were told they were attempting to make some special arrangements for all those going to San Francisco. About an hour before our arrival at Palm Springs, we were told that a special coach would take us from Palm Springs to Bakersfield, hopefully in time to catch the Bakersfield to San Francisco train.

We duly arrived at Palm Springs, and those of us going to Bakersfield alighted and were shown to a coach, which was pretty full. I was lucky enough to get

Two scenes seen from the coach from Palm Springs to Bakersfield

Mountains we had to cross from Palm Springs

Wind farm on mountains round Palm Springs

a front seat and was able to talk to the "spare" driver, with whom I had an interesting conversation, so my diary says! It also says that one of them would email me. As I never got that email, I have no recollection of this! I did take many photos (luckily from my small camera) of the country side from the coach, from the valley sides covered in windmills, to the more raw beauty of the hills and mountains. Oddly enough, the two carriageways of the motorway "swapped" sides going up this pass, and before the descent to Bakersfield and the rolling plains of California they resumed their correct positions. We arrived in good time to catch the train that we should have caught!

These trains were the usual two tier trains, and I found myself sitting near some students playing cards. I asked them what they were playing, because it resembled Rummy! It was their version of Rummy (there are many versions of this card game!) and they kindly invited me to join in. What friendly people they are in the USA! Anyway I was glad to join in. It helped pass the time, for outside there appeared to be miles and miles of vineyards. My new friends departed before my stop, and not long afterwards the train pulled in at Stockton station, 2 minutes EARLY. Somehow I had missed seeing most of the stations along this route, but apparently I passed through Wasco , Corcoran, Goshen, Fresno, Madera, Merced, Denair, and Modesto! This was the first USA train to be <u>early</u>! Not bad considering the day had started 4 HOURS late. Wonders will never cease! I had phoned Kami to confirm that I was to be there on time, and not 4 hours late!

Kami was the second Internet friend whom I had met once before, a few years previously, when she and her parents visited London, and Dilys and I had taken them around parts of London one summer's day. Kami arrived a few minutes later and took me

A Nodding Donkey, pumping oil

The extensive Californian Vineyards

back to her flat which she shared with her boyfriend. We had a long interesting talk till just past midnight! Another long day over for me.

Chapter 17

Kami in Stockton, California.

{Kami}

The last time I had seen Kami was in London, when she was a 16 year old girl, with her parents, and Dilys and I had spent the best part of a day showing them round parts of London (Hyde Park and two Museums). She had grown up since then, but still seemed the caring young person I had got to know in a couple of Yahoo groups. Stockton is a town (city) near to San Francisco and was near to where Kami was at University studying music, eventually hoping to be a teacher of music in schools.

Anyway 11th November was a Saturday, so she had no classes. After my late 7.30 am (for me!) getting up for some fruit breakfast, Kami and Jimmy took me out to Stockton malls and a Trader Joes (where you can get some excellent organic and high class health foods). We ate at two different restaurants; I had salad at the first (lunch time) and a vegan Sushi at the other. Then in the evening Kami took me to her university, to a classical concert where they performed Stravinsky's Petrushka and Rite of Spring. This was very enjoyable. Kami is very knowledgeable in Music (well, she ought to be, as she wants to be a music teacher!)

Next morning we all rose late and went shopping for food, to enable me to cook my stir-fry for their lunch, which they seemed to enjoy. In the afternoon Kami took me to a peaceful area, where I gather she liked to come to relax from the bustle of the world. There was a lovely lake near woodland and hills around. The lake was low, due to low rainfall recently. We saw many birds, and I took several photos of the scene and Kami, but I never saw these photos - see the Argentina chapter for the reason. On the way back to Kami's we saw a couple of coyotes which crossed the road in front of us, in the dark. That night it was early to bed (well, normal for me!) after deciding what music to use for Kami's grade 6 class next morning. Kami had asked me to bring a few CDs of English Music of differing types.

Monday 13th was another rather strange day! I seemed to be getting a lot of them. But it was MOST interesting. Kami and I got up early to drive to the Don Riggio School. I had to have a pass as a visitor. Kami was a student teacher of Music at this school to a class of 11 year olds. I had about 15 minutes to tell them a bit about my trip round the world and to do the UK/USA words. This list was becoming VERY useful! The class teacher was busy noting down all the words, as she didn't seem to know most of them either! I never thought I would ever be teaching people of the USA anything, let alone pupils, teachers and University Students and lecturers about ENGLISH! This was a subject, when I was in school, that I was not very good at, and I needed to take my 'O' level exam three times to reach a pass standard! But that was a long time ago. After the pupils had enjoyed this lesson, Kami used some of my CDs to play them some Beatles, John Rutter and Elgar. Later we went to another school for Kami to observe a music class (Hoover Elementary, again I had to carry a pass round with me). Most of the pupils here were Spanish speakers, having classes in English.

Next was to Kami's University for a Singing Lesson in English Composers; the teacher there was very friendly and allowed me to sit in and listen. After that I was able to surf the net and check emails on a computer. After that we went to a long teacher training lecture, which most of the students appeared to think was useless, reminding me of my teacher training year in some respects.

Then Kami dropped me off at my hotel in Stockton (a Howard Johnson Hotel) which was near to the railway station. This was a slight change of plan, as originally I was to have stayed my last night with Kami, but she needed the time to do some unexpected work next morning and would not be able to take me to the station from her flat. We had a big hug and said our final goodbyes. So ended a jam packed three days with Kami and her boyfriend, days which will be engraved on my memory bank. Kami is a lovely young lady and I am sure she will do well. I hope that she too will pay another visit to UK.

Chapter 18
Here I come LA!

There's a fog upon L.A.
And my friends have lost their way
We'll be over soon they said
Now they've lost themselves instead.
Please don't be long please don't you be very long
Please don't be long or I may be asleep
Words from Blue Jay Ray by George Harrison - The Beatles

(S.L.T., Domitila}

When I arrived at the Stockton Railway station, after a quick early breakfast and a walk lasting about ten minutes, I discovered another anomaly in Amtrak. There were TWO stations, and I had been staying in a hotel near the OTHER station! I had arrived at this one, but I had to depart from the other one! Luckily there was a bus connection, which got me there in time, and I eventually went back to Bakersfield station on this train, passing through the fertile lands of California, and from Bakersfield the normal coach took us up and over the mountains and down the long descent to Los Angeles and its railway station. The "Days Inn" Hotel was within easy walking distance, up a slight hill from the station, and I checked into my pre-booked room for a couple of nights on the 4th floor. Well, it was a different level at the back and front, it seemed, being on a hillside; the front seemed to have three extra floors! Luckily there was a lift. There was free internet access there and I spent a bit of time catching up and rang SLT.

SLT was the person I had come to LA to meet, the second friend I met from Zorpia. SLT might sound a queer name for a delightful young lady, and it is not her real name, which is Domitila. Domitila is from Guatemala, living in Los Angeles, California. SLT actually stands for Sexy Latin Tiger! Well, she turned out to be rather on the small side, so there was only a little roar from this tiger, but she was a BIG person in Zorpia. Very mysterious, and intriguing. I certainly considered it an honour and a privilege to meet her the next day. I had spoken to her only twice on the phone before I met her, once about a week ago and tonight.

That evening I went on an exploratory walk about, and in a very Spanish area with outdoor markets I found a delightful vegetarian café "Casa de Sousa Coffee House.

Here I had a lovely fresh Vegan salad, followed by Vegan Ice cream. I can strongly recommend this to all, especially vegetarians and vegans. In the evening I made several phone calls and checked with the airline that I was to have vegan meals from California to Argentina, and booked my Howard Johnson Hotel near the airport in California, which ran a free bus shuttle service to the airport.

After a reasonable night's sleep, the next morning, after phoning Dilys, I was excited at the expectation of meeting this so mysterious SLT. At 11.20 she finally arrived in her car with a work friend, Fred, who drove her car and took us to a lovely restaurant **The Cheesecake Factory** in LA, and I had a another salad. We had an interesting talk over the meal, and yes, she was small, and Latin, but no tiger; her roar was more like a purr, and she was aMEWsing. She was such a nice person, I really was so glad to have met her. We were next taken to the Santa Monica beach and I walked on the hot sands and paddled in the sea with SLT, in the oh so warm Pacific Ocean! Luckily her

friend Fred had his camera with him, and I have a record of this meeting. It is amazing how many lovely daughters and granddaughters I have "discovered" that I have around the world, who have had nothing to do with me till I met them on the Internet! Sadly the pair of them had to return to work, to make up the time they had taken off to meet me. But it was worth coming all this way for those few hours. That evening I returned for another salad at the Casa De Souza, and a takeaway ice cream! Yummy! That evening I talked to a few people to check final arrangements for meeting in the future part of my trip.

I now had in effect two long days of travelling, with meeting interesting people on the journey to San Francisco, but that is another story!

Chapter 19
Back to San Francisco and goodbye to USA

Before I left my hotel I was able to phone Dilys, and in good time I walked with my heavy luggage back to the railway station, but more easily than coming because it was downhill. I caught the 10.45 am Amtrak coach to take us to Bakersfield, to go on my last Amtrak train of the journey. We left Bakersfield at 1.20. This line seemed to be much better at keeping to time that other Amtrak trains. But as "normal" for Amtrak, although I had booked to go by rail from LA to San Francisco, the first part and the last part were both by Amtrak coach!

On this train, after catching up on some lost sleep, I woke up to find an interesting conversation going on between a mother, a Spanish lady, a Yugoslavian lady and a young lady, Caroline (about 22), who was dressed in a uniform-type long dress, and carrying and reading her Bible. I thought just how like my friend Kim (from Antigonish) she was in profile. They were actually talking about Home Schooling, which is a much bigger and better organised way of education in the USA than in the UK. Caroline, it turned out, was one of the many groups of "alternative" Christians, called Mennonites. We were talking about a variety of subjects, including home schooling, religion and cats.

Caroline was telling us a bit about the Mennonites, and how everyone has to be dressed modestly, and to us a bit old fashioned in appearance. After I returned home, I looked up on the net about the Mennonites and found this simple information: *"At the centre of Mennonite teachings is the need to believe in Jesus Christ as the one who died and rose from the dead in order that people could live in union with God. Mennonites believe that the life and teachings of Jesus guide our daily living. They believe that the church should keep Christ's life and ministry alive in the world, just as though Christ was still living on earth: that's why they refer to the church as the "body of Christ". Mennonites believe that the church is made of people whose sins have been forgiven and who choose to follow Christ's teachings. Mennonites believe that Christians should try to relate to each other and the world in the same loving, forgiving way that Jesus practised."*

They certainly believe in a more simplistic way of life, and a dress and appearance code. Women usually wear long dresses with hems no higher than half way between the knee and feet, and covering their arms, and a headdress or small hat to cover most of their hair. The men wear a beard but not a moustache, and hats and old fashioned type clothes.I am glad that I met this young lady; she was really open and friendly.

We passed the Stockton Station (where Kami went to University) and at Martinez we had to change to an Amtrak coach to complete the journey to San Francisco. I asked the driver if he went anywhere near the airport, and he said no, that was out the other side of the City. I asked if there were a bus, and he told me that I would probably have to get a taxi. We passed over the famous bridge at night and reached the final stop on the journey. The driver then asked me to wait behind and asked me exactly where I needed; I told him the hotel and its address. He told me a taxi would probably cost me about $40. Then he surprised me by saying that he would take me to the hotel. I told him I hadn't got much money left, in fact it was about $25, and I would need about $5 for various things at the airport, so he said "give me what you can afford", and I gave him $20; and he very kindly took me a longish way out of the city, couldn't find the hotel, and stopped at least twice to ring it on his mobile to ask for directions. Eventually he pulled up right close to the hotel, thus proving to me that in North America, in both Canada and the USA, there are people who care and will go out of their way to help. My first day in Canada I was helped, and my last day in the USA I was helped, by people who had no public duty to, but did so anyway.

So my only night in San Francisco was at the Howard Johnson Hotel near the airport. After a reasonable night I had some of the free breakfast that these cheaper range hotels offer, a self service choice of foods, juice, tea, coffee, cereal, toast, etc.

So my last night in the USA was 16th November, the 58th day of my journey.

Chapter 20
Don't Cry for me Argentina! (Evita …..)

It won't be easy
You'll think it strange
When I try to explain how I feel
That I still need your love
After all that I've done
You won't believe me
All you will see
Is a girl you once knew
Although she's dressed up to the nines
At sixes and sevens with you

I had to let it happen
I had to change
Couldn't stay all my life down at heel
Looking out of the window
Staying out of the sun
So I chose freedom
Running around trying everything new
But nothing impressed me at all
I never expected it too

I was about to do something else that I had never done before: go and stay in a country where I cannot speak or understand the language, and go on my own. Luckily my internet friend I was going to stay with, with her family in Buenos Aires, was a keen and proficient English speaker, as was her fiancé. But I was still 24 hours away, and had a long journey to take part in first, and not without its dramas!

My first part was getting up in good time, packing and eating the Free Breakfast before being whisked away by the free shuttle bus service which toured all the local hotels in the area to get us to our flights on time. There was in fact no hurry! The plane arrived 1½ hours late, which meant it was that late leaving too! We had a reasonable time at Dallas/Fort Worth airport for the flight to Buenos Aires. But I was anxious all the time in case we were late. We are supposed to be there at least an hour before the flight leaves. I had checked in at San Francisco and it didn't need the all the security measures going through again, but we had 25 minutes to change planes! Which we just about did! THANK GOODNESS! I must mention something else here. At the check in at San Francisco I found that one of my bags was overweight, but the rucksack could be heavier, so using the scales, I made the case just at the limit and put the Camcorder and a few other heavy things into the rucksack. It was all done in a bit of a rush. As we were limited in the number of hand luggage, I had put the camcorder back in the rucksack. I wished now that I had not had to do this.

At Dallas/Fort Worth (yes, I was back again in Fort Worth!) I was also worried about the luggage being transferred too, as we had no way of knowing! My flight to the Southern Hemisphere and to a totally foreign speaking country was now in operation. I was looking forward to meeting my Internet daughter Lisa (in the sky with Diamonds) and her family who were so kindly going to put me up in their home for 6 days. Lisa was a massive Beatles fan, and into 60's music and a lot of things English. We had met in a Beatles and a Vegetarian Yahoo group.

Still some drama to come though.

Yes, the drama of nearly missing the Argentina flight was small compare to what happened later. The plane took off only a few minutes late, at around 2pm and headed south towards the southern continent and over the equator. By the time we reached Buenos Aires I was, in time, 4 hours closer to home as well. When it was time for the main dinner, I found that being Vegan was not a priority on this flight, i.e. we veggie people didn't seem to get served first! When most people had had their meals, I eventually stopped one of the flight attendants and asked about mine. Some time later, when most people had finished their food, a very apologetic man came and told me that in error they had given my meal to someone else, a Vegetarian! He asked me what I did and didn't eat. Later still they came with a large plate of salad and a few other things and a fruit drink. It was a meal that a business class person had ordered as a vegetarian, but he had missed the flight. They had had to take off the dairy produce, but otherwise it was fairly satisfactory. In fact in some ways better than I would have got as a standard flier. After I had eaten the meal, their chief flight attendant came to apologise again and offered me a voucher for 1000 Air miles free as a compensation token. To me this was purely a token, as I could not hope to use them, as they applied to American Airways only! (I found out later.) Anyway I got about 4 hours of restless sleep and early breakfast was OK as we approached Argentina over Paraguay. It was a long dark flight. I felt that American Airways service had deteriorated. The last time that I had used them was in 2002 to go to Phoenix to meet Jess for the first time. Their air seats were definitely not as comfortable as the trains.

The good news though was that the flight was about 15 minutes EARLY!

So started a lovely and interesting stay with my Argentinian friend, whom I had been dying to meet for some time, one of my "internet daughters" Lisa. Though I was made entirely at home by her lovely family, this next episode was not without its dramas. Worse was still to come. It was now Saturday 18th November, 9.15 am Argentinian time! And I was nearer the South Pole than the north for the very first time. I was about to experience life in a loving caring home in a non English speaking country.

Chapter 21

Buenos Aires, the home of the Tango and Mate Tea

{Lisa, real name Melisa.}

And of the lovely family of Lisa. I had known Lisa as "Lisa In The Sky With Diamonds". I came across Lisa in two Yahoo groups. One was a group for Beatles fans run by Rachel Brown from the USA, who came over to the UK for a year and spent a few days with us at Christmas in 2003, in between terms when she was in College in South London. The other, also run by Rachel, was called "Lettuce Leaf in the Sky With Diamonds". Later I found Lisa ran her own Yahoo group, based on her love of George Harrison, which she ran with the help of her friend in Montreal (Maud), whom I met earlier in the trip. She also had a Yahoo group for Synaesthesia, a condition I had never heard of before, which she had. Synaesthesia is where one sees colours associated with certain words, sounds, or music. It can be associated with smells as well.

I had got to know Lisa quite well, and we had often talked in MSN or Yahoo messengers as well as her Yahoo groups. She was still at school in the early days, and a kind of "Father/daughter" relationship grew. I found her command of English very good. And so Lisa was very keen for me to come to Argentina, and she and her family very kindly invited me to stay a few days with them in November. She would have preferred a week or so later, when she was fully on holiday, but it was so difficult to arrange to be at any country when it was the best for everyone. In those 6 lovely days Lisa did have a fair amount of time to show me around Buenos Aires, in between a few classes she had to attend. In spite of the three events when things went badly wrong, those few days are certainly one of my most

Lisa's Tortoise

Sebastián's 18th Birthday party

Cutting of the cake, with firework!

pleasant memories of this trip.

The love and kindness of Lisa and her family towards me began on my arrival at the Airport. I knew that her Father would be in the arrival area, as he worked at the airport, though not in this department; he did have the pass to enable him to meet me before I went through customs etc. He saw me first, I believe, because I saw an official looking man waving to me as I came through the "gate". Ernesto was not as good at English as his daughter, but we managed to exchange greetings and he kindly showed me through the customs and arrival places. I feel sure I got through much quicker with his presence, than I would have done had I been on my own. After going through about three check points, we finally collected my luggage, which to my great relief was there, and then I met and found myself being hugged by Lisa. Her father was not working that day, so he quickly took us to their car and after quite a long drive we arrived at their home. It was about an hour's drive, further from the airport than I had expected.

I was introduced to the rest of her family. Her mother not only speaks English, but teaches English privately to a number of after school pupils most days, including Lisa's brother, Sebastián. Later I met her grandmother, who seemed to spend most of her waking life here, but lived with her sister in another house a few streets away.

One of the first things we did was go to the local shops and find a phone card that allowed me to phone people anywhere in the world cheaply, via a landline phone. We talked a lot as well as catching up with my emails etc. The first surprise was that it was her brother's 18th birthday party that night! One of the guests was Javier, Lisa's then fiancé, (that relationship has ended) who also spoke good English and was keen to speak it like an Englishman. We had exchanged a few messages in MySpace, of which Lisa was also a member!

One (very) nice kind of surprise was that, when meeting family and friends of the family, male and female, it was the custom to give a hug and touch cheeks. Lisa's brother's friends coming to his party seem to consist mainly of young attractive girls! So I quite enjoyed this kind of greeting; it took a little getting used to, especially with males, but it was fine. Some of the males knew that there was a difference in the UK and used the English custom of shaking hands. The party didn't seem to start till about 10 pm! His girl friend brought him a lovely Birthday cake. Lisa had made sure that there was enough vegan food for me and her. She was the only vegetarian in the house. I was lucky enough to have a dance both with Lisa and her mother, which was nice; it reminded me that when I went to the wedding blessing of another great Internet friend in Phoenix Arizona in Nov 2002, I had also had a dance with my friend Jess and HER mother!

The party went on till at least 4 am - well, that was the time that I eventually got to bed! A long day! AND I had had only 4 hours sleep the previous night!

First we had to make up the bed. Originally it had been planned that I would sleep in Lisa's bed in the room she normally shared with her brother, but eventually we decided that it would be best if I slept in the bed made up for me in the front room, because I was an early riser, and it would have meant me possibly disturbing Lisa early (for her) by having to go through the room in which she was sleeping in the mornings.

What I have failed to mention was the first absolute disaster that I "discovered" not long after my arrival. I was keen to show Lisa my camcorder, the one that takes such lovely photos, close-ups and distance shots as well as movies. When I was in San Francisco I had

Central Buenos Aires

Lisa's "George" tree, planted in the memory of George Harrison, in the garden

Central Buenos Aires

taken the camera and its heavy case out of the suit-case and transferred it to the rucksack, to even up the weights, so as to avoid extra payments. The camera case carrying the camcorder was put below other things so as not to be obvious. When I opened up the rucksack at Lisa's, I pulled out the camera case, and thought it seemed lighter, and found the camera GONE! All the other things appeared to be present. Just the camera appeared to be missing. And nothing else was missing either, or so I thought at the time. All the spare cards, lenses, battery , battery charger, were still there. I came to the only reasonable conclusion, at the time, that I must have left the camera out at the hotel, or it had fallen out of the case, when at the airport and I was changing it. So I left it till the Monday to start making enquiries at the hotel and airport. Luckily I had my little Sony camera still, and got some nice pictures of the party.

Sunday had already come long before I retired to bed and slept! But after a late rise Lisa took me to the City centre. A wonderful day, marred at the end by a second disaster, for me.

To get to the city centre we had to travel by bus, train and metro. It was when travelling on the train that I found out one of the differences that one can expect in Buenos Aires, the constant salesmen selling their wares on trains. At practically every other station a man would get on and work his way through every carriage one by one, first of all giving everyone one of the objects he was selling. It might be a hair product, or a photo, or a rhyme or a cleaner, almost anything not very large, which he can easily carry lots of. He would then stand at the end of the carriage which most of the passengers were facing and tell us (wholly in Spanish of course, so I was never tempted to buy! what he was selling): it might be a straight forward sales or some sad story about someone needing help.

After his talk he would then collect up most of the objects, and on making the very occasional sale he would take the money offered, Some of them had a young child with them who would do the giving out and collecting. Lisa of course was able to explain some of what the things were or supposedly helping in a charitable way.

Lisa had rather excitedly got a list of about four veggie restaurants in Buenos Aires, and being latish we made our way to them one by one, only to find them all closed on a Sunday. Eventually we found an Italian restaurant which would provide us with a vegan salad. I know how disappointed Lisa was, as she had gone to some trouble to find out where the places were. She then took me to see a few historical sites in Buenos Aires. It was here in the early evening in a pedestrian precinct that we saw a demonstration of the Tango. Buenos Aires is the home of the Tango. I never knew that before. As they say, we learn something new every day. I am sorry to say I cannot remember very much about the importance of each of the buildings she told me about, and I photographed in the early evening darkness. This may be partly because the next disaster which was about to occur took place.

We retraced our journey of Metro, train and bus. Apparently fewer people offered their sales once it was dark! Nothing untoward happened on the steel wheeled transport; it was the rubber wheeled transport that shook me! We waited in the bus queue, and got on, Lisa seeing to the tickets; what seemed odd was that the ticket machine was behind the driver. Whilst Lisa was putting her coins in the machine, I was about to grab hold of the vertical bar for steadying passengers, when without warning, with a queue of people still waiting to buy their tickets, the bus lurched, not only forwards but also sideways as it pulled out to pass the parked car in front of it. All I remember was grabbing the bar, and then finding myself collapsed on the floor, and with much pain in my right ribs. Unknown to my brain memory cells I had missed the bar and crashed into it, due to the rather violent lurch, and I must have hit hard my right ribs, and this knocked me out for a few seconds, long enough for me not to remember anything from just about to hold the bar to being on the floor. Lisa was of course very concerned, and I said I was alright, well, alright enough to continue the journey home. It was of course rather painful, and once in the house I found the arnica cream and arnica homoeopathic pills I had brought with me to try and cover all eventualities. I am glad I had the foresight to carry such stuff with me. I rubbed much cream into all the painful areas, and took the pills. I also had some ice to put over the area. There was nothing broken; it was just a bruise. I also found a small cut on my elbow, for which I had a suitable cream as well. Trying to get to sleep was not easy, and after about an hour I got up and put on alternate hot and cold compresses on the worst areas. Eventually I got to sleep till 8am with a COLD compress on the spot. Lisa's mum was very kind in helping to get me these hot and cold compresses during the night.

The next morning I had breakfast in the morning sunshine in the garden. I wrote up my diary, put more arnica cream on the bruised areas, answered emails and took a few pictures in the garden, including Lisa's pet tortoise and her famous "George" Tree, planted in memory of George Harrison of the Beatles. We had lunch after Lisa woke up, about midday! After lunch Lisa took me out to local shops to purchase some foods to make the stir-fry the next day, and a wok to cook it in, and a couple of cake tins.

On the phone I managed to talk to someone at the

Hotel in San Francisco to see if I had left my Camcorder there. I did the same to the San Francisco Airport. They said they would let me know in the next few days if they had found it or not. I explained that I would only be at that address till the 23rd.

Later Lisa and I played Chess. She put up a gallant effort, but after 2 hours I finally beat her! I phoned Rhiannon (in New Zealand) to check with her re my visit, and discussed the possibility of staying an extra two days, because she wanted me to stay longer. For the rest of the evening we all chatted till 1am!

Next morning the pain in my ribs had subsided, and we went shopping for more food for the stir-fry and the cake I was making them that night for all 5 people. It was whilst out shopping that I realised that there were many stray dogs hanging around the streets most of the time. They seemed quite harmless, and sorry looking.

This was my first time cooking in the southern hemisphere and the stir-fry was stirred in the same direction as in the north. It worked well for this, but the cake was a disaster! It seemed OK when being mixed, but when cooked it went flat almost like a biscuit. Must be the wrong way I stirred it! In fact, I found out why: it was the wrong type of margarine that I used. I had got Lisa to check that the ingredients were all vegan, but forgot that it could be a low fat marg. They are 50% water! The stir-fry was a success, and Ernesto took many pictures including a video on his camera, which is up in Zorpia in my Video collections.

That evening Lisa had to attend her Music school, for a rehearsal for the concert the next day.

Later that evening, after Lisa's return, we talked on the phone to Rhiannon, the first time the pair had talked to each other apart from in the Yahoo Groups.

I was now exactly half way through my trip. This was the end of my 64th day, Tuesday 21st November

The eating of my Vegan Stir Fry

Lisa

The Tango at Airport

The chocolate "cake" that turned out to be a biscuit

2006.

The following day Lisa took me out for the day to a lovely riverside place, normally about an hour away from her home, but we had to wait over an hour for one bus. We also travelled part of the way by train.

It was in the station shop that the third disaster struck; this time it was poor Lisa who was affected. We came out of the shop and then Lisa discovered that her wallet was not there, anywhere in her bag or pockets. We went back into the shop and I looked around on the floor and the shelves of goods for sale and Lisa asked the shop assistant, but we found nothing. We had noticed a few youngsters in there at the same time, but had thought no more about them. We saw a police woman in the station, and Lisa told her about the theft, but the police did not seem to think they could do much. What was so bad was that in the wallet was not just her cash, but also her identity card, the actual and copy! And other cards like library cards etc. We made our way to the local police station and found them just as unhelpful as the policewoman on duty. Apparently unless there had been a hold-up with violence or violence threatened, they said there was nothing they could do. Lisa was able to leave her name, address and phone number and a description of what was in the wallet, in case any parts of it turned up, because only the money would be of use to the thieves. We returned to the shop and left them the same details.

Naturally Lisa was terribly upset. I did my best to console her with listening and talking and hugs. We then found a nice spot by the river on the other side by crossing the bridge, and had our picnic lunch.

After returning by train and bus to home, we went out again because that evening it was Lisa's big evening at her Music School We travelled by bus (I was very careful to make sure I had one hand on a support all the time!) to the hall, and Lisa introduced me to some of her friends there. We used the usual Argentinian friendly greeting, and I saw the whole concert. Lisa sat with me during the parts she was not performing in, and explained a bit about the chorus singing she was doing. I took a few photos and videos of this event on my small camera. After the event Lisa was certainly more cheerful again, and she was so pleased that I had come to watch her show. I really had enjoyed it.

First thing after breakfast Lisa had to get sorted out getting herself new ID cards, and I printed off my car hire agreement, from an email, for my days in New Zealand. Lisa took me out by bus and train. We changed trains at one stop so that we could meet up with her fiancé, Javier, who was to be with us for most of my last full day. As I needed to get my flight from Wellington to Sydney changed from Nov 30th to Dec 2nd, we had to find the B.A. Office, which we did, and then we made our way to Lotus Neo Thai Vegetarian Restaurant This was one of those that Lisa had tried to take me to on the Sunday. I can recommend this to any vegetarian/vegan, It was nice to know that such places exist in Argentina. We really enjoyed our meal there. After eating we made our way back the BA office to finalise my ticket change. Then we caught a train to stop off at some beautiful Rose gardens, before saying my final goodbye to Javier. I was really pleased to meet him. We then returned to Lisa's home and I spent most of the time packing up ready to leave fairly early the next morning.

I want at this point to thank Ernesto and Susanah for their great kindness in having me to stay for 6 wonderful days. Susanah was the perfect hostess and tried her very best to look after me in a strange country (for me, with different customs and language). For

My few hours in Chile Santiago airport

instance, I was brought up to always help and lessen the work that the host has to put in to have visitors stay, and as my bed was in a convertible settee I always tried to do the packing up and putting out each day. But Susanah was not used to this! We amicably agreed to help each other! THANK you so much for making me so very welcome. Ernesto was due to work at the airport the next day, but in the late afternoon/ evening; in spite of this he very kindly and generously took me to the airport early in the morning, which meant he had to return home to take Lisa back and then come back to work later. The long drive from their home was an eye-opener on how varied is the life in Argentina from rich to very poor. At the airport Ernesto was taking many pictures of Lisa and me , especially when we had a final hug. Lisa now has two fathers - Ernesto, of course, and me, her internet father! My days in Buenos Aires had been so happy, inspite of the three disasters.

I now had a two hour flight to Santiago, in Chile, and there I had a wait of 11 hours for my flight to Auckland, New Zealand. We were given a free complimentary meal at one of the restaurants. I found my mobile would not work in Chile! This was my shortest visit to a country on my trip! We finally took off on Friday November 24th at 10.45 pm, after I had taken a few photos of the sunset.

I arrived in Auckland at 3 am on November 26th after an extra long night, much longer that the apparent 4 hours! But on the other hand it was much shorter than the apparent 27 hours.

WHAT HAPPENED on November 25th?

.

Chapter 22
"A Day Not In My Life"

Sunday, Nov 26 2006, 11:02:06 PM

Nov 25th 2006 (A day not in my life!)

What ever happened to THIS day,
I thought, as I in bed did lay.
The day before it was still to come.
The day after I was all struck dumb.
For the day after November twenty fourth,
Twenty five never came forth.
Instead twenty six became a fact
Twenty five I certainly lacked.
By plane I left Chile, feeling hot
Cold definitely I was not.
By plane I arrived in New Zealand,
Pretty chilly, but a pretty land,
But somewhere over the ocean
November twenty five was lost in motion.
The International Date Line
Caused this day to resign.

Now I am in New Zealand!

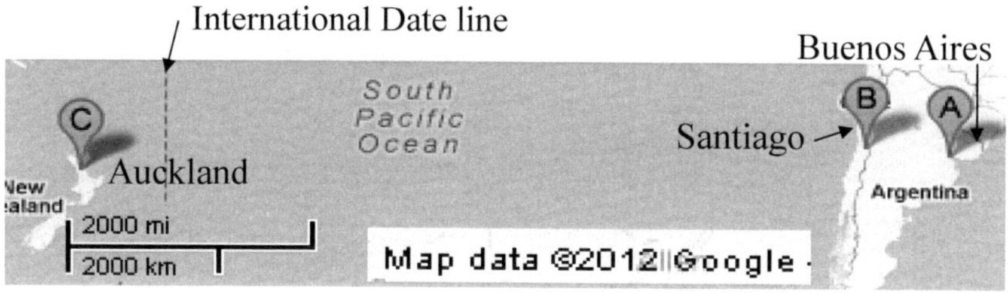

Chapter 23
NEW ZEALAND Nov 26th, the 69th day

{Rhiannon}

The intercontinental plane touched down in Auckland at 3.30 am on Sunday 26th November, NZ time. At no time had I been anywhere on the 25th, hence the poem was written for that day on the early morning of Nov 27th. But a lot was to happen before that, little of it as expected. Anyway, I had arrived in New Zealand, upside down to Dilys back home. It seemed odd that we were now walking with our feet pointing towards each other, through the centre of the Earth!

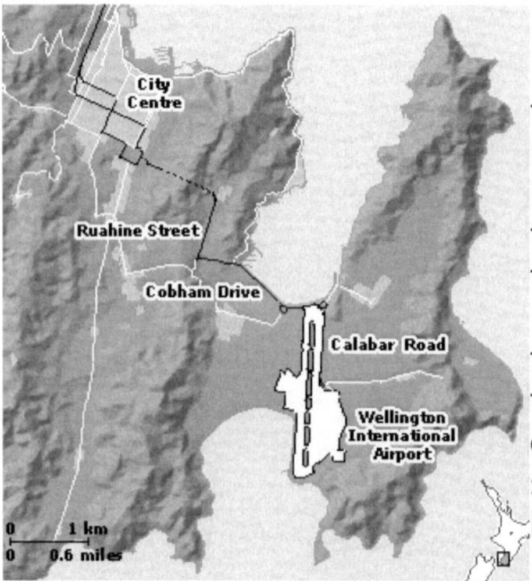

This map shows the reason for the difficult approach to Wellington Airport.

Well, walking was the first thing I needed to do, and I had plenty of time to do it as my short hop to Wellington by plane didn't leave till 8.05am. But no one had told me, before, that it was not from the SAME airport. I had to make my way to the local airport, which was about 15 minutes walk away. I was given a street map, and in the early morning light as day was breaking I found my way to the national airport from the international airport. I actually arrived before they were ready to open the doors. I had passed through the customs without any problem, having eaten up any FRESH food that I had still got, as it was illegal to bring in any raw uncooked food. We had several video warnings on the plane about this! After I had waited outside for about 30 minutes, the doors opened and we could get into the warmer air, and a bit later we could check in. The procedures were much simpler, as it was not an international flight. Eventually we climbed aboard a smaller plane and we were on our way to the most horrendous looking landing by any plane that I had been on. I had been warned by Rhiannon what was about to happen, so there was that reassurance beforehand that it would be OK, but it was still scary. The position of Wellington's airport allowed only one way in, from the seaward side. We came in low, lower, and it appeared for ages that we were about to become a boat; then suddenly the land appeared and we sharply slowed down and finally came to a halt after a short but fast retardation on land! Nerves calmed as we taxied to the berth. Birth was the right way to describe the "docking" as it was like being re-born! The music that was playing on the arrival tannoy system seemed MOST appropriate. "Help!" particularly the words ".........Help me get my feet back on the ground...." I wondered if they chose that song on purpose!

I found the kiosk for the my car hire, and phoned Rhiannon to let her know I had arrived safely, and picked up a white Siron Daihatsu (DLN 204). Now another new experience, driving upside down! But here we were back to the normal side of the road, at least! I had a 2 hour drive to Palmerston North. I had street maps and signs to follow and make my way. There was quite a steep climb to get out of Wellington, over the surrounding hills (which made the airport so difficult to approach), and soon I was speeding on my way

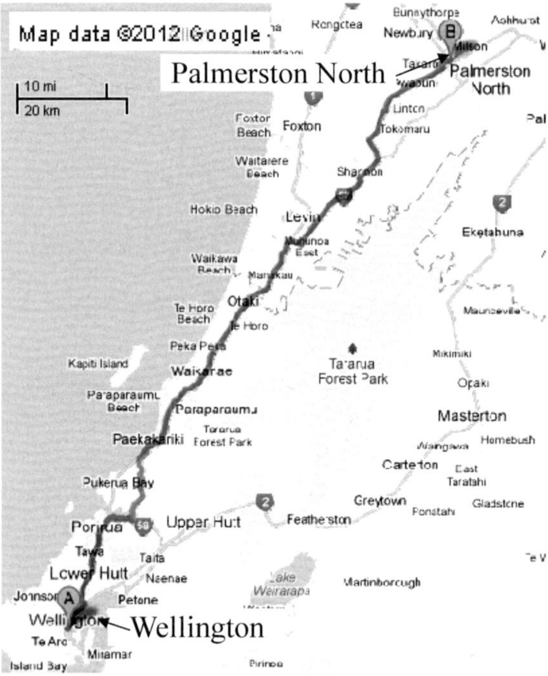

(not really speeding!) to the flatter plains inland. Once in Palmerston North (Is there any other Palmerston in New Zealand, I thought?) I got out my maps and tried to find out how to get to Rhiannon's address, but with one way systems and new roads and traffic lights it took me longer than I expected to arrive, in spite of Rhiannon's helpful directions (I meant that, I was not being sarcastic!)

I pulled up in a kind of lay-by opposite her house and dragged my luggage out and walked across the road and was greeted by an enthusiastic lovely hug by Rhiannon. After many years of knowing each other on the net, and by phone and letter, we had met at last. Rhiannon, after I had settled in with my luggage, then took me round a few local shops to get some food etc. and a phone card. We had a long chat about many things, including her fiancé, who was in Australia. Rhiannon was saying that he would love to meet me when I was in Sydney. Later Rhiannon's mum returned home from work, and after more talking we decided that today was the best day of my planned stay to make my stir-fry for them. I found out that being upside down to home the food did stay in the frying - pan! And after an hour we all sat down to eat. They seemed to enjoy it, as had everyone so far! Anyway we all lived!

After the meal Rhiannon showed me some of her stamp collection; many of the items were ones I had sent her over the years, and she showed me some other things I had given her as well, including the record by George Harrison "My Sweet Lord" in a frame. Later we started planning our trip to the geysers in Rotorua. It was to be a two day trip, staying one night in a hotel/guesthouse. Talking with Rhiannon before, I had learnt that she hardly ever got out and about, so the idea being to give her a memorable and enjoyable couple of days out for a treat, as she seldom got out of Palmerston North. Her Mum seem quite enthusiastic, and said she wanted to come too! We discussed other, more local, places to visit as well. Eventually we retired to bed after making up their sofa in the sitting-room for my bed. We had decided to start the trip on the Tuesday, so we had a day to plan.

Next morning I got up and tidied my bed away, as I was in the sitting room, and had breakfast. Rhiannon rose later; she told me she was not feeling too good, and I got a bit of lunch, and then went for a walk into town and took back the phone card that that I couldn't make work. It was unlike any others I had had in other countries! I found a new one in another shop which made sense, and I found a new camera, my now precious Canon Powershot S31S. I bought it out of the money I thought I would get from the travel insurance, which I hoped to get from the Camcorder's loss. The day before, Rhiannon had talked with enthusiasm about getting a new camera one day, and when in the camera shop I saw the price of decent digital cameras had come down, so I thought I would take her to this shop on the last day of my stay and buy her one of her choice for her birthday. I was quite enthusiastic about this, because she told me she was wanting a new camera, and had often in the past told me that no one seemed to celebrate her birthday! Anyway, I was pleased with my purchase and returned to Rhiannon's house, and her mum had by now got home from work. It was then that Rhiannon told me that her Nan had to take her to a family event the next day, so she would have to miss the two day trip to the famous geysers. That was a pity, because I thought Rhiannon was looking forward to the trip, but it wasn't possible to change the days etc., so I decided to go anyway. Later her Nan came round, and I was glad to meet her, because I had heard so many nice and good things about her from Rhiannon.

Her Nan also explained that my visit wasn't working out from Rhiannon's point of view. Nan also explained why, and I am indeed very grateful to Rhiannon's Nan, for without her I would have been lost as to the reason. Apart from my one return night in two days' time, I would need to find other accommodation.

Next morning Rhiannon's Nan came early for Rhiannon, and I left just afterwards and drove to some of New Zealand's lovely countryside, seeing snow capped mountains in the distance (Tongareiro National Park), and fields that looked very English. What did seem strange, though, was that everyone thinks of New Zealand as sheep country, but I do not remember very many sheep at all! Were they avoiding me? But I did see many cattle in the fields. I drove by Bulls, Taihapw, and Walouru. By afternoon I arrived at the Sulphur Valley region; one did not need to see anything, as the scent in the atmosphere was constantly lingering. I found Wai-o-Tapu Wonderland, one of the places where you could see this wondrous land of rainbow coloured, bubbling, steaming and gushing waters. There were pools of yellow, orange, green and blue lakes, holes emitting steam and mud glubbing blobs sprouting from a mud lake. There were deep holes, small holes, paths alongside these lakes and streams,

Interesting Scenery on the way to Rotorua

Mount Ruapehu

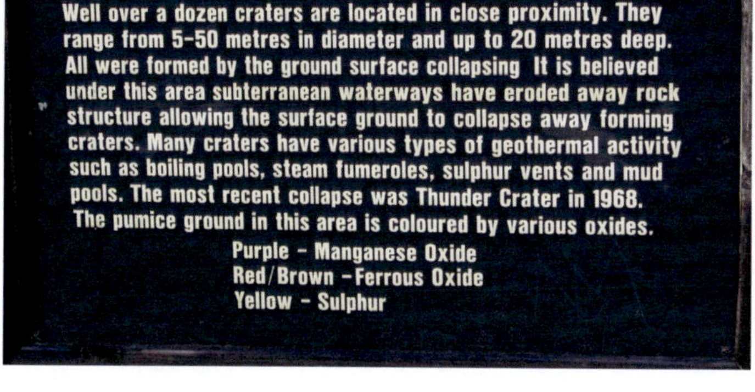

and of course the ever present highly scented sulphurous atmosphere. It was just impossible to get away from! I took many pictures; it's such a pity I could not record the clinging scent as well! I found out that to see a real live geyser I would have to return tomorrow morning at 9.45 am. It crossed my mind, "How did they KNOW at what time a geyser would gush?"

Anyway at closing time I made my way to Rotorua and found a nice small B&B place, on the outskirts of the town, and walked into town to look for a restaurant. I found a Thai restaurant that provided me with an adequate Vegan meal. (I was finding that Thai Restaurants were quite good for Vegetarians!) I was also able to spend a few minutes at an internet café to check emails. I returned and slept fairly well.

Next morning I was up early enough to arrive at the Geysers to witness their eruption. Hundreds of people were sitting in ancient theatre style seats partly around this little volcano-like structure, and then a guide explained all about this area, its history and geography, and then on cue it gushed, at 10.15 am! It was, however, explained, and we were shown, how it did this dead on time every

Various scenes from Wai o Tapu

day at 10.15! But I think I will leave this little mystery as a mystery so as not to give it all away and spoil the show before you, the reader, visit the place. It is quite spectacular, and worth going to if nothing else to learn about why and how it all happens. I took many pictures on my new camera, but was still very much learning how to use it! I also saw something else, a kind of field of mud where every now and then a big bubble would burst with a loud plop. I managed to capture a few of these on camera.

Leaving this sulphurous valley, I drove over the Te Urewera National Park, for 99km of which the road was of unsealed surface, reminiscent of the Yukon, very bendy and hilly. I hadn't realised this from the map, so this journey took a whole lot longer than I expected. Rhiannon's mother had said not to hurry back, but this slow pace was not what I had expected. I stopped for my packed lunch, and often took some pictures of wonderful scenery. Most other drivers drove carefully, and they were few in total, but some left a cloud of dust behind them that enveloped everything for a few minutes! Eventually I reached the end of the dusty road and was back to full speed, and after driving via Napier, Hastings, Waipukurau, Dannevirke and Woodville I arrived eventually at about 10pm. It was dark, and I was entering Palmerston North from an unfamiliar direction. I had tried several times to phone both landline and mobile to let them know I was on my way, but I got no answer or the engaged tone each time. I was so sorry for being so late and explained to Rhiannon's mother roughly what happened. I decided to leave at the same time as she went off to work at 6am, as it was obvious that what Rhiannon's Nan had told me was true and there was no point in staying. I want readers here NOT to feel badly in anyway towards Rhiannon. She is not a bad person - please accept that.

I also want to thank Rhiannon's Mother, Joanne, for so kindly allowing me to come and stay; she made me feel at home.

Obviously I was deeply upset, and left unhappy, especially after such a promising start. It was simply pouring down with rain on my departure. It was still quite dark, and I eventually found my way on the road back to Wellington. I was also heavily sleep-deprived, and had to pull up into a lay-by and grab some sleep in the car, before finding my way to Wellington.

The day brightened up and I found my way around, where the airport was and its car park, and then I searched for a guest house on the outskirts of Wellington in Johnsonville. It was a nice place, a motel, and had its own kitchen unit. After settling in, I walked around the town area, found an internet café and managed to talk to Madam Boo, my other friend in New Zealand whom I had planned to meet. Shirley is her real name, but in Zorpia she was well known then as Madam Boo. I had not known her for very long, but she said she had wanted to meet me, so we arranged to meet at 10 am the next day. I also phoned Mellissa (in Toowoomba) where I was going to stay for Xmas, and she told me that a scan of her baby was OK, baby was the right way up, and no apparent complications. I

The Geyser

& the V shaped Falls

also phoned Chris Yardley, my only ex school friend I was meeting on the trip, and Dilys to explain what had happened. There was a huge amount of dust that had accumulated in the car, from the drive on the dusty roads; I cleaned it out to the best of my ability! It was amazing how the dust had filled the smallest of crannies. I hoped that I had got rid of most of it. I managed to get caught up on sleep, and had a restful time, enjoying the better weather.

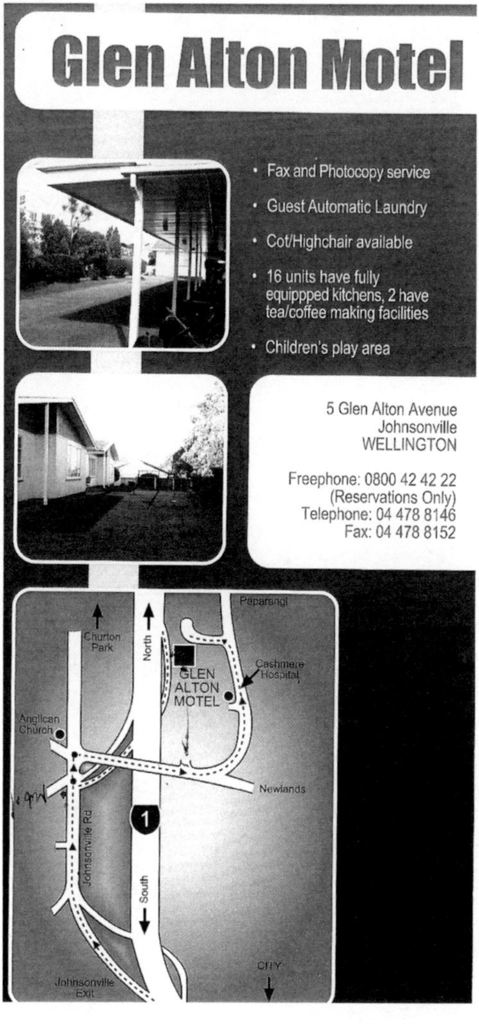

Chapter 24

A day with a Zorpian in Wellington.

{Madam Boo}

I must admit I did not know Shirley very well. Yes, Shirley is her name. But by the end of the day, I certainly knew her a lot better. Before I met her I managed to phone Lisa to let her know what had happened earlier, and explained that I had forgotten to pass on the CD she had made for Rhiannon's birthday. Lisa understood.

At 10 am, outside the Te Papa Museum in Wellington, I finally met the great Boo! Shirley was the third of my Zorpian friends whom I met. Here she gave me a present of some CD's; how naughty of her! Te Papa is New Zealand's national museum, offering visitors a unique and authentic experience of this country's treasures and stories. Over five floors, you can explore the nation's nature, art, history, and heritage - from the shaping of its land to the spirit of its diverse peoples, from its unique wildlife to its distinctive art and visual culture. There was too much to take in in this one short visit, but I was glad to have been taken round and to increase my knowledge of New Zealand's heritage and culture. Shirley is herself a Maori, the first ever Maori I had

Plants seen in the Wellington Botanical Gardens

met. We then found a nice restaurant where I was able to get a decent salad, and then I was shown round a little of New Zealand's capital city. Then Shirley realised that she had left the present she had given me, along with a bag of her own stuff, somewhere. So we hurriedly retraced our steps to the Te Papa and restaurant, and luckily it had been found and we recovered our things. We then found where I had left the car parked and drove out to Shirley's home in Lower Hutt. Here her "ex" was looking after her two lovely children; he had made some tea for us, and I had a chance to get a short nap and catch up on emails on Shirley's computer. I left around 11pm. What a wonderful end to my short stay in New Zealand, to have met the real

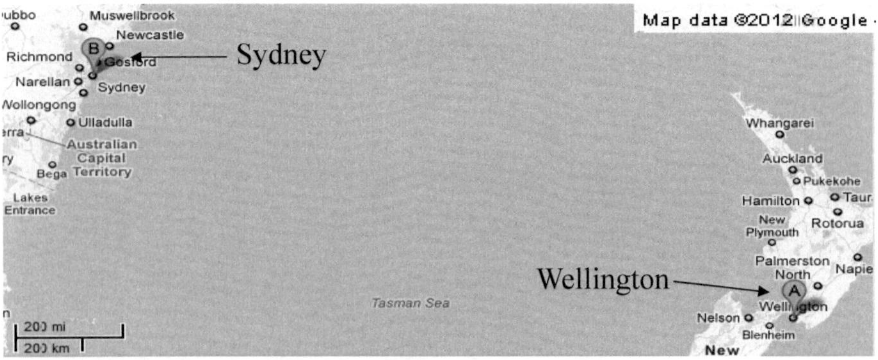

Boo, and her delightful children. On my drive back to the airport car park, I was asked to stop by the police; they were checking people at random for drink drivers. Luckily I had not had any alcohol at all, so I passed and arrived around 11.30 pm at the "Thrift" region of the airport car park. Everything seemed to have shut. I slept part of the time in the car, and read a bit. My flight to Sydney Australia was at 6 am. At 4 am on Saturday 2nd December I left the car locked up, took all my stuff, and passed over the keys.

This was when I had my next shock!

Chapter 25
THAT BIG ISLAND!

(Arun & Jayshree; Mike Dodd)

Before I arrived on the big island, one of the bigger shocks was at the Wellington Airport, when checking in. The airport was gradually opening up when I finally left the car in the correct area of the car park, passed the keys over to the correct place, and then started going through the process of leaving New Zealand and clocking in at the gates. Here I got my shock! Somehow, although I didn't remember the One World airlines system telling me that I would need visas (and so far, except when I paid for one on the Canada/USA border control, my Passport had been good enough), I suddenly found I needed one to enter Australia, of all places. This seemed odd, as Argentina had not required me to have one. The good news was that there was an Australian office only a few minutes' walk away where I could buy my visa! So I did that, thankfully with no trouble. Then a smaller shock was there were airport taxes to pay too! I thought my tickets had covered that! Oh well...

On the plane I thought I must check the visa requirements of Philippines, Hong Kong, Singapore and India, once I got to Australia. The short hop from Wellington to Sydney (well, relatively short) was soon over and I was now in this great continent with strange and weird animals, found nowhere else on Earth.

I was now in the land that my Father always said we would end up in if we dig deep enough on the sands back in England!

It was in this part of my world tour that I met three people whom I had known before the internet. Chris Yardley was the first that I knew, then Arun, followed

**Sydney's Olympic Games Stadium &
the famous Royal Opera House**

**Sydney Harbour Bridge
& Old Post Box**

by Sandra; all for different reasons, which I will explain when I get to their part of the story.

I had previously arranged by phone to catch a train from the airport to Chatswood, where Jayshree met me, as Arun was on his weekly golf game, and I was whisked away to their lovely house in the quiet suburb of Belrose. One of my memories of Arun was after I had left Swansea University, when I went to my interview for my second teaching job in Edmonton. Arun was living with his parents in Enfield and they kindly put me up for the night, when I came from my then abode in Doncaster. I remember especially the meal that his mother made, a real Indian meal. Although very spicy and full of tasty foods of many kinds, it was not the mouth burning heat that I had found in "Indian" restaurants. This was much more "restful" and tasteful eating. Arun, I remember, explained that the Indian restaurants made their meals extra hot because that is what they thought the British expected (or something like that)!

Jayshree was one of the traditional Indian food preparers, and I really enjoyed my lunch with them. After I was settled in and properly introduced, they took me in their car to see the sea and beaches, but the weather was poor. I forgot to mention that it had rained on my arrival. Later I found this was a normal occurrence when I arrived in a new city, in Australia!

That evening we talked about old times back in Swansea (1963/4) as lodgers in Dilys & William Thorne's home, Tavistock Road, Sketty. We were both still in touch with Helga, Dilys' daughter, and had been until fairly recently with Dilys. A few years previously, my Dilys and I had been back to Swansea for a few days and had stayed with Dilys. That was a weird experience, being in the same house as TWO Dilyses. Anyway, back to Arun and our reminiscing. There was the University, the Singleton Park, the Thorne Family and their dog lolo. Then we caught up a bit on what had happened to us after then. Later that evening I got in touch with Mike Dodd, Sandra, and Chris Yardley, on the phone, and fixed up my meeting arrangements with them. I tried a few times to try and meet up with Adam Chapman, but failed to get any answer on the phone, sadly.

That evening Arun took me for a drive to beaches nearby and we ate out at a restaurant.

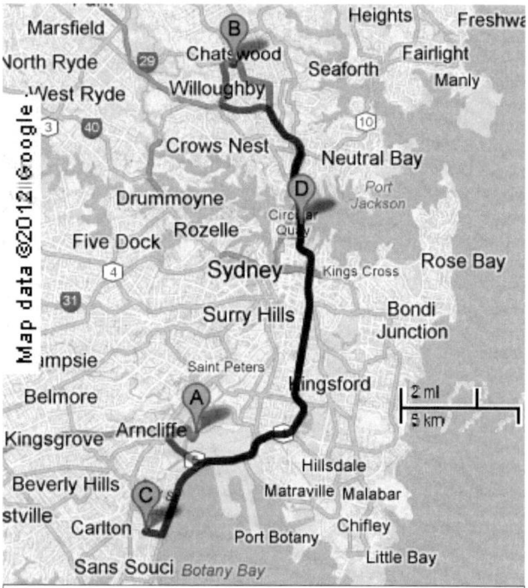

A) Sydney Airport; B) Chatswood; C) Scarborough Park; D) Sydney Harbour Bridge & Opera House.

The next day, Sunday 3rd December, Arun took me out to more areas of local interest in the Sydney area, including Scarborough Park, where Arun kindly videoed me walking on a bar in front of the Scarborough Park sign, to prove I had been there! This was the second Scarborough I had visited on my journey; I had two more to see in Australia later. We also saw the famous Sydney Opera House and Harbour Bridge, the site of a past Olympic Games, in 2000, and finally the B'ahai Faith Temple. This is religious organisation that was intended to unite all faiths, and to live in Peace. That evening I cooked my stir-fry, for the first time in this great "island" continent, and it seemed that they enjoyed it as well. Anyway we were all still alive next morning!

The following day I was introduced to Arun's son, his wife and their daughter (15 months old); Jayshree

Some nature seen in Sydney.

looked after her three days a week. I caught up with emails, and wrote and posted in Zorpia, Mystical and My Space the 4th episode of my trip. I also booked a bed at the Backpacker hotel in Alice Springs and a two day Adventure Tour to Uluru (Ayres Rock), for my trip to Central Australia, in a few day's time. Later that afternoon Mike Dodd came to fetch me and took me out to his ranch a few miles away; he showed me around his lovely place, and we viewed some of his gems in his stamp collection. Afterwards we had some tea, ably assisted by his daughter, before he returned me to Arun's home. Arun thought that he might well have met Mike in business before! Mike was one of the four Stamp Addicts Yahoo Group members I was to meet on my trip.

The following day I took an early train into Sydney to book the rest of my train journeys in Australia, the Canberra and Brisbane journeys; I had already booked the long journeys to Alice Springs and Perth. I also went to the Indian High Commission to get my Indian Visa, but there was a HUGE queue, so I decided to leave it to when I was in Perth and was there for a longer time; I was told it took a few days to organise. I also found out from a local travel agent that I may need visas for the Philippines and Singapore, but not Hong Kong. I then had a pleasant walk around the Sydney Botanical gardens and Hyde Park. It was here that I saw in real life something I had only seen before in one of "The Eagle", Dan Dare stories: an overhead metro train. "Eagle" was a boys' magazine (comic) whose front pages ran the famous Dan Dare Pilot of the Future stories. It was first started in 1950, and was set in the period 1995! And here was one prediction come true, overhead railways!

I found a nice sandwich bar that made lovely salad sandwiches in which one can choose one's own fillings, and they had separate tools for the ingredients,

Typical bush regions of South Australia

so the fillings which were not vegetarian or vegan did not contaminate my food. That evening back at Arun's I prepared for my trip to Alice Springs, leaving my main suitcase to be collected in 2 weeks' time, after the first of my two Great Train Journeys in Australia.

Arun kindly took me to Chatsworth station to get the train to Sydney, but before this I posted off some of the stuff that I had gathered up on my journey that was making my case too heavy. Also I posted a book for Dilys for a Christmas present, and the claims form for my lost camcorder.

For such journeys one had to book in an hour in advance of departure. As with all of the long journeys I booked in a sleeper service only if I was spending more than one consecutive night on a train. This first part was one night to Adelaide, then I had to stay in a hotel before catching the famous Ghan train to Alice Springs, which again was a one overnight journey.

It was on this train that a strange coincidence happened. On a journey such as mine a few coincidences are bound to happen, I suppose! But this was one of the best, at least I thought so.

I found my seat (all seats were booked), and not long after I made myself comfortable in my aisle seat a young girl (upper teens) took her seat next to me. Before the train departed, she got up and "disappeared" and a little while later a man arrived and took her seat, explaining that their family had been split up by accident, and his daughter was now sitting with her Mum. Later still he told me that the train guards had sorted out a set of seats for the family to all sit together, so I now had a free seat next to me for most of the journey, very useful for overnight journeys!

Unlike most trains, these long distance ones had lounges and restaurant carriages. That evening, passing through the Blue Mountains, we were entertained by some terrific flashes of lightning, and the accompa-

Human Nature

Human Nature is an Australian pop vocal group. They formed in 1989, originally as a doo-wop group called The Four Trax, while the members were school-mates in Sydney.

After signing with Sony Music and renaming themselves **Human Nature,** they released their debut album Telling Everybody in 1996, and have charted 17 hits in Australia's Top 40, and five hits in Australia's Top 10.

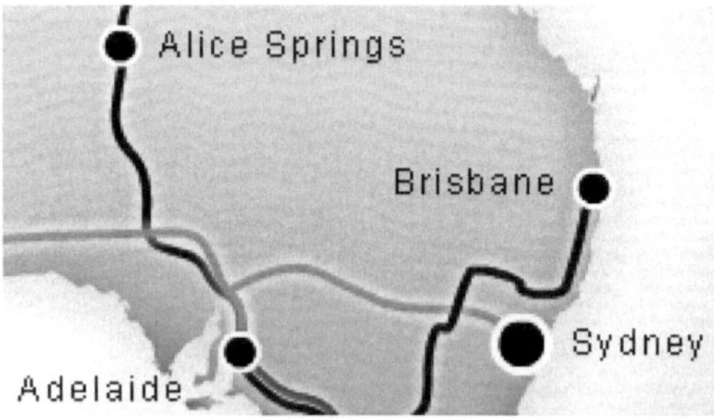

nying heavy rain, something I saw very little of in Australia. I spent my free time doing Sudoku and reading my books and looking out of the windows for photo opportunities. In the lounge cars we could play games, read or just stare out of the windows. This part of the journey was in fact the first of a three day journey to Perth, which I would be returning to after Christmas.

I got some sleep on the train. Before our arrival at the first stop of the day I saw some kangaroos bounding away from our train, the first ones I had seen in the wild. Later we stopped at Broken Hill, an outback town; here we had 90 minutes to look around etc. Here was the first treat. This was a "special" train journey when the Australian group "**Human Nature**" were travelling the whole way across Australia, and giving open air concerts at each major stop on the station. At Broken Hill there were crowds there to welcome them on this event and one of the local primary schools was lucky enough to sing with them for a few songs. I took a short video and a few stills of this event. It seems that the Indian Pacific Railway did this kind of thing every year to give a show for the outback towns on this prestigious 3 day journey.

Travelling then through the parched wheat lands of South Australia, we eventually arrived at the Adelaide Keswick station at 3.40 pm. At Adelaide I had to spend one night in a hotel to wait for the twice a week train to Darwin. I asked at the information bureau about reasonable hotels, and they gave me the name of the Ambassadors hotel, and a map. I was able to book the last room available at $A60 B&B, and it was bang in the centre of the city. I also booked two nights for my return journey, 13th & 14th Dec. It was an old hotel, with what seemed like the original manual self operated lift from Victorian times. After I was settled in, I wandered round the city centre and found an internet café and spent an hour there, and later eventually discovered where the Vegetarian "Sprouts" restaurant was. This was one of those I would have gladly highly recommended, but since returning home (to the UK) I learnt that it had closed. Sad, because the food and service was so good. I went to bed knowing that the next chapter in my adventure was going to be so different, yet not knowing how different, or in what way.

Prior to British settlement in 1788, groundwater levels were in equilibrium. Seasonal recharge, and year round utilisation of ground water by deep rooted native vegetation resulted in ground water levels remaining static. Land clearing in Australia has resulted in a loss of this native vegetation, replaced largely by agriculture and pasture crops. These are often annual plants and shallow rooted, and thus, unable to intercept, and adequately absorb stored, and rising ground water. This creates an imbalance in the hydrological cycle, and results in dryland salinity. Salinity is classified as a dissolved salt content of a substance like soil or water. Salinity can prevent crops and other vegetation from growing leaving land empty.

Salinity in South Australia is a problem in all principal agricultural areas, with 370000 hectares of land and wetlands impacted. At current rates, this is expected to increase by 60% by 2050 It is expected to cost the state around $47million per year in lost agricultural profit, and is expected to taint more than 20% of ground water to levels above those safe for human consumption.

Salt patches are appearing in many places in South Australia, devastating farmlands

Chapter 26

When Thinking of Central Australia... "ALICE" Springs to Mind!

The day started fairly normally: I partook of the free breakfast, simple yet sufficient, and the choices allowed me to have an all vegan one. After that, leaving my luggage in the hotel, I wandered round Adelaide. I visited the Aboriginal Art Exhibition, which showed me how artistic these original native people are. I then found a wonderful open market which sold a huge variety of fruit, vegetables and nuts. This market has recently been depicted on a set of Australian stamps! And not far away was the **Organic Vegetarian restaurant, "Bliss".** I think this was my second favourite restaurant on my world trip, after Spiral Diner in Texas. Anyway I really enjoyed my meal here. Lovely people and food. They provided a lovely fresh salad.

I also discovered the FREE BUS SERVICES of Adelaide. They had two circular services, that passed most of the attractions and services in the city, and they were regular and FREE. No wonder the city was not choked up with traffic. I recovered my luggage from the hotel and used the shuttle free bus back to the railway station for a departure at 5.30 pm, in temperatures of 38C, on the famous Ghan Railway. This is one of THE most famous railway journeys in the world, going from Adelaide to Darwin and back, twice a week, through the very centre of Australia, through desert lands where temperatures reach well over 50C in the sun and little shade is found. The train service acquired its name from the fact that when originally built it took over from the camel trains that went from north to south. The camels were imported from Afghanistan, as the camels there were used to the searing heat and dryness. Hence the name the Ghan Railway.

I was going only to the very centre of Australia,

and not to the north in Darwin. My journey would take one day, and drop me off at the famous town which is in the middle of a desert, but with huge reserves of underground water, that has seeped there from the mountain regions to the East. Why famous? Because of Neville Shute's book telling the story of an outback Australian who met an English girl in Japanese occupied Malaya in World War 2. Several films and TV versions have been made of this story, which was very moving, though actually it has very little to do with "A Town Like Alice", which is in fact Alice Springs. Back in those days it was just a small village, and it has now grown to a considerable size. Coming to Australia I just had to visit the very centre, as ALICE Springs to mind when I think of Central Australia, and that wonderful story. There is still another strange coincidence to tell of, and that is about to emerge on this exciting railway journey.

The train left on time at 5.30 pm. As it was only a single overnight journey I had not booked a sleeper service, but as on other long distance trains there were public lounges and restaurant cars. The train's temperature was kept at a cool 20C. I spent most of my waking time in the lounge car. There I found the same family whom I had met on the train from Sydney to Adelaide. Father and daughter I had met on the other train, and now I met the mother; they too were going to Alice Springs. The daughter was organising the card game 'Cheat'. About 7 of us joined in at different times; the mother, the daughter, a lady Jen and myself played mainly though . How she did it, I don't know, but the younger lady seemed to WIN every time. It was whilst playing Cheat that I discovered her name, that was to stick in my mind for ever! YES, she was called ALICE!, and she was going to Alice Springs! I had with me my Neville Shute book "A Town Like Alice", which I had brought all the way from England to

Remains of the old original track for the Ghan Railway

Typical scene from Ghan railway in Northern Territory

take with me to Alice Springs! Just one of those strange things that some human beings like to do! Anyway we played mainly Cheat, and Alice won nearly every game. But we also played Rummy, which she didn't win, so guess which game we played most! Another couple were playing Scrabble, some of the time.

For this journey I had brought with me fruit and nuts to eat, for my meals. All fresh food had to be eaten before leaving the train if one left the train in a different state from that which we had departed. This was a "safety" measure to try to prevent crop pests and fungi from crossing borders. So one had to eat up everything that was fresh food, or it was dumped! I got little sleep that night, and saw the sunrise. After I had my fruit breakfast, Cheating resumed, and I then asked Alice's parents if it were OK to ask Alice to sign my "Town Like Alice" book on Alice Springs Railway station. Alice was delighted to do this, and I have photographic evidence of this event! I also played Scrabble with Jen and Peter, a couple from Lancashire.

The train pulled in at Alice more or less on time at 11.55 am Dec 9th.

After the "signing" and wishing the family a happy Birthday outing for an elderly relative (the close family were all descending upon her near Alice Springs as a surprise), I found the special shuttle bus waiting to take people to various hotels including the **Alice Lodge Backpacker**. This was my first experience of a backpacker hotel. It was in fact a kind of Youth Hostel, and sleeping was in Dorms of 4 or 9. I opted for the 4 bed room; at $A20 per night B&B, that was less than £8! They even had an open air swimming pool, and by gosh that WAS needed! Unfortunately I found I had left my swimming shorts in the suitcase at Arun's! So I walked into Alice Springs town centre, in the searing heat of 37C in the shade. But no sweat! The atmosphere was so dry that one never got wet sticky

Lounge area of Ghan Trains

Alice Brown and her parents

Alice holding my book "A Town Like **Alice**" which she had just signed on **Alice** Springs Station

clothes! I had brought with me my sun glasses, and for the first time some sun block cream, which was needed in this part of the world. I eventually found a shop that sold swimming shorts, and then a restaurant that would give me a decent vegan salad meal. The Vegetarian one appeared to be shut. I walked back itching to get cool in that pool! Eventually I found my way back (I had a map!) and got changed, and wondered why others were not using the pool. It was so cool! This was the first time I had swum for YEARS, it being too cold in UK waters!

I went to bed fairly early, 9.30 pm, after having been talking to a young chap, called David, who was telling me how to beware of the spiders and snakes, some of which are deadly poisonous. It was great that a young man should be so informative and helpful to me. Basically one has to respect the wildlife and normally no harm will come to one. It was a pity that I couldn't get to know more of him. We were talking out in an open field surrounded by houses, interrupted only by lovely parrot-like birds, and other birds.

The early to bed was because the next day started at 4.15 am, to be ready in time for the Adventure Tours, Australia, bus.

The next two days were going to be jam packed with learning and adventure, such as I had never experienced before.

Uluru was to be blessed with more visitors.

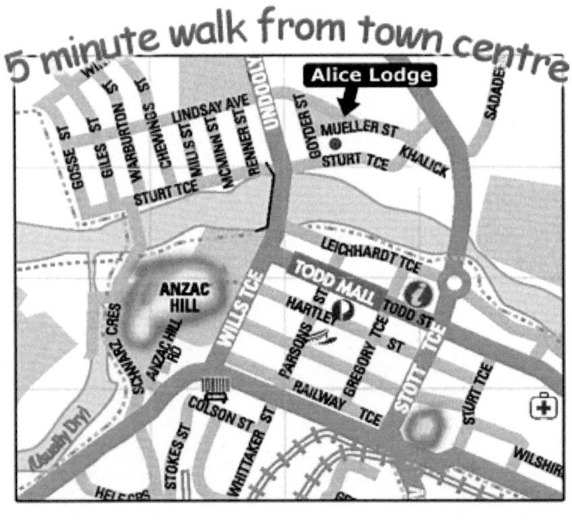

Chapter 27
"Uluru - You Rock"

Promptly at 5 am the shuttle bus arrived, and three of us from this backpackers hotel were taken to the centre of Alice from which all the various tours departed. The other two were going on a different tour.

I was booked with "Adventure Tours, Australia" on their two day "Red Centre, Highlights Tour". It was more expensive than similar tours, but the only one with vacancies and taking only two days. It had to be only a 2 day tour as the trains back to Adelaide were only twice a week. The tour was advertised as a "small" groups operator, up to 24 in group. It turned out that there were only 7 of us. There was one Irish girl, who had been before and wanted her boy friend to see this incredible part of the world; he was from London, but also Irish; then there was an older (in his 40's) chap from California, USA; two 19 year old Japanese girls, who previously did not know each other; and finally there was a chap from Rugby UK who turned out to be the other vegan on the trip. He knew I was vegan because I was wearing my Vegan Camp cap. He said that he had never met another vegan in his life before! Anyway when I booked I was assured that they would cater for Vegans at all meals. The trip included 4 meals. Travel was in a 24 seater minibus, so with 17 spare seats we were comfortable! It was air conditioned, thank goodness, because the heat outside was overpowering, though bearable because of the absolute dryness. On our tour we were very lucky, as not only did we have a tour guide leader, Gareth, but also a trainee leader, Anthony. Gareth did the driving and Anthony did most of the tour guiding and talking.

We had a LONG drive on what seemed an endless straight road. Anthony often told us about interesting landmarks as we drove by; then suddenly we slowed up as he spotted an eagle gorging itself on a dead kangaroo on the road side. I got my camera out, but got only a couple photos of it flying away, as it took time to get the camera ready. This straight road was one used by long “train” lorries (Trucks), which cannot stop quickly, and are the main cause of the dead kangaroos littering the road sides. Later we turned off this main road and stopped for lunch. Later still we arrived at Kings Canyon, and pulled up at the official car park and ventured outside. Anthony then told us that we were now going to walk up “that” hill, and pointed to a steep hill that looked like a good scramble, which in the English Lake District would have been a nice warming-up climb. But this was quite different: there was little sign of life, a few trees dotted about, and bare red rocks. The shade temperature was just over 40C, ahem! WHAT shade?! The actual temperature was well over 50C! Then we were informed of the name of the hill, and we were asked if we still wanted

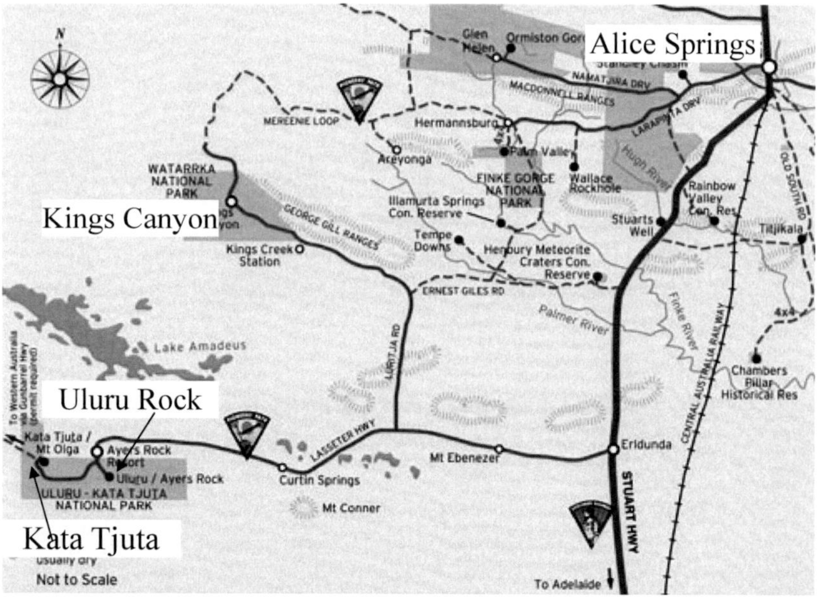

Sign Post in Alice Springs

Parrots like this would eat from the grass all around you, in Alice Springs

Dried up river bed in Alice Springs.

Now wild Afghan Camel

KINGS CANYON

to go on this climb. We all opted to give it a go, in spite of its name **"Heart-attack Hill".** I happened to be very much the oldest one on this trip; most, except the Californian, were in the teens or twenties. We had been told we

Kings Canyon is the beautiful centrepiece of Watarrka National Park (Kings Canyon), in the George Gill Range, south-west of Alice Springs.

It can be reached along the sealed Lasseter Highway and Luritja Road from Uluru/Ayers Rock or Alice Springs, the unsealed Ernest Giles Road from the Stuart Highway, south of Alice Springs or the Mereenie Loop through the West MacDonnell Ranges.

The park preserves a number of features, from the canyon to fascinating rock formations, woodlands of desert oaks and other diverse and rare plant and wildlife species.

EXPLORING ON FOOT

It is important to remember that daytime temperatures can be high, particulary in summer. Walkers and climbers should carry and drink two litres of water for every hour they are active and plan any strenuous activity in the cooler, early mornings. Remember to only walk on marked tracks and, if you become lost, stay where you are.

NEEDED at least 3 litres of drinking water for this climb, and they were right! One of the Japanese girls managed half way up, and one of the leaders stayed with her, and the other leader, Gareth, stayed near me as he was obviously concerned that my age (68) might be a hindrance. I made it to the top with very little trouble, stopping often for sips of water. I always find it easier going up than down. Once up there it was fairly flat, and most of the group then went off on their own to go round the top of the canyon. I decided to take a rest and return back down to the base. After a while, as often seems to happen in going down long steep hills, my legs started feeling "rubbery", so I had to slow down. I know now that Gareth was getting worried, not realising that it was just my legs doing what they normally do in descending long steep hills. Yes it was HOT too, but though that added to the effect, my main problem was the "rubbery" feel I normally get on such descents. Half way down we met Anthony and the Japanese girl and Gareth returned to the top to wait for the return of the others, and we slowly descended to the foot of the hill and to an open air shelter to get out of the searing heat. I finished up my 3rd litre, and lay down on the wooden seat and dropped off to sleep (my mid day nap! That was also what was hindering me, just being overtired, I usually had a mid day nap.) On awaking after about ten minutes I looked up into the apex of the shelter and saw a couple of largish white spiders, and also a tiny black one with a red spot! I took a couple of photos using the zoom, and even at that distance I got a fairly credible picture of two "Ghost" spiders and a Redbacked Spider. Both are poisonous; the tiny one was possibly one of the most deadly spiders. Eventually the others of the group returned and we then drove off to see the incredible rock called Uluru, the real reason why most of us had come on this trip. It has a mystical and religious significance to the native Australians, the Aboriginals.

Before we got there we stopped to view the "false" Uluru, a rock formation that at some angles resembles Uluru, but is of quite a different type of rock. It is in

fact called Connors Rock, and only in the far distance is it mistaken for Ayres Rock. It is the third most important rock formation in the region. Each of the three are of quite different rocks.

Eventually we arrived at the camp site that belonged to the company that ran the tours. There, there was a kitchen, and three or four heavy duty tents and a store room and a large open space in the central area.

The toilets and wash rooms were in the main part of the site, surrounded by many small camping sites.

We had arrived in time to view Uluru at sunset, but unfortunately for us the only opportunity was missed because of cloud; nevertheless it was still an awesome sight. After we had dinner, we sat round the camp fireplace (but no fire!) and we were taught to play the Didgeridoo by Gareth, who had brought his own with him. He demonstrated some sounds, and explained that the real players could keep playing this mystical instrument for an hour at a time, by circular breathing, something he was learning to do, and could only keep it up for a few minutes. He then let us all have a try, explaining that it was very difficult. Never having played this before, I was the second to try and believe it or not I managed to get some notes out of it, but

Eagle flying away from eating a dead Kangaroo on the roadside

Uluru at sunset time from the camp site

Uluru at sunrise

Info re Central Australia.

Near the heart of Australia, from the parched dry plains of the Northern Territory, rises the biggest monolith in the world, the colossal Uluru (previously known as Ayers Rock). Called Ayers Rock by settlers, the ownership of the rock was transferred to the Aboriginals of the area and it re-gained its Aboriginal name of Uluru, which means Great Pebble.

Uluru is one of earth's great natural wonders and encountering it for the first time is quite an experience. Consisting of mineral rich sandstone, Uluru measures 2.4km (1.5 miles) long and 1.6km (1 mile) wide and rises up to 867 metres above sea level.

Aboriginal rock paintings

Uluru is a sacred site for the Aboriginal tribes, and has great spiritual meaning. Each feature of the rock has a meaning in 'Tjukurpa' or Dreamtime, the traditional Anangu law that explains how the world was created.

The caves in the rock have been decorated with Aboriginal paintings and prehistoric art, some of which indicate such things as the whereabouts of water and other vital information, others were painted for religious purposes and as a means of both storytelling and for a culture with no written language to teach and record its history.

Ever changing shades of Uluru

Apart from the sheer imposing size of Uluru, what can make viewing it so memorable is the fact that as each day passes the rock changes colour depending on the light and atmospheric conditions, and never remains the exact same permanent hue.

Sunrise and sunset are perhaps the most magical, and it is easy to see why the native inhabitants held this area in such high regard. It is hard to come away from Uluru without feeling enriched by its calm spiritually and sense of permanence.

The geological story can be found here. Some of this was explained by our guide Anthony.

http://www.environment.gov.au/parks/uluru/nature-science/geology.html

Martin & Helena trying to play the Didgeridoo

Our transport for two days

Me, Helena, Martin, Gareth, Michael, Californian, 2 Japanese girls

not with circular breathing! Helena was able to do it as well, but her boy friend Martin just could not do it! I then asked Gareth if it could be played at both ends. He assured me it could not. So I did!

That night all of us, except the two Japanese girls (who opted for the tents) slept out in the open in

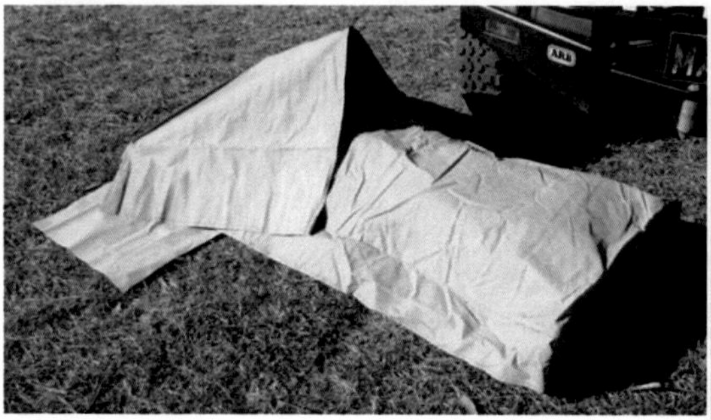

swagbags (or Swags). It was so warm that I was in pyjamas in just a sheet sleeping bag till about 3am, when I zipped up the cover. I also covered my head with a net to keep off any biting insects. This was my first night of sleeping out in the open, and what a magical place to do it!

We did not get much sleep as we were woken at 4am for breakfast, and drove early to a site inside the Uluru National Park to see the sunrise's light on the colossal red rock. I took many pictures as the sun rose. The

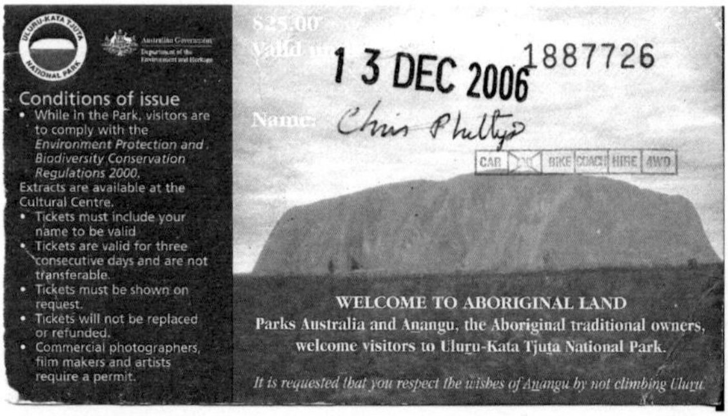

clouds had now dispersed; the sun was not a particularly deep red, but nevertheless it was spectacular. Later we were dropped off and walked the 9 km round the rock. The cavern and cracks were awesome. Many

Two of the features on Uluru

of these we were not allowed to photograph, as they were sacred; the few photos I do have I believe were in the allowed areas. (There were obvious sign posts telling us the parts of the rock where photography was banned.) One of the most important and interesting parts was the water hole where wild life came to drink.

After this excursion we were whisked off to the second most important rock outcrop in this region, Kata Tjuta (Olgas) rocks. These were also red, but of quite a different kind of rock and were not so smooth. In between the rocks was a canyon into which we walked. Anthony continued his fascinating commentary on the rock's geological and Aboriginal sacredness. I asked him if he had studied Geology at University, because he seemed so knowledgeable. I was surprised by his answer, that he was a school drop-out! He had never been to 6th form college or University. He said he had been learning everything from books and internet, as part of his training for being a tour leader. It just goes to show that being a school dropout doesn't mean you have no brains!

Our next port of call was to the Aboriginal Art & Heritage exhibition, not far away. There was certainly a lot of interesting and fascinating history of these original natives of Australia who had learned to live in and manage this land of contrasts, most of which was desert and red sands. The life here is very fragile, and the Aboriginals knew how to protect it. Luckily the European settlers are now becoming more and more aware of how fragile this wonderful land of rare and strange life forms is, and at least in part there is now a much greater respect being paid to the Aboriginals' way of life.

We finally drove back the long way to Alice Springs via the "Fools" rock and saw a few small sand twisters, of which I tried to take a video. We got back in the early evening and I had a glorious swim again in the back packers swim pool. A group of us walked into town and went to various places, and I went to a reunion meal with our Tour Guides and others of the party in their hotel. Believe it or not, I got my meal FREE! The kindly man there thought he could not provide me properly with a meal, and I got some nice fresh salad, FREE. This was at Malinky's. I also want to thank our two tour guides for their care and help in making these two days so enjoyable

Kata Tjuta (The Olgas)

Chapter 28
Back on the Ghan to Adelaide.

After two days of very early risings I was able to stay in bed till a more normal getting up time next day as the train was not till 12.40pm. What did seem unusual was that the dorm of 4 this night was mixed; the first night it had been an all male room. After breakfast I had a wander round the area on my own till the shuttle bus took me and a few others to the station. I gladly boarded the train to get into a cooler atmosphere. I had a long chat with a UK Photographer, who was taking a series of Ghan Photos for a slide show. There were several places that we could see from the train where the line had been rerouted. I thought that I would try the restaurant fruit salad as I had not stocked up with new fruit. We were informed that the other Ghan train had had a derailment up near Darwin. There are only two trains in service. I decided, in case it was mentioned on the national and international news, to send a few texts to home and other places where I was expected shortly to let them know it was not MY train. That night I decided to try sleeping on the floor of the train instead of the seats, allowing the other passenger two seats to sleep in. It was not a good move, but I did get some sleep, though the floor was rather hard!

I was up early and took many sunrise photos from the train. I had a restaurant breakfast of fruit, cornflakes and toast. The train arrived 10 minutes EARLY at 9.20 am. I caught the shuttle bus back to the

Adelaide getting ready for Christmas

Bliss Vegetarian Organic Café, Adelaide

Ambassadors hotel. I couldn't get over the old fashioned lift! An olde world place in the centre of modern life! I was able to leave my luggage there before check in and spent the day wandering round the incredible open market and visiting, again, the Bliss Restaurant near by.

Such a lovely atmosphere there at Bliss, and good food. Then I found free Internet use in the Library, caught up with stuff, then went by (FREE) bus to the botanical gardens. I went back by bus and had a lovely meal in "Sprouts" Veggie Restaurant. (Sadly this has now closed!)

Then went back to the hotel, washed a few things, had shower and relaxed.

Next morning after the free breakfast I took the free bus to the library to check emails, but for some reason my email company had a bug that day and I could not reach them. I then decided that it would be a good idea to visit the **Cleland Wildlife park**, so I caught the bus that went near there. The day had started bright, but a little cooler than usual. Gradually we got cloud cover and by the time we reached the wildlife park it had also got cooler still, and I was still in my hot-weather summer shorts. There was a hint of rain. In the park one of the first parts I went to was the Koala compound where we were allowed to have communication with one, with the keeper present, but only in small groups of up to 4 at a time. Being on my own, I was allowed to talk to and stroke its back whilst the keeper fed it. The keeper also kindly took a photo of me stroking the Koala. There were many unusual birds in the water birds enclosure, and in a picnic area

Life seen at Cleland wild-life park

Kangaroo who fed from my hands

My hand stroking Koala

there were a few kangaroos who would come up to you to take food from your hands. One could buy food to feed the animals and birds. That was the only food we were allowed to feed any of the animals there. I also saw a Tasmanian Devil. Then the weather really changed and it rained; luckily there were indoor exhibits of snakes and other reptiles and insects and so on.

Because of the change in weather I did not stay as long as I expected and returned to Adelaide by bus. The rain had eased off by the time my return bus arrived. I had my 3rd and last lunch at "Bliss" and went to my hotel for a nap. In the early evening I had my last of 3 meals at Sprouts. There were other veggie restaurants in Adelaide as well, but I didn't get round to going to them. I also managed to have a short phone call to Dilys.

After an early morning breakfast at the hotel, I caught the free shuttle bus back to the station. For some reason the one I had booked failed to turn up, so I had to return to the hotel to book another. The weather was getting warmer again. Eventually the Indian/Pacific train arrived from Perth and after a while we were allowed to board, and we departed more or less on time at 10 am. We stopped for 2 hours at Broken Hill. The heat had definitely returned. I had time to wander around this outback city and found a

More life seen at Cleland

small health food store café, and had a nice cup of herbal tea. That evening I finished reading the book I bought after attending the Oklahoma University with Reggie: "Beloved". I started on the famous "The Da Vinci Code" I slept on the double seats, but not too well. As we were crossing a state border again, I ate up all my spare fruit and nuts for breakfast. The weather next morning changed again while we were travelling through the Blue Mountains, and much rain fell and it was misty. Unfortunately our train got stuck behind two freight trains and instead of arriving back in Sydney at 10.15, it was 11.20 before we could leave the train. I spent a lot of the spare time doing Sudoku or reading "The Da Vinci Code".

Mural seen at Broken Hill, station

Chapter 29
Avoca Beach.

{Sandy}

It was now day 89, and Saturday Dec 16th. Thanks to FriendsReunited.com I had got back in touch with one of my very earliest pupils, who was a lovely bright little 11 year old when I first taught her, at Edlington School (near Doncaster) back in 1965. So 41 years later I was now going to meet her again; she herself obviously was now an adult and also a mum of older teenage and young 20's daughters. I never got to meet them unfortunately. But I did, of course, get to meet Sandy (Sandra Cameron as I knew her) and she kindly invited me to stay a night with her in Avoca Beach. I changed trains at Sydney and was picked up by Sandy at Gosford station.

We had a lot of talking to do catching up over the past. Strangely enough our last meeting was in a café in Cornwall, when I was on my honeymoon with my first wife Christine. We had called in at this café and, surprise surprise, were served by Sandra and Christine (her older sister, whom I had taught in my very first

Some life seen at Sandy’s house!

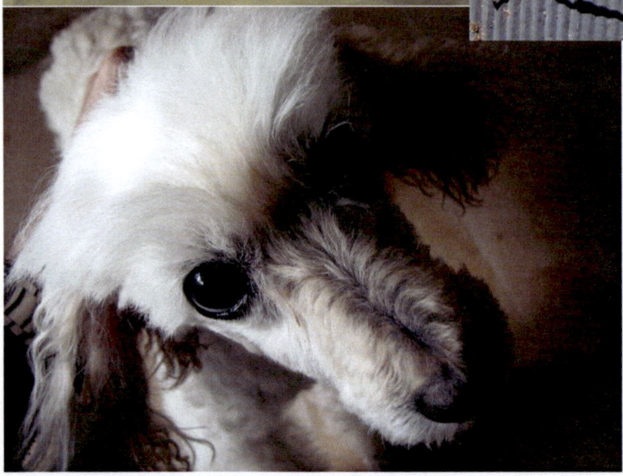

Sandy’s little dog.

year at Edlington; we had not got on quite so well as Sandra and I had, but she was friendly enough!) Sandy remembered that at lunch time, when we teachers had to sit with the pupils at octagonal tables for lunch, I had explained to them that they needed to chew each mouthful at least 30 times before swallowing! I wished I had kept that piece of advice myself!

After a lot of talking, Sandy took me by car to the famous Avoca beach and we heard the ear-splitting cicadas in the trees as we passed. On the wonderful beach, with sands and rocks, we had our photo taken, and I saw a large 'fly' dead on the sands. This is when I learnt that Cicadas are flies, not grasshoppers! I was amazed at how big they were. I always say that we learn something new every day and that pupils and ex pupils often teach their teachers! I slept below the main house in the spare room, which was a kind of lower flat. The house was built on a steep slope in woodland, and there were beautiful birds coming to her bird-table, some of which allowed me to photograph them. Sandy really lived in a lovely part of the world.

Next morning Sandra drove around many of the nearby areas and showed me beaches and sea and hills, and we heard the ever present, but unseen, cicadas. We spent time catching up more on our past lives and I found that her sister, Christine, was also living in Australia, but in the only island state, Tasmania, one of the two states that I did not visit at all, sadly. Later Sandy took me to Gosforth station to return to stay one more night at Arun's, and to finally pick up my large suitcase, which they had so kindly allowed me to leave in their safe keeping for 2 weeks. It was really lovely meeting Sandy again and seeing how a bright cheerful small pupil had developed into a bright cheerful adult mum. Now we are keeping in touch via Facebook.

Scenes from Avoca Beech

Rock Face

I was staying only that one night at Arun's this time, so sadly there was so much I didn't have time to talk to them about. I hope that on their next visit to the UK they will come and stay with us. Just as I hope any of the people I met will, and especially those I stayed with on my trip.

I had booked a taxi for 6 am to take me to the station, as it was too early to expect or ask Arun to take me. I said my final farewells to Arun and Jayshree, and thanked them so much for making me so welcome. And so to my next destination, to meet the third and last person from my past, and in a state that I had not yet visited, the smallest of all the Australian states, and the only one completely surrounded by another, which was formed about 100 years ago in 1913.

Canberra *is the capital city of Australia. With a population of over 340,000, it is Australia's largest inland city and the eighth largest Australian city overall. The city is located at the northern end of the Australian Capital Territory, 280 km (170 mi) south-west of Sydney, and 660 km (410 mi) north-east of Melbourne. The site of Canberra was selected for the location of the nation's capital in 1908 as a compromise between rivals Sydney and Melbourne, Australia's two largest cities. It is unusual among Australian cities, being an entirely purpose-built, planned city. Following an international contest for the city's design, a design by the Chicago architects Walter Burley Griffin and Marion Mahony Griffin was selected and construction commenced in 1913. The city's design was heavily influenced by the garden city movement and incorporates significant areas of natural vegetation that have earned Canberra the title "bush capital". Although the growth and development of Canberra were hindered by the World Wars and the Great Depression, it emerged as a thriving city after World War II.*

As the seat of the government of Australia, Canberra

is the site of Parliament House, the High Court of Australia and numerous government departments and agencies. It is also the location of many social and cultural institutions of national significance, such as the Australian War Memorial, National Gallery of Austra-

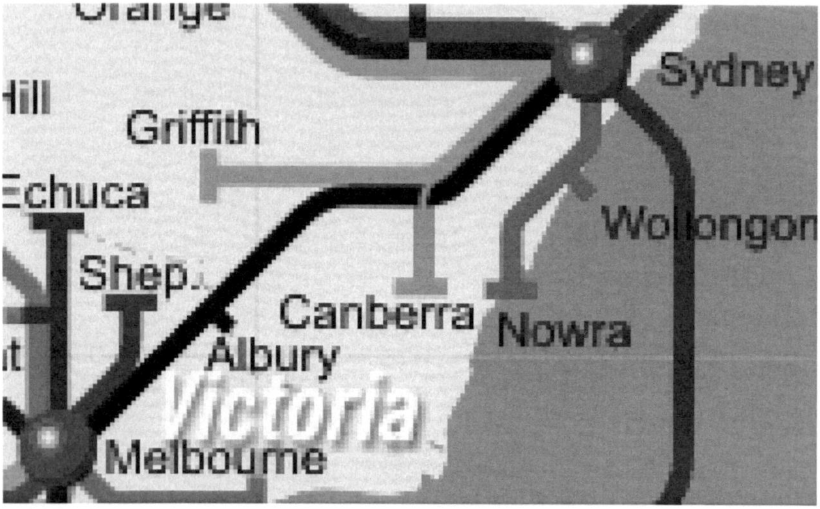

lia, National Museum of Australia and the National Library of Australia. The federal government contributes the largest percentage of Gross State Product and is the largest single employer in Canberra.

Chapter 30

Same name, street, school, hobby but not met since Summer1958

{Chris & Audrey}

Chris Yardley moved to Tunbridge Wells when I was in the 5th form at The Skinners' School at Tunbridge Wells, Sept 1954. I believe he came from South London. He was in the same form as I was, and the form master was...my father. Later I found out that he was living in our street, Newlands Road. He also had a younger brother and a sister. Sadly his brother Michael died a few years ago, but his sister still lives in Tunbridge Wells, as does my sister. At different times all three of them enjoyed the Newlands Road Philatelic Society. This was the club that I was asked to start by the boys and girls in our street for them in April 1953, not long before the Coronation of Queen Elizabeth II. This club, though having a slow start, did actually become quite famous in Philatelic circles, and survived for almost 14 years. It was never ever run by adults. Once a member became 21 they had to leave. The three founders, Robin Grey, Colin Fowle and myself, did become Honorary members at that age, but the committee was always made up of under 21s. This story will be the subject of a different book, as soon as I can get down to it after this one.

To be quite honest I had forgotten Chris had been a member, and was surprised to learn that he had a WONDERFUL collection of New Zealand, especially of the early "Chalon" heads, as well as of Machin head issues of GB. He also had a an interest in other areas, and found for me a list of the Post Office Training School stamps. (Ordinary British stamps, but overprinted Training School or with plain black lines). He

Botanical
Gardens
Canberra

also had some of the NRPS First Day Covers. The club ran a FDC service for all new issues from 1957, to raise funds to run the club. Anyway back to THIS story!

I left Chatsworth station and changed trains at Sydney, catching the 7.45 am train and arrived in good time at Canberra, at 12 noon, and was met by Chris. We did a short tour of the Parliamentary area before driving to his home in Holt. He and his lovely wife Audrey made me feel so at home for the next two days. That afternoon we had a lot of catching up to do. One of the most interesting facts that I learned was about David (Lofty) Day. He was the tallest chap in our year at our school. His father was a policeman, and Lofty followed in those footsteps with the Kent Constabulary. During his career Lofty was stationed at Chartwell, Sir Winston Churchill's private residence in the village of Westerham. It appears that on some lonely evenings Sir Winston would invite Lofty to spend time with him in the house. As a souvenir of those evenings Lofty acquired used cigar boxes from his host, some of which he padded and returned to the great man - who subsequently used them as 'gift boxes' for other guests.

That evening Chris kindly took me out to the Tidbinbilla Reserve, a wildlife park. We saw plenty of kangaroos and emus and I had fun photographing the insect life, but I was really hoping to see a platypus. The resident warden told us that one needs to go early evening at dusk as that is when they often emerge. But nothing persuaded them to do so for me, sadly, during the two hours we watched for them. This was the one creature I really wanted to see alive, in the wild. It was good to know that wildlife parks like this were there helping to keep the natural wild life going in Australia. I was grateful to Chris for taking this trouble taking me to a place where platypus were

Canberra ,
Capital city of
Australia,
seat of the
Commonwealth
Government

known to be.

Audrey made us a LOVELY Vegan meal that evening.

Next morning, early, the bird chorus included the deep throated song from an Australian Magpie which I was able to photograph and record. Audrey showed me how to cut open a mango, one of my favourite fruits, when ripe. The trouble is that most in the UK are picked too early (to be transported from far away), and don't seem to ripen properly. I had a lovely fruit breakfast. Chris and Audrey live in a beautiful part of Canberra on the edge of a golf course. That day Chris and I did some of the tourist tour of the Capital. We visited the Parliament buildings (not in session), the National Museum, and the Botanic Gardens. Many photographic opportunities were taken, and flashes of moments of beauty are for ever recorded in my albums. That evening they took me out to a Thai restaurant where I was able to get lovely vegan meal.

Chris has a really marvellous collection of the famous (philatelically) Chalon Heads of Early New Zealand, and he showed me some other collections.

I had a long day's travelling the next day, and I had to say goodbye to Chris and Audrey in the early hours as my train left Canberra at 6.37 am. Chris very kindly got up early and deposited me at the station in good time. It had been really good seeing Chris again after a gap of nearly 50 years! I arrived back in Sydney at 11 am. I left my heavy luggage at the luggage office and went on a walk to re-find the Gourmet Salad bar where I had had such a lovely salad sandwich before. I ate one there, and bought an extra one to have on the train, an overnight 13 hour journey to Brisbane. Before I left Sydney at 4.20 pm I booked myself in at the Metro Central Hotel, for the night of 29th December when I needed to be up fairly early to catch the Indian Pacific Train to Perth, on a three day journey right across Southern Australia, another of the GREAT TRAIN journeys. But that is 10 days ahead. I was about to have the most different Christmas ever, for me.

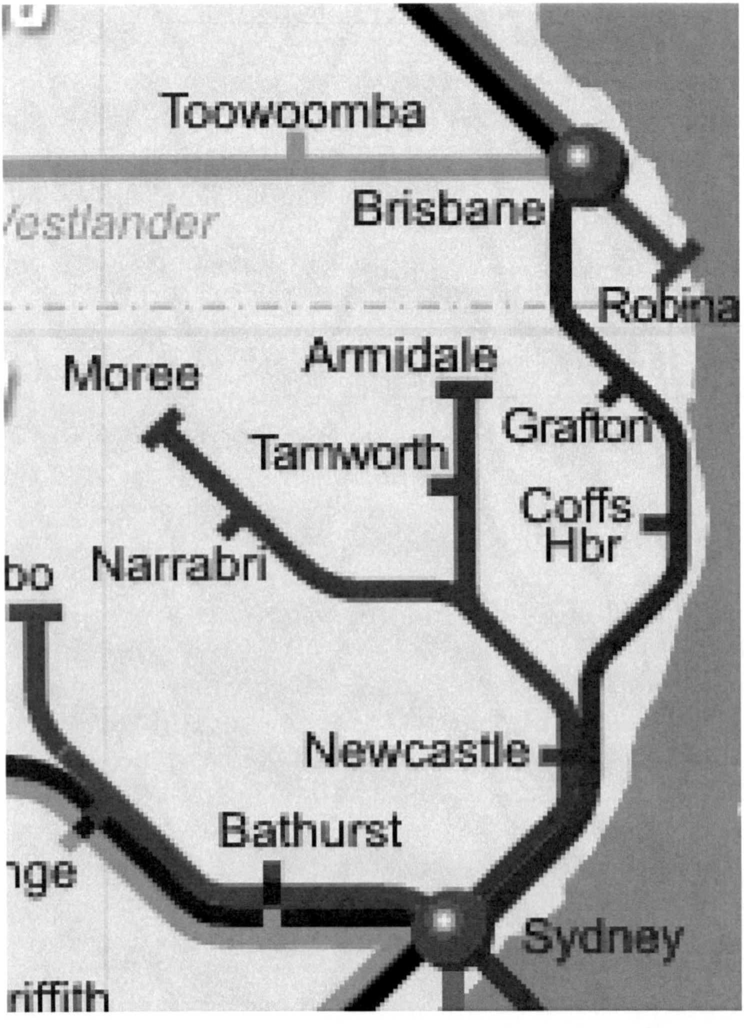

Chapter 31

Summer Christmas in Toowoomba 2006

Meaning of Toowoomba

There are a few theories about the origin of the word 'Toowoomba'. The name may have come about from a number of aboriginal words which relate to the original swamp land which Toowoomba was built on. Apparently, the aboriginal word 'tchwampa' means 'the swamp', 'choowoom' was a native melon which grew on the banks, and 'woomba woomba' meaning 'reeds in the swamp'. We don't know the precise origin of the word 'Toowoomba' however it would be safe to say that it was inspired by the swamp land that the Aboriginals called it.

{Mellissa & Josh}

My train to Brisbane left Sydney at 4.20 pm and gradually wound its way up the coastal route to Brisbane, passing through a mixture of English and Aboriginal sounding town names. The terrain changed quite a lot on this journey, but was green and hilly most of the time. I saw some rainfall. But most of this journey was in the dark, and I had a bit of sleep on the train seat. There were no lounge cars on this train, but I was able to read and play Sudoku and eat my sandwich and fruit, which I had to finish up before leaving the train at Brisbane at 5.30 am on the 21st Dec, the 94th day of my journey. By now I was getting more and more excited about meeting my lovely friend Mellissa and her husband Josh. I had known Mellissa for about 6 years in Yahoo groups, mainly in helping to run a group for people with de-

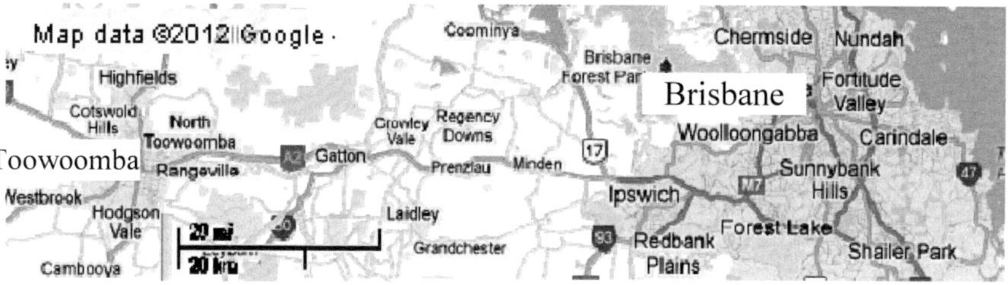

pression, and learning how to cope with it, but Mellissa was also a frequent user of Danielle's Group Mystical Dreamland, for writing and fun. It was in this latter group that I had made the closest friendships with people on the internet, and I was meeting or had already met many of its members on this trip.

At Brisbane, the capital of Queensland, I caught a bus to Toowoomba at 07.10 (which left about 40mins late) and arrived at 09.30 in Toowoomba centre, and then a local bus to the region of Toowoomba where Mellissa lived and arrived at 10.30. The temperature was like a really hot English summer! It certainly didn't feel as if Christmas was coming in 4 days!

Of course we had a big hug, though I had to be gentle as there was a large bump in the way - Mellissa was due to give birth in a couple of weeks or so.

Another friend of Mellissa's happened to have called in, Steve, whom she had not seen for a while. Somehow we got talking about where I had been, and I mentioned Alice Springs and seeing the red-backed spider and taking its photo by zoom. The he said "OH! I have one in my car under the bonnet! Would you like to see it?"

So we went out, he opened up the bonnet and lo and behold there it was in its web, upside down, a tiny little black spider with a red back. How could such a small creature be so deadly? Well I braved the experience and got really close to the spider and took a lovely picture of it, from only about a foot away! That picture was one of my best, and was in fact used on the cover of the programme of the play that my

Drama Society performed the following summer "The Spider's Web", an Agatha Christie Play.

After her friend had departed, Mellissa and I had a lot of talking to catch up on. We had known each other 5 years and it just seemed like meeting an old friend whom we had not met for a time, whereas in fact we had never met in person before. Mellissa's mum was there too and the three and a half of us went shopping for food, mainly for fruit for me. I had been told about her mum, and was so pleased to meet her as well. The things I had been told were all good, and I saw nothing to disagree with that.

Later Josh returned home from work, and as Mellissa had explained, he was a lovely fellow. That evening we all went round to Josh's parents for a pre-Christmas gathering. Eventually we all went to bed. It had seemed such a long time since I had a proper bed, but in fact I had only missed one night, the one on the long distance train from Sydney to Brisbane.

As well as a Christmas Card (How could it be Christmas ? It was so hot!) from Dilys, which had come by post with the "CLIPS" which for the first time I had not done most of, was a nice poem from Dilys, our first Xmas apart since we had married. But there was also a lovely card welcoming me from Mellissa.

Next day Josh went off to work for the last time before Xmas; he had 4 days off. I went for a walk to the nearby shops to get some food to make the stir-fry that evening. Mellissa had to have a fair amount of time resting, being so close to giving birth to her first child. She did a lot of reading or watching DVDs. Anyway both Josh and Mellissa both seemed to enjoy my meal. Afterwards I played our first ever game of Scrabble with Mellissa, which I only just won. We now play a Facebook version regularly on the internet, which though I often win, she has been known to win a few times.

Butterfly on my fingers

Other life seen in Toowoomba

On my 95th day, Saturday Dec 23rd, in the heat of the day I took a bus into Toowoomba and went shopping, for more foods, and found a nice Organic restaurant. That evening we played the Drawing Game and the Rhyming Game. Mellissa had heard about these pencil and paper games from our regular discussions in "Mystical Dreamland". Now Mellissa and Josh found out how much fun they were.

Next morning Josh and I got up at the crack of dawn and he took me out for an early morning walk to climb the local mountain, Table Top Hill. What wonderful views! Obviously I did record some of them, but the camera can't take in the real beauty of such scenery, when you can see so far away and in 3D. It was on the descent when going through some woodland that, with the help of the camera zoom facility, I was able to take a movie of a cicada, singing! There were not the huge quantities here that there had been in Avoca Beach, but before I had only seen a dead one. Now I had a live one safely digitalised in my camera!

It was very kind of Josh to take me on this wonderful walk, and it was one of the highlights of my visit. It was just a pity that Mellissa was too near to giving birth to be able to join us. Later I walked into the local shops again and did a bit of final shopping for Xmas, and on my return I made two Vegan cakes: a sponge cake and a fruit cake. It was now Christmas Eve. It still seemed so weird being in shorts and T-shirt and trying to get cool, when back home we'd be wrapped up well with heaters keeping us warm. Mellissa's family were coming next day, so it was to be a big gathering.

Christmas Day in Toowoomba found me up earlyish making a nut roast and custard [My notes in my diary say that this was for the "cake" crumbs, but I cannot remember that, except that I took a photo of the jug in which it had overflowed in the microwave cooking !] and the topping for the sponge cake. Then Mel-

Scene near Toowoomba, Table Top Hill

Cicada, singing

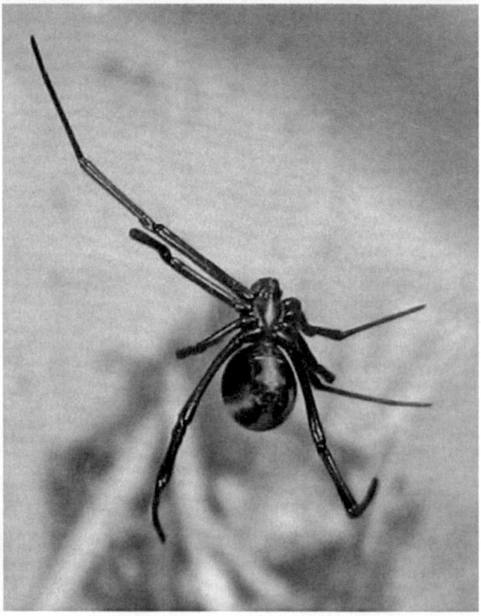

The Redback Spider

lissa's family arrived. Her mother, her grandmother, her brother, and his wife and their two lively children who were, naturally, excited. After the present opening session I read the two children my book "Miss Chief", which they seem to enjoy. Christmas dinner was had later and a few did try a bit of my nut roast and cake.

After the family had departed, Mellissa needed to rest and I caught up with emails on the net and phoned Dilys, where it was now morning. Later that evening Mellissa was again beaten at Scrabble!

Two days prior to Christmas, I remember Josh taking us all to see their vet re their little bird who was not well. I remember the vet was a nice man and he explained that the bird almost certainly needed a bigger enclosure, so we went hunting for such a cage, but didn't find one, so he ordered one. I heard later that the bird fully recovered by being given a larger cage.

Two other important members of the household have yet to be mentioned. To me the most famous was Darcy. When I first met Mellissa on the net, she called herself "Elizabeth Bennett" and her cat was Darcy! Now the reason why this was important was that it was this which had helped us get talking, as I had only a few years previously been the Rev Collins in the stage version of the famous story, "Pride and Prejudice" by Jane Austen. The other important family member was their husky called Gypsy, who was not allowed in the house, partly because of the cat and bird and fish! Darcy seemed to spend most of his time sleeping. And sadly not very long after I had departed I heard that Darcy. had passed away.

So my first Christmas away from the UK was upside down to my wife Dilys! Certainly it was topsy-turvy also in the weather! The next day, there was a sudden change and it went cloudy and cold and RAINED. It does rain here! But never for two days in a row, which it DID do in fact for 2½days! So Boxing Day was quite a contrast to Christmas Day. Christmas day had been hot and humid, but today was COOL and wet. It certainly rained all morning. Josh played in a big tournament-like game on the internet (rather like a Dungeons and Dragons game but with many people on the internet). Mellissa did a lot of sleeping. In the afternoon I went for a local walk to the nearby lake and took several photos, including one of a small butterfly that liked walking on my hand. Later Mellissa and I played another game of Scrabble, but this time we had a two letter list to help us! This did result in both of us doing better, but sadly for Mellissa I still won.

The next day was even colder, and I just had to change from shorts to long trousers. Josh was back at work, and Mellissa needed to make up sleep that she found difficult to get at night, so I spent more time on the net. Mellissa's keyboard was such that with a lot of use the letters had worn off, and most of the keys I could not see! Not being a touch typist and only using one finger, meant that it took me longer than normal to type! I also read my book and played Sudoku. In the afternoon Mellissa and I watched the DVD I had bought them for Xmas. GUESS WHAT IT WAS? One of the film versions of "A Town Like Alice". I wished I could have got them the DVD of the BBC TV serial version, a much better version that kept much more closely to the book.

That was the last full day staying with Mellissa, and in the evening we all played the Star Wars version of Monopoly. Somehow I managed to win that too! (That surprised me, as Josh was the best player, I thought!) So ended the 100th day and sadly the next day I had to leave Mellissa and Josh, to go and stay a night in Brisbane as my train to Sydney was rather an early one.

But in a way my hundredth and first day was quite unusual.

Chapter 32

And on the 101st day I reached Scarborough!

December 28th was a sad day to start, sad because I had to say goodbye to Mellissa, Josh, her “bump” and Darcy and Gypsy. Josh had to leave earlyish for work. It was still cloudy with a little rain. But gradually it brightened up, and the temperature had risen sufficiently for me to be back in shorts. I hugged Mellissa and kissed the baby (well, as near as possible!) and walked to the local bus to take me to Toowoomba Bus station, and then the Greyhound bus to Brisbane.

Of course the three of them will be MOST welcome to come and stay with us, if they manage to get to Scarborough, UK! I have to stress the UK Scarborough, as today I was going to Scarborough, Queensland! I caught the local train from Brisbane to Brunswick, and walked to the **City Palms Motel**, where I was staying , booked in and left my luggage, then found a bus going to Redcliff district and the Bay area that was called Scarborough. It was about an hour’s ride, and the weather was pleasant again. This was the third other Scarborough that I had visited on my trip. It was certainly the nicest of the ones named after my own. Like the UK, original, Scarborough, it had two beaches, separated by a kind of cliff (red sand-

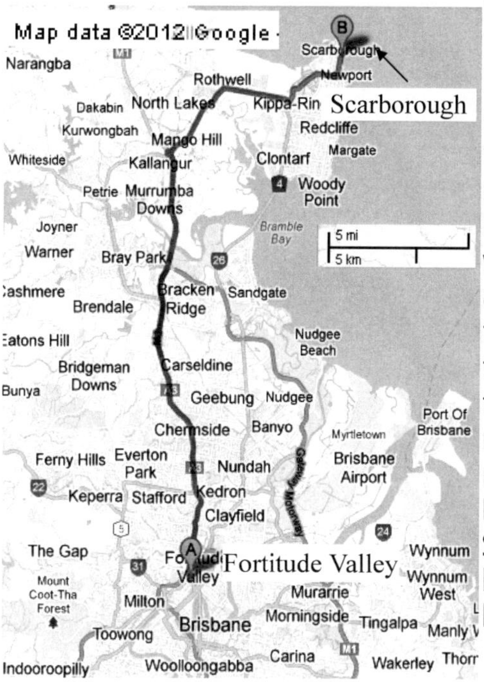

Scarborough, Brisbane

stone). Although it looked nothing like the original, it was certainly pleasant, and I would not mind spending more time here. I took many photos of the beach and rocks, then walked round the north bay and caught the return bus back to my Motel. I then bought some food for the journey, and relaxed by reading and playing Sudoku as it was to be an early rise next morning.

I had my breakfast of fruit at 4am, and booked out of the hotel at 5 am. I walked to the local train station, and caught the train to return to the main station in Brisbane. My train left Brisbane, to return to Sydney (a 15 hour ride) for the last time at 6.30 am. I hadn't gone far when I realised to my horror that I had left my green bag and a Tesco bag of FOOD on the local train or at the station! I wondered what would be the fate of this bag! Would it be blown up in a controlled explosion in case it was a bomb? But my main thought was what a waste of food, and now I would go hungry. I was just thankful that the only contents of those bags was food, and a nothing special in the way of souvenirs from my trip.

40 minutes late, the train arrived into Sydney and I made my sleepy way to the **Metro Central Hotel** that I had booked when I was travelling the opposite way a few days ago. This was probably the most expensive hotel stay ($134) of all, and I was spending a very short time, arriving late and getting up early. But it gave me time to book in my luggage for the journey and time to walk around Sydney for the last time, purchasing some new food to eat on the journey. I didn't have time to walk to that lovely Gourmet sandwich bar so I had to make do with food from shops on the station. I eventually climbed aboard the long train, for one of the longest train journeys ever for me. The train was a little late in getting away at 2.55pm. Next follows a thrilling journey, another great rail journey of a lifetime.

More views of Scarborough Brisbane

Chapter 33
Indian/Pacific rail journey, Sydney to Perth - Crossing the great Nullarbor Desert

This was to be my last long distance great train journey on my world tour, and I had booked the Red Kangaroo sleeper service. This did not provide meals, but there was a choice of eating one's own food and or using the restaurant or the bar. And there was a lounge carriage as well. I had

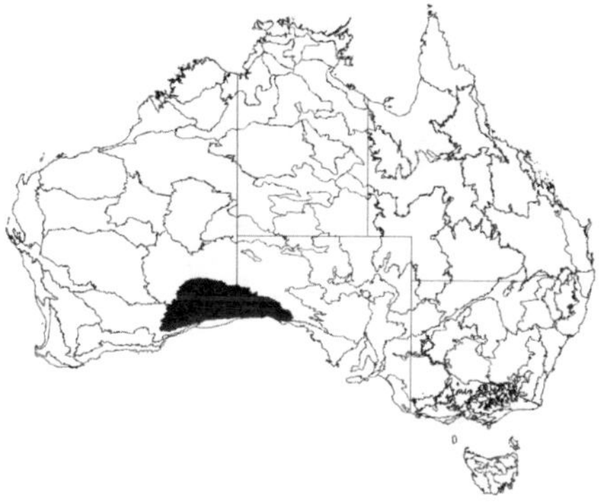

opted for the Red, rather than the Gold service, as it was considerably cheaper, and it was easy to obtain one's own food at the stopping off points on the journey. Gold Kangaroo included free meals in the restaurant. This train travels only twice a week each way, but it seems pretty full. I had hoped that my cabin would not have to be shared, as had happened in my two previous trains with sleeper service, but for the first day I shared with a "seasoned" Gold Kangaroo traveller, as he had booked too late, and had to travel red for the

The Trans-Australian Railway railway line crosses the Nullarbor Plain from Port Augusta. to Kalgoorlie. Construction began in1917, when two teams set out from Kalgoorlie in Western Australia and Port Augusta in South Australia, meeting in the centre of the Plain at Ooldea, an uninhabited area noted for a water supply. This original line suffered severe problems with track flexing and settling in the desert sands, and journeys across the Plain were slow and arduous. The line was entirely rebuilt in 1969, as part of a project to standardise the previously disparate rail gauges in the various states, and the first crossing of the Nullarbor on the new line reached Perth on 27 February 1970. The Indian Pacific is a regular passenger train crossing the Nullarbor from Perth to Sydney via Adelaide.
The railway line holds the record for the longest straight section of railway in the world (478 km), while the road contains the longest straight piece of tarred road surface in Australia (146.6 km).

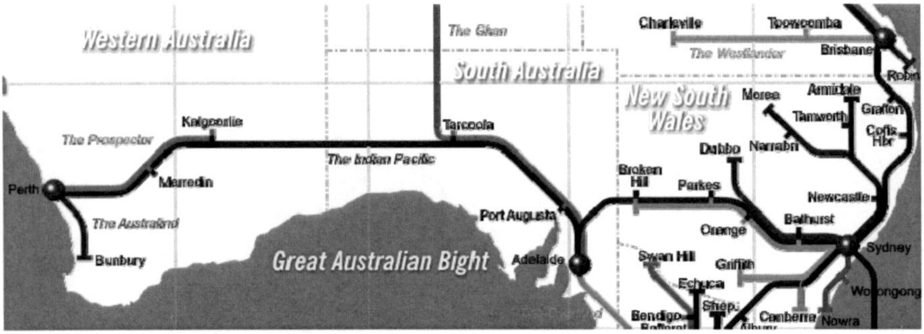

THE ADVENTURE THAT SPANS AUSTRALIA

The Indian Pacific is a fascinating adventure that spans the massive continent of Australia, from coast to coast, ocean to ocean. This certificate acknowledges your trip in Gold Kangaroo Service aboard the Indian Pacific, one of the world's greatest and longest train journeys.

Tony Braxton-Smith
Chief Executive Officer
Great Southern Railway

Gold
KANGAROO SERVICE

Date travelled
2006

CERTIFICATE OF CROSSING

PHOTO BY STEVE MADEX

THE BEARER OF THIS CERTIFICATE HAS CROSSED THE NULLARBOR PLAIN. ON THE LONGEST STRAIGHT STRETCH IN THE WORLD. COOK IS A GREAT PLACE TO VISIT AND HAS A POPULATION OF 7 PEOPLE.

1 CAT 20 CHOOKS 30 DINGOES

1 DOG 3 MILLION FLIES.

SIGNED...........................TOWN MANAGER

first day. He was a writer, from what I remember and seemed an interesting man. We left Sydney a little late. This first day was in fact a re-run of the earlier trip to Alice Springs. One of the main differences was that this time I had sleeper service and the weather over the blue mountains was fine, and I did get a more comfortable sleep than in standard service! The next morning when we stopped at Broken Hill I went on the organised trip to see the Royal Flying Doctor Service station, which was operating from near Broken Hill. This was something I had heard about, mainly because it was commemorated on Australia postage stamps, so though it cost extra I just HAD to go. I think about three coaches full took us out and we had a proper conducted tour, telling us the history of this service for supplying the outback towns villages and settlements. Broken Hill itself, although an outback town, was quite large and had a decent shopping centre and an art gallery. We re-boarded the train and later that afternoon we pulled in to Adelaide, my third and last time to see this clean city. We stopped long enough for me to walk into the wonderful market area and top up with more food for my journey; I would not see any more sizeable places till we reached Perth in two days time. On returning to our cabins, as promised my Gold Kangaroo friend had found a place in the Gold service for the rest of his journey, so now I had the double cabin to myself. I said goodbye to Adelaide and then we pulled away, on

Irrigation on the way to Adelaide

Royal Flying Doctor Service, hangar.

Adelaide

Broken Hill

to new territory for me after Port Augusta. Whilst sitting in the lounge area I got talking to an Argentinean student who was about to start doing a PhD in Statistics in Perth University. Later I joined in playing a different form, to me, of "rummy" with a couple.

Seeing in of the New Year at its fastest.

When we re-boarded the train at Adelaide the staff were all dressed up as if in party mode! So we thought that the seeing of the new year would be in a party mood! Anyway we played rummy in the lounge car and nothing special happened. But for me this was definitely the fastest that I have ever approached and entered a new year. In the past I had always been in one place, and not travelling. But on this train travelling at 85 Kph into the new year was certainly faster than I was used to. We drifted off to bed around 12.30 am. I was up 6 hours later to watch the first sunrise of 2007. Not too long after breakfasting time (for most people!) we pulled in to the famous town which has been a "watering" stop ever since the railway existed. It is in the middle of the desert. It now has the distinction of being the town where the whole resident population of human beings turns out to greet the four trains per week that pass through and stop for a couple of hours. I have the authenticated certificate (laminated!) that boldly states that the town has 7 People, 1 cat, 1 dog, 20 Chooks 30 Dingoes and 3 MILLION FLIES!. The certificate also boldly states that we are going to be crossing the Nullarbor plain on the longest straight stretch of railway in the world.

DIFFERENT GAME OF RUMMY

In this version you cannot lay down till you have at least four of a run in same suit or four of same number. When you pick up the whole of the discard pile you must be able to lay-down at least the top card showing from that pick up. The cards point values are 5pt for 2 to 9, the rest are 10 pts. Those laid down count positive, those in your hand negative. 1st to reach +500pt is winner.

4 Signs at Cook

2 views of the Nullarbor

Kalgoorlie

Only 477.14 Km! They have a bold notice telling people to "GET ILL! The hospital NEEDS YOU"! And other such stupendous claims. One such claim, that must always stump them is that they have a cricket club!

The town used to be a LOT larger when the trains really needed to stop and refuel and take on water. They even tried to get trees to grow there; there was, several years ago, a big drive to start a small woodland. There really was a hospital, school and cinema and several shops. In our two hour wait here in the searing dry heat, we wandered round the derelict town buildings and saw the sights, and visited the one remaining shop that sold us all the possible souvenirs that they could possibly think up for such a historic town with the smallest population, in which the shop opened 4 times a week for a couple of hours to hundreds of souvenir collectors of "rare" material. I think some food was available, but only in the sweet shop format. The daily newspaper had plenty to report. The only thing was that the news was the same every day!

We then all piled on to our long refrigerated boxes on wheels, thankful that the heat inside was not so great, and continued our crossing of this famous railway line and *straight* away Rummy was resumed . Later, in the early evening, we were at the end of the straightness and were deposited for a two hour break at Kalgoorlie, where we found that the heat outside was still unbearably hot, even at 10 pm. Many of us were highly disappointed that we could not go on the advertised coach tour of the gold mines, because being a Holiday the train company could find only one coach willing to work, and all the places were taken up by the Gold Kangaroo passengers. Anyway those Red Kangaroos of us who were the Rummy contingent went for a wander round Kalgoorlie and we were looking for a cooling off place and eventually found a hotel bar open to non residents and we ordered our drinks.

Inside the India/Pacific train

Inside the refrigerated air was TOO cool and being in shorts I was beginning to shiver! After a while we wandered out again, grateful to be back in the heat, but by the time we were back at the train we were so glad to be able to get back into the cool train. Luckily it was not as cool as the hotel!

The scenery outside the train was, as expected, mainly the same, but there was real life out there, both plant and animal who survived the harsh hot conditions and very little rain. I believe that it is less than 7 inches a year and most of rain falls in one or two spells of short duration. I know that on the news on TV when I was in Perth a few days later I heard of much flooding even in the Kalgoorlie area. Anyway as it was an early arrival in Perth next morning, we went off to bed. Coming off the high Nullarbor plain occurred during the night and the contrast of the scenery as we pulled in to Perth was great. It was much more Mediterranean, and there were clouds to greet us.

Before our arrival we had to declare what foods we had, and the health inspector made sure we had no fresh fruit or veg with us before we detrained! They did on this train allow me to keep my cashew nuts, as they are in fact partially cooked. Breakfast was all the remaining fruit I had, and I gave away a couple of apples!

We alighted from the train, and guess what? It RAINED. Not heavily, but it RAINED! Why was it, I asked myself, that in practically EVERY Australian city I visited it RAINED, often on my arrival? I thought about hiring out my services to the cities that needed rain (free accommodation would do) just for me to go and visit them and bring them much needed rain! Another English traveller was also remarking on the same thing! Anyway the rain was not much, just a little fine rain and I decided to walk to my hotel, under my trusty umbrella.

Now I was at last in the city where I was hoping to meet one of my first Internet friends. We had been friendly since we first became acquainted in her Yahoo group “In The Veggiepot”. What an adventure I had had because of making so many young friends around the world. Now the last stage of my Australian adventure had at last begun. I was staying put in Perth for ten full days. This was to be the longest stay in one place on my whole journey.

Free Transit Zone (FTZ)

Within the Perth city centre travel on public transport is free. The boundaries of this free travel zone are defined at the Transperth web site. To travel within this zone you can simply hop on any train, bus or CAT. You are not restricted to the amount of times you can use this service and no tickets are required. The FTZ includes City West and Claisebrook on the Fremantle, Midland and Armadale train lines, the start and finish of the FTZ are clearly marked, on the train stations and bus stops. If you board a train or bus inside the FTZ and intend to travel outside of the FTZ a valid ticket must be purchased and fares apply from where you first board to your destination.

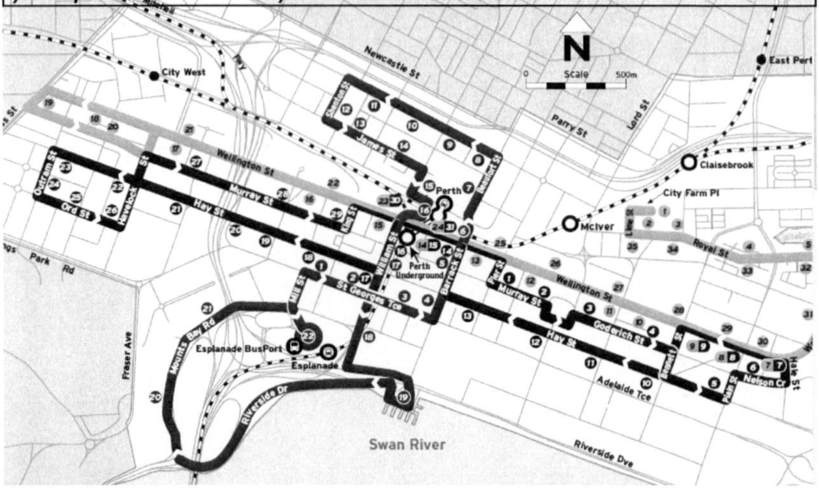

Chapter 34
PERTH,
and on Rottnest Island I went QUOKKAS!

{Mike Enjo}

I arrived at my hotel **Kings Perth Hotel**, which had been booked earlier on the internet. I find that often one can get much cheaper rates booking hotels on the net! I arrived, and although I was booking in early, my room was ready and I was able to go and get settled in.

By this time it was quite late (for me) for lunch; using Happy Cow I had a list of Veggie places to eat in Perth, and using a map I eventually found **Govinda's** Restaurant. I had a nice plate of salad with rice, and it was only $2! It was, though, quite a way from the hotel; later I found nearer places to eat, or I ate my own fruit. I found an internet café, not far from the hotel. And after having a late mid-day nap, I had dinner at the **Lotus Vegetarian Restaurant**, where I had a decent meal for only $12. It was on my way back to my hotel that I met, quite by chance, Ian and Janet and 2 of their New Zealand friends, and later still the other couple of Rummy card players from the train journey. They were driving all the way back across Australia in their Vauxhall car. Life is full of surprises! I then returned to my hotel, room 617 which was on the 6th floor. They had a key safe so one could leave one's keys when one went out. Now here it was that I saw the rather strange notice (to me), about clothing standards in the hotel. The wearing of Thongs was banned! At the time this puzzled me. "How would they KNOW if you were wearing a Thong," I said to myself. This conundrum was not sorted out till I met Mike; I felt a bit shy at asking about this at the hotel!

I had a decent night's sleep, and went shopping for

fruit for breakfast and booked the hotel for the further 6 nights, as I found it was satisfactory! It was cheaper to do this on the net! Luckily I could stay in the same room.

I then decided to check up on Visa requirements for going to Philippines and Hong Kong. Hong Kong definitely did not require one, and nor did Philippines, as I was staying under 21 days. I went to the Philippines Embassy to check this. Later I went to the Indian Embassy, but found it closed at 1pm! So I had to put that off for 2 more days, as I planned to visit Mandurah all day the next day. I then found Gelare, very close to my hotel, and had a lovely Vegan Smoothie. This place had been recommended to me by Danielle.

I got around Perth making use of two of the three CATS. What a useful thing is a CAT! There are three FREE bus services going on intermingling circular routes around Perth. At each bus stop there was an automatic digital sign telling one how long one would have to wait. And as the service was every ten minutes, you never had to wait very long. No wonder the traffic was not clogged up as people USED this service instead of cars. More towns and cities should have this system. I also found out that EVERY bus in Perth offered free transport within the city centre. *[http://www.lookatwa.com.au/Transport/cats.html]*

With not much to do, I now relaxed back in the hotel and used the internet café. I had a longish journey lined up for the following day, to Mandurah. Ever since I met Danielle in her VeggiePot I had wanted to visit Mandurah.

Thursday Jan 4th was the day I needed to start taking daily the South Eastern Asian Homoeopathic medicine as a precaution to help prevent me catching several diseases that can be found in the region I was going to next after Australia. One tablet I had to take 3 times a day and another once per week.

After breakfast I caught the free bus to the bus station and then two other buses to reach Mandurah centre. On the long distance bus, I was about the only passenger, and suddenly the roof window blew wide open and rattled loudly. One of its fittings had broken! So for the rest of the journey I held onto the roof window handle, to prevent it blowing right off. I learnt that soon this bus service would be replaced by a new train line service, connecting Perth to Mandurah.

When I was deposited in the centre of the town I walked around the Performing Arts Theatre area, along the Estuary, the Mandurah Plaza, the Mandurah Museum, and Pinjarra road to the centre and wasted 50 minutes trying to use the internet (free) at the library. A couple of teenage girls on the other computers, obviously having slow working computers as well, were making remarks suggesting that old people should not be using computers. This seemed rather surprising, and am not sure why they were feeling like that! I just ignored them. Though one was polite enough when I asked her something about the library.

I think I just managed to READ some of my emails, but it was far too slow to reply. So after having a nice vegan salad at **Baked 'N' Buttered,** I returned to the bus stop, walking back to the estuary.

Scenes at Mandurah

I had taken several photos in this area, including several water birds. I returned to Perth by buses, with no memorable mishaps. That evening Mike phoned to arrange for him to meet me the next day at 8.30pm and for all day Saturday to take me to my fourth and last Scarborough.

The first thing I did was to take the bus to the Indian Consulate to arrange my Visa to India. But after a long chat and filling in of forms I found that they could not process it in time before I left for the Philippines, with no settled addresses ahead of me. So the next thing was that I had to go to the Quantas air line building in Perth, and change my flights so that I stayed an extra day in Singapore and returned home from there direct to London on the 26th Jan, arriving early morning in London Heathrow on the 27th Jan. I had been going to stay in India for about 5 days, in a flat belonging to my friend Geeta, but they had sold it recently, so I was instead going to stay in a hotel. And also I had hoped to meet up with my son Tim in Delhi. (There were no Indian Internet friends there to meet at that time.) So it was very disappointing not going to India, as I had not seen my son for a few years, although he lives in UK, mainly because he is so busy at work. I use his company as internet service provider.

Anyway this took me till 1 pm. I then checked my emails and found one from Danielle agreeing to meet me for lunch on the Wednesday, if she was well enough. She was experiencing great pains in her spine. I then had a late lunch, and a latish tea and Mike called for me in his car and took me to a café, where he ate whilst I had a drink. We had a good chat about his life, and Zorpia, for whom he now worked full time. We also talked about my trip and the people and places I had visited. Then he took me round Perth by car to see the Perth lights, including Perth from the hill side (Kings Park) to look down on its night lights.

Perth at night from Kings Park

In and around Perth

Mike deposited me back at my hotel, arranging for him to pick me up at noon next day.

Scarborough (again!) Beach.

Before Mike arrived to take me out for the afternoon I made use of the time to catch up with emails etc on the internet. At 12 noon Mike arrived with his lovely wife Aya and their baby Grace, and whisked me off to Scarborough Beach, which is on the coast and a suburb of Perth to the north West. So now at last I had visited 4 Scarboroughs on my world journey. There are 14 around the world, and I had now been to 5 of them. Scarborough Beach seemed to be nothing more than a long sandy beach running South to North. I did paddle there and have photographic proof! Then we drove about 30 to 40 miles north and went to the lovely Yanchep National Park. It appears that there are several national parks in this area of Western Australia where wild life is allowed to thrive with as little interference by humans as possible and yet people can view and enjoy nature.

We saw birds, and Koalas, and went on a wetlands trail (2 km) round Lock McNess. On this trail we passed a sleeping Brown Snake. This snake is one of the most renowned poisonous snakes in the world. In fact there are several varieties in Australia. The one we passed is deadly poisonous, but treated quickly enough one can be saved if bitten. The Western Brown Snake is smaller and less dangerous than the Eastern

Yanchep National Park
offers you a choice of nine interesting walk trails ranging in length from 500 metres to 55 kilometres. Along the way you will witness spectacular scenery and panoramic views from the sea to the scarp.
Yanchep National Park, National Park Road, Yanchep, 6035
Phone +61 08 9561 1004 Email yanchep@dec.wa.gov.au
Website http://www.naturebase.net/yanchep

Mike & his daughter

Perth Bell Tower

one. I attempted to take a picture of it, but it slithered away into the grassland and undergrowth before I could get the camera ready. *(The picture shown is not mine.)* I know that Aya was quite upset by the experi-

ence, particularly because she was pregnant. I was just pleased that I had seen one in the wild, but disappointed that I had not got its photograph. We actually passed it only about three feet away! We were on a proper pathway.

Later we passed an area where Koalas were sleeping high up in the trees and I saw and photographed the famous kookaburra, but even using the zoom, I was unable to get a sharp picture, as it was quite well shaded in the woodland area. It was wonderful meeting Mike and his family; I was so pleased to have found out about this intelligent and interesting man and especially to have met his lovely wife and daughter. When I first met Mike in Zorpia, he seemed pleased that someone actually wrote in sentences and spelled words "correctly", and used punctuation! Mike was then a full time employee on Zorpia. I was privileged to have met him.

Later I was returned to my hotel and I caught up with things on Internet again, and on my walk back to my hotel I happened to look inside another one in passing and saw to my amazement Ian and Janet and a friend of theirs in the hotel restaurant. I joined them for a while and caught up with our respective news.

That evening I managed to make contact with Tricia and Roger Walmsley from the Perth Friends Meeting (Quakers) House. *[West Australia Regional Meeting, Friends Meeting House, 35 Clifton Crescent Mt Lawley, Perth, WA 6050 +61 8 9272 1268*] The next

Osprey Nest

My visit to Rottnest Island

The totally adorable friendly wild Quokka

morning they very kindly came to pick me up and took me to the meeting. This was, I think, my first ever experience of attending a Quaker Meeting out of the UK. I brought to them greetings from Scarborough England, and was asked to return them. Roger and Tricia kindly returned me to my hotel and after a nap and lunch I spent time wandering round Perth City taking photos. I was particularly interested in the Swan Bell Tower, the largest musical instrument in the world.

In the evening I went out again to take photos of the night lights of Perth, still very Christmassy! So ended day 111.

NO PLATYPUS

As you know, one animal I was keen to see was a platypus. This was the last chance I would have of seeing one, and several people suggested that I might see one in Perth Zoo. On taking a bus to the zoo, I discovered they had no platypuses, but I did see an echidna.

The echidna is best known not only as a mascot of Sydney Olympic Games 2000, but also for its amazing biology. Like the platypus, this unusual mammal lays eggs and suckles its young. The echidna and platypus are the only members of a primitive group of mammals known as monotremes. The one I saw was curled up fast asleep. I saw many other interesting animals from Australasia, as well as the more familiar Zoo animals like Giraffes, Elephants etc. The enclosures here

were larger than some of those I saw in Fort Worth, and they all looked well cared for. Of the two zoos I visited I preferred Perth's. It was less commercial too.

I spent some time on the internet both AM and PM.

Interesting fact: The name '**Monotreme'** means 'single opening', because members of the order of Monotremata all just have one opening when other female mammals have three (vagina, the urethra, and the anus).

Even in this day and age, still a lot of people think that these creatures are inferior, believing that these are the ancestors of the "superior" mammals. Modern studies have almost proved that the modern monotremes are survivor of a long-ago division of the mammal world.

Going back to the eggs, these are maintained for some time, and Monotremes lactate, but nipples are absent. The milk comes out from the mammary glands through holes in the skin, and not only that, these Monotremes have long lives, with low levels of reproduction.

Monotremes' jaws are built differently from the other kinds of mammals, and its jaw muscles are different too. The small bones are totally merged to the skull, and not lying from the jaw as in pre-mammalian synapsids. The outside opening of its ear lies at the jaw's base. They have additional bones at the shoulder area, which other mammal forms do not. They have a reptile-like movement, legs are at the side of the body and not under it. A male Monotreme's leg has a spur near the ankle, and this holds a strong venom.

The internet was cheaper in the library, and nearer the hotel, and it was coin operated. The Internet café I found was reasonably cheap, and was open longer hours, and you paid for your time at the end of your session.

When I first met Mike, and he was telling me of interesting places to go and see, he asked me if I had seen a Quokka. At first I thought this an Australianism for Crocodile. But it wasn't. What Mike told me made me really want to meet one. It was an endangered species, and was now only found in one place in the world, in the wild. I had to go there. I did go there.

It meant getting up early, which is what I did on

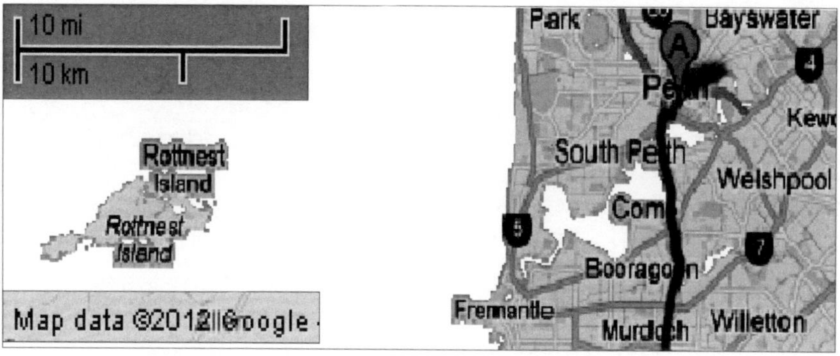

Tuesday Jan 9th, at 5am. I took a train to Fremantle 7.10 am, and a boat at 8.30 am and arrived at the jetty at 9.20. The boat then returned to Fremantle. I was now on an island just 20km northwest off the coast of Fremantle, Rottnest Island, a popular vacation spot and day-tripping destination for Perth's population and visitors. Famous for the quokka, a small marsupial unique to this region, Rottnest offers a relaxed holiday atmosphere and brilliant water-based activities and historical attractions. Willem de Vlamingh discovered the island. He was a Dutch mariner who thought Rottnest's quokkas looked like giant rats. When he landed in 1696, he named the island 'Rat's Nest Island', or in Dutch, Rottenest Island. This low white sandy island is quite small, measuring 11km long and 5km wide.

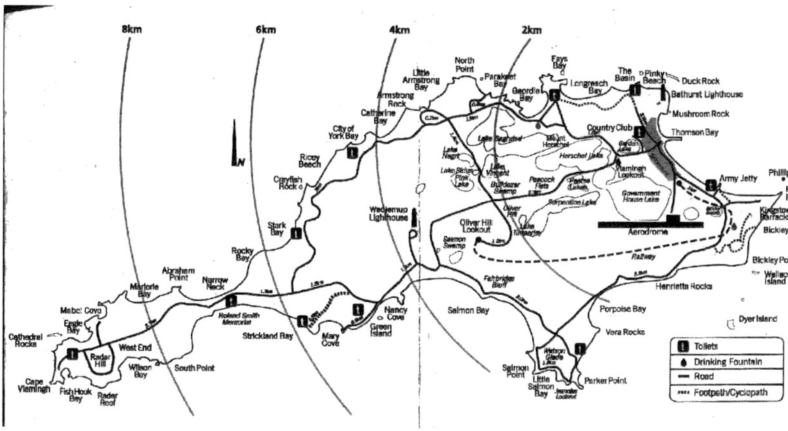

Rottnest is covered by grassy plains, woodlands and scattered salt lakes; its low-lying scrub and bush vegetation is very hardy. Rottnest Island Pines and Rottnest Island Tea Trees are native to this area and dominate much of the landscape. Rottnest's coastline is very attractive; there are numerous secluded bays with clear water and soft, white beaches to rival any island in the world. The surrounding sea is a marine sanctuary that protects a wide variety of fish and other marine creatures. No pets, guns or spear guns are allowed on Rottnest Island. Visitors are not allowed to bring motorised vehicles, only bicycles. There is a regular bus service going on a circular tour stopping almost anywhere people want. There is also a train.

The main reason for my visit was to see a Quokka. The Quokka (Setonix brachyurus), the only member of the genus Setonix, is a small macropod about the size of a large domestic cat. Like other marsupials in the macropod family (such as the kangaroos and wallabies), the Quokka is herbivorous and mainly nocturnal. It can be found on some smaller islands off the coast of Western Australia, in particular on Rottnest Island just off Perth, and Bald Island near Albany. A small mainland colony exists in the protected area Two Peoples Bay, where they co-exist with Gilbert's Potoroo. The Quokka has no fear of humans and it is common for it to approach them closely, particularly on Rottnest Island. It is, however, illegal for members of the public on Rottnest Island to handle the animals in any way.

When I did finally see one close up, I fell in love with it. I decided mentally that this is an animal I would love to have as a pet! But I know that was impossible. The Quokka is such a sweet animal. I took its photo as still and as movies.

I took many photos of beaches, scenery and wildlife.

The island itself was amazing. The beaches were out of this world. Things were so clean and fresh. I did in fact use the bus to see several beaches, and at one such beautiful beach, which was a good 40 minutes walk away from the nearest bus, I did see slithering below me a brownish snake. I managed to photograph it, all except its head because it was so quick to hide! This snake, the Dugite, is a venomous snake, part of the Brown Snake family. This snake's bite can be deadly, especially to young children or elders.

Again, like most venomous snakes they will only bite if they feel threatened. Be careful when walking through the bushes throughout Rottnest. Watch your step and if you do come across this, just respect their habitat.

At the end of a long day of walking I took the boat back to Fremantle and train back to Perth. The day was not quite over: I had another surprise in store in the early evening!

When I arrived back at the hotel, I noticed two strange looking cycles, which had a double seat trailer attached. They were obviously for transport. Later I came out again and saw a youngish couple of men there. I got talking to one about them, and he explained it was a new public transport system, for clean taxi services in towns and cities. They were actually power assisted cycles, and were being trialled out in different parts of Australia. I was offered at FREE trial, and it was an interesting experience. Something like this needs to be offered in all major towns and cities. I wished them all the best. Now it was time for bed before the day I had been waiting for, and the person I was about to meet, one of my earliest internet friends, the one I thought of as a daughter.

Quokka

Power assisted cycle taxis

Chapter 35
Mystical Dreamland.

{Danielle}

Danielle was definitely one of my earliest internet friends, whom I will always remember, as my first internet "daughter". When we talked in the Yahoo groups and on MSN and Yahoo messengers, talking together just seemed so natural. The age different was BIG. I was old enough to be her grandfather. She was the one to first point out that our ages were the reverse of each other, and worked out that this would be the case every 11 years. She was 16 and I was 61, but this was for only a few months of the year. From this I developed the terminology of being a "Reverse Teenager!" and in several Yahoo Groups this was how I was known as a joke. In July 2010 I was again a Reverse Teenager of "17" and year later our ages were in reverse again, when Danielle was 27, for part of that year.

Apart from her being, as she described herself, a lonely Vegetarian, she was also very much into green politics. She was also interested in many aspects of life and geography and astronomy. But apart from our finding it so easy to talk to each other, she did actually TEACH me something, and that I will also treasure all my life. I had never considered myself a writer of anything much, even though when at school I had rewritten a 6th form Xmas time sketch, filling it with some of the most 'awful' puns on the teachers' nicknames, done in such a way that though obvious who was being mentioned, they could not complain! When I went to college, again in spite of my having failed English O level twice before passing it on the third attempt, I started the twice yearly College student magazine "The Badger" (the college Mascot!) Later I started the 5 times a year "Newspaper" which when published sold for 1d, and was very popular: it sold out on the day of issue! This was called “McOft” (Medway College Of Technology) and included real news and “scandals”. When I finally became a teacher of Maths I nearly always started up a form magazine issued two or three times a year, to raise money for charities, but the children mainly wrote these themselves! Sandra Cameron, whom I had met in Avoca Beach earlier in this journey, was one of those who helped produce her form’s magazine.

The one thing I had never done was write poetry, and never considered it, as I felt unable to do so. Now Danielle was often writing her inner feelings down in poetry. At first I had not really realised that her poems were from her heart and feelings. I assumed that they were just *interesting.* But she encouraged me to write poems myself. It was not long before I was writing all sorts of them. Funny ones, serious ones and purely ridiculous ones! I found that my young friends on the internet enjoyed them, and this encouraged me further. And though I do not write so many now, I do still do so. With having practice I think they are better written now, well Dilys says so. I still can’t spell, and don't really understand poetry construction from any grammatical perspective, but there is one thing I am absolutely sure about and that is the fact that without Danielle’s encouragement I would never have started writing in this way. I found it easier to write in this form when feeling emotional about something. This also led me to understand better what Danielle was writing about, and today I was going to meet MY TEACHER.

She confirmed the time and place by email and I waited outside Gelare hoping that I would recognise her, because it was a long time ago since I had seen a photo of her. I saw this prettily dressed young lady approach the café, and thought that can’t be her! I knew her only wearing jeans. But this lady was at the right time, she was about the height I expected, and I followed her in and she turned and we both asked each other "Are You........." and yes we were. I bought her a chocolate ice cream (VEGAN of course and I had a smoothie, I think, or I may have had the same, I cannot remember!)

I was so happy to be meeting my "daughter" after all these years, and she was not only the nice friendly person I knew, she was so pretty too. To look at her one would never have guessed the real pain she was suffering in her spine. We talked for over an hour in the café, about many things. One was that she had not realised till very recently that Adam (from Sydney) had a deep crush on her, although they had talked soooooo much in those days. She told me a lot about her family and her feelings and her time soon ran out and we walked together to the bus stop where she caught her bus to take her to see a surgeon to discuss what would be needed to do.

In an email she had warned me before that, because of what had happened many years previously when at school she had been molested by a teacher, she was not able to give and receive hugs from older men, and that even applied to her grandfather. Anyway, whilst waiting for her bus we asked a passer-by to take our photo together for my photo records. And, as her bus was about to arrive, I asked if it were OK to shake hands and we did, and then just as she was about to get on the bus she suddenly turned and gave me a short but meaningful hug, which I of course returned. I felt so happy, even though our meeting had been so short. Afterwards she told me (in an email) that the pain had been increasing in that time. I was so sad that such a lovely person should have to be suffering so much, it did not seem fair. All she gave out was love and kindness.

Later that day I posted off another parcel of stuff home as my suitcase was getting so heavy with souvenirs and leaflets etc. This was the fourth such parcel. This was also my last day in Perth. Happy at meeting Danielle whom I cared about so much, and sad that we would probably never meet again.

Next was my roundabout journey to a multi island country in S.E. Asia, The Philippines. In my early days as a stamp collector, being a Phillips I wanted stamps from The Philippines, and strangely enough the first friend I ever had in The Philippines was a stamp collector!

(*The last I heard from Danielle was a couple of years later, after she had had her spinal operation, so she survived. But not having heard from her since, I*

A Unique Attraction – One of its kind.

An outstanding landmark location linking the City and River, the **Bell Tower** is a unique attraction – a musical instrument of considerable historical and cultural significance. Here bells and clocks from all over the world, from all through the ages, have been carefully restored, preserved, interpreted and are now celebrated by visitors daily.

The Bell Tower is a GOLD MEDAL Major Attraction for Western Australia.

This historic ring of bells was gifted to the people of Western Australia as part of the national Bicentennial celebrations.

The Bell Tower includes the twelve bells of St Martin-in-the-Fields, in Trafalgar Square (London) which are recorded as being in existence from before the 14th century and recast in the 16th century by Queen Elizabeth I.

They are one of the few sets of royal bells and are the only ones known to have left England.

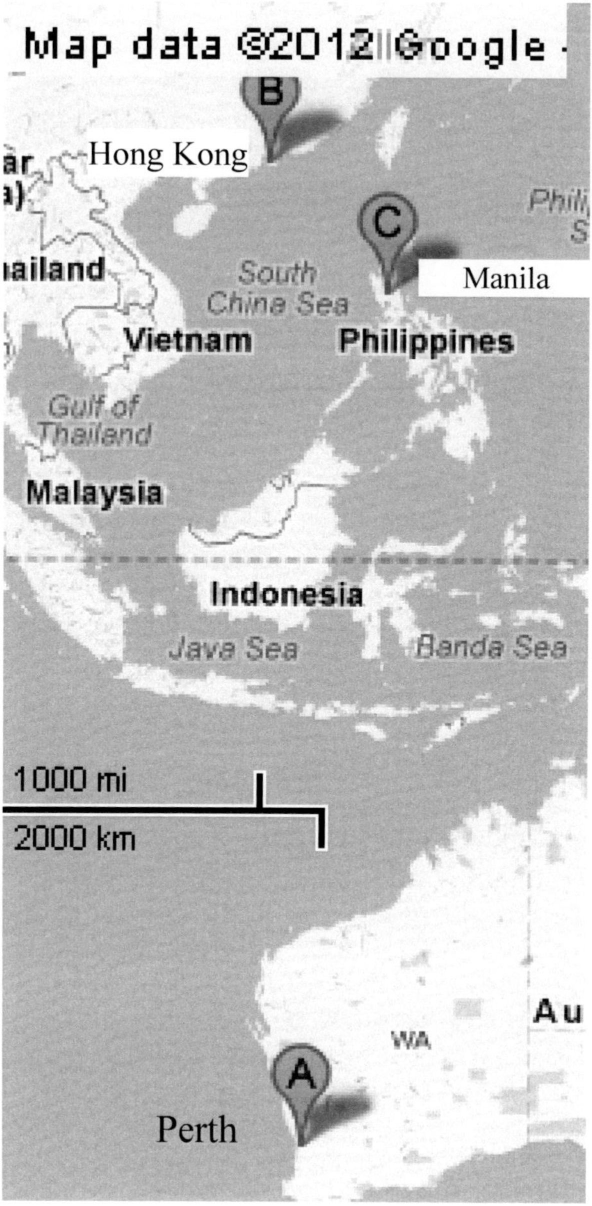
Map data ©2012 Google
B
Hong Kong
C
Manila
Thailand
South China Sea
Vietnam
Philippines
Gulf of Thailand
Malaysia
Indonesia
Java Sea
Banda Sea
1000 mi
2000 km
WA
A
Perth

Chapter 36
Long day to Manila

(Dee and Monica}

For some reason there were no direct flights on the "One World" flights system to take me to Manila from Perth; I had to go via Hong Kong. So in the morning I packed up everything, had a last go on the internet for 50 minutes, caught the free shuttle bus to the airport at 10.30 am and boarded the HUGE plane. The seats were 2 - 4 - 2. I had a window seat, thankfully, from which I was able to take a few photos of Northern Western Australia. The plane took off promptly at 1.50 pm and arrived at H K at 8.35 pm. This meant a wait till the early hours to catch the Manila plane, a short 2 hour hop leaving HK at 8.05 am. I had decided to "sleep at the airport!" using the seats. Luckily I found that in the airport there were a few places, near seats, when one could use the Internet for free. Officially one was allowed only 15 minutes at a time, but as so few people were about time was unlimited most of the time. So that night I spent the time eating, sitting sleeping, reading, standing (at the internet connection) and going to the toilet.

Luckily because the flights were booked as a single journey I had only my "hand" luggage with me; the main luggage was transferred automatically. Eventually the time for boarding, 6am, arrived and I was on the plane to the multiple island country in the South Pacific, which kind of bore my name. The country of which I wanted to collect the stamps when I was a boy because it was called Philippines! A country in which I was about to meet two young ladies (plus Monica's friends): Monica whom I had "met" in The Yahoo Group "Stamp Addicts" when she was 14, 5 years earlier, and I had helped her add to her collection, who was now at University of the Philippines-Diliman Campus, Quezon City; and Dee, whom I had met more recently in Zorpia, who was now a paid employee of Zorpia. I had known Dee only just over a year, and had helped encourage her through a very difficult personal time.

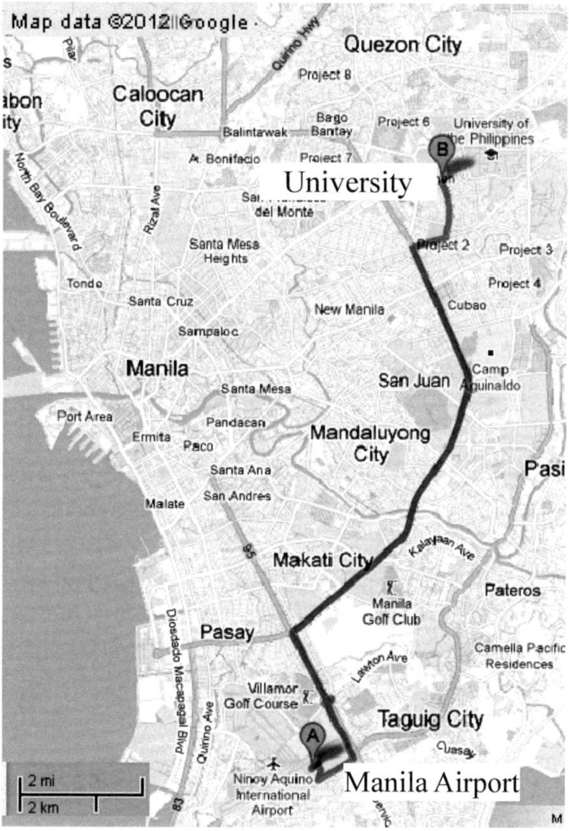

Because of university lectures Monica was unable to meet me on arrival so I arranged to meet Dee at the airport and we went out to a restaurant for a meal. We had great difficulty in meeting up at the start because of the difficulty I had in hearing anything on my mobile phone, and Dee had gone to the wrong terminal. Eventually that was sorted. The noise level at that terminal was so loud, and the constant blaring of announcements. (It was these that drowned the phone conversations!) We went by taxi to Bill Mall and I had a nice salad and fruit lunch. We took photos of each other together and chatted a lot. Luckily we did get a chance to meet up again. Dee kindly returned me to the airport and waited for Monica. Monica eventually arrived a little late with an instructor friend of hers, Andy (Ferandre), and we all got into a taxi; we dropped off Dee part of the way to her home in Quezon City. We finally arrived at the **University Hotel**. My place had been kindly booked for me by Monica's mother, who was a university professor, in the University of the Philippines-Baguio Campus. She is also the Chancellor of that campus. After dropping off all my luggage in my room, we went to a veggie restaurant, but as it was near closing time and they had sold all the food, we went to another nearby one. We bumped into a lecturer, who knew Andy well, and when this man got to know that I would be writing this book about my trip we found if difficult to be by our selves. He was obviously trying to be helpful, giving me advice and names of agents and publishers, because he had had a book or two published. Eventually I had to explain to him that I had only just arrived and was very tired and had not met Monica before in person, and we needed to talk. Eventually he understood and Monica, Andy and I found a quiet place to talk before we all went our separate ways to bed. So ended a very long TWO days which was like one day!

I slept well eventually and was sufficiently rested for another long day, which was to be so interesting, and so full, that I hope that I do not miss out too much.

We met up at the hotel after breakfast, and I was introduced to Agnes (instructor of political science), and Andy again, and two Japanese students (from Tokyo) who were in The Philippines for a short while on an exchange system. I had my first experience of trav-

University Hotel, Diliman

San Agustin Church

Fort Santiago

Manila

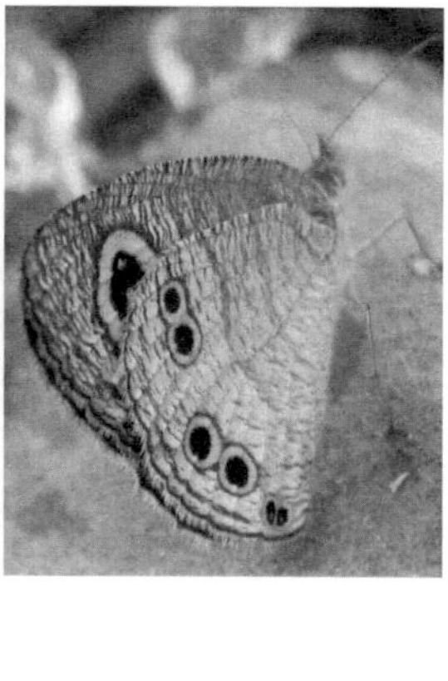

elling by Jeepney.

Jeepneys are to Manila what rickshaws are to Beijing! The way to get around cheaply. Anyone who has not been in one or seen the traffic in Manila, has missed out on their education in public transport. Jeepneys are in fact a glorified Jeeps, originally left over from WW2 when the USA left hundreds of them! Now these stainless steel and chrome masterpieces are a colourful and most prolific form of transport. They carry about 10 people in a kind of minibus with two long seats down each side; the door is at the back. People pay their fares one by one by passing their money to the front, and the driver whilst driving passes the change back, all one by one! Once in the crowded streets of central Manila the fun begins! Apparently once one vehicle has gained an inch in front of another at either side, they HONK HONK and they then have the right of way to change lanes in FRONT of the other! Very hair-raising at the time! What English people who DRIVE here think I have no idea! But I never saw one accident.

This took us part of the way into the Manila City Centre We completed the journey by a large taxi. They took me to inside the old city walls and toured the remains of Fort Santiago.

{This fort has a lot of history much of it not pleasant for the Filipinos. It is situated at the mouth of the Pasig River, which flows into Manila Bay, and was first built to keep out

Ant hill

Nature as seen in and around the University area

Cockroach

The Oblation

the pirates and other marauders. The Spanish then took control in the 1500's. It was the Spanish who rebuilt it as a stronghold fort after they defeated Rajah Sulayman; instead of wood they used stone and it is a formidable and imposing structure.

The Spanish in those days wielded unforgiving power from Fort Santiago. Not only was it used to house the military and Spanish officials, it was also a prison, with its infamous dungeon. Jose Rizal is one of the most famous heroes of the Philippines. He spoke 22 languages, was an academic, artist, scientist and surgeon. But he had nationalistic beliefs and his writings depicted the cruelty of the Spanish over the Filipino peoples. On 26th Aug 1896 he was amongst several who were rounded up and thrown into the dungeons. This date was the start of the Filipino revolution. It was whilst he spent his final days there that he wrote his famous Poem Mi Ultimo Adios, (My Ultimate Goodbye) The full English translation can be read here www.philippines-travel-guide.com/mi-ultimo-adios.html *Jose Rizal was executed by firing squad on Dec 29th 1896, aged 35, for nothing more than writing the truth. A true hero of an oppressed people.*

Not long after this the USA "defeated" the Spanish in a kind of mock battle, to save the Spanish "Honour" and then the USA found a long bloody battle on their hands trying to wrest control over the whole of the Philippines.

The Philippine Revolution against Spain began in April 1896, culminating two years later with a proclamation of independence and the establishment of the First Philippine Republic. However, the Treaty of Paris, at the end of the Spanish-American War, transferred control of the Philippines to the United States. This agreement was not recognized by the Philippine Government which, on June 2, 1899, proclaimed a Declaration of War against the United States. The Philippine-American War which ensued resulted in massive casualties. Philippine president Emilio Aguinaldo was captured in 1901 and the U.S. government declared the conflict officially over in 1902. The Filipino leaders, for the most part, accepted that the Americans had won, but hostilities continued and only began to decline in 1913. U.S. colonial rule of the Philippines started in 1905 with very limited local rule. Partial autonomy (commonwealth status) was granted in 1935, preparatory to a planned full independence from the United States in 1946.

Preparation for a fully sovereign state was interrupted by the Japanese occupation of the islands during World War II. With a promising economy in the 1950s and 1960s, the Philippines in the late 1960s and early 1970s saw a rise of student activism and civil unrest against the corrupt dictatorship of President Ferdinand Marcos who declared martial law in 1972. Because of close ties between United States and President Marcos, the U.S. government continued to support Marcos even though his administration was well-known for massive corruption and extensive human rights abuse. The peaceful and bloodless People Power Revolution of 1986, however, brought about the ousting of Marcos and a return to democracy for the country.}

I have included here this brief modern history of The Philippines, because so little of it is known outside of the area, and it touched me so much that they have had to suffer so long. It was while touring the Intramuros area that I felt I had to learn more. The construction of Intramuros (Walled city) was started in 1571 by Miguel Lopez de Legaspi, a Spaniard. The walled city covers an area of about 160 acres. Intramuros was a fortress city with walls 6 metres high and a commanding 3 kilometres in length. It is no wonder it was impenetrable.

We found a place to eat lunch within the Intramuros. It was a nice little restaurant and I was able to get a decent vegan meal. I had noticed that hanging around were lots of small cats; the vast majority are feral cats living mainly off scraps, more or less in the same way that in Buenos Aires there were feral dogs wandering or sleeping around. Sometimes these feral cats did get adopted, as Agnes told me she had adopted one back at the university.

After lunch we all went to the St Augustin Museum, which is housed in the oldest church in the Philippines. It dates back to 1670, when the Spanish built the first building, mainly in wood. There was a long history of rebuilding several times and a longer history can be found at this site

San Agustin Museum

SAN AGUSTIN CHURCH
Intramuros, Manila
Tels. 5274060 / 5274061 / 5266793 / 5266794
FAX # 5274060
E-mail Address: samuseum@nsclub.net.
OPEN DAILY
8:00 A.M. - 12:00 NN. 1:00 P.M. - 6:00 P.M.

http://en.wikipedia.org/wiki/San_Agustin_Church,_Manila

San Agustin Church was one of four Philippine churches constructed during the Spanish colonial period designated in 1993, by the UNESCO as a World Heritage Site, under the classification "Baroque Churches of the Philippines". It had been named a National Historical Landmark by the Philippine government in 1976.

Later we found an internet café and spent about an hour there. There was a group of male youngsters there who were obviously having a great time, but for me they were so loud I couldn't concentrate. We then decided to stay and watch the firework displays. The area near the Bay was getting more and more crowded, so as it was some time before the displays were due to start we moved away from the area a bit and found a café for drinks and food.

Eventually the first display began. This was the 2nd World Pyro Olympics. It was hosted by The Philippines at The Esplanade at the newly completed SM Mall of Asia. 9 countries took part (two displays per day), and Philippines, being the host country, were not in the competition, though they did a display on the last night. We first saw the Chinese which was very precise and beautiful, but for interest and general 'watchability' I MUCH preferred the Philippines display. The Chinese display did win the award for technical precision, but afterwards we learnt the UK display was declared the overall winner. After this magnificent aerial show of pyrotechnics we found ourselves in

4 Flowers, seen in Hotel garden

A Jeepney

the midst of a huge milling of people all wanting transport. All we wanted was to be far from the madding crowd! It took us ages to find a suitable taxi driver willing to take us all back together in one vehicle to The University. Andy was the one who knew best how to negotiate. Eventually after much searching we found one, 6 of us squeezed in a four seater taxi, and eventually 6 squashed bodies alighted at the university hotel gates. What a relief! My friends then had a short walk back to their quarters, and I slept soundly after one of the most interesting days of my life.

The next day I met Monica for lunch at her student hall, along with Andy, Agnes and 2 or 3 others of their friends. Before meeting them I had spent time wandering round the hotel grounds taking photos of plants and insects, and one of the famous Jeepneys. I could have filled a photo album with a large variety of styles and shapes. They all had plenty of chromatic beauty.

Monica had very kindly made me a salad, which had been intended for me on my arrival, but we had been diverted by eating out instead. But it was still in a fresh state, and I was most grateful to her for going to that trouble. We then went for a walk in a more countrified area and went to a museum and saw the famous statue of the naked man at the front of the University building. This called the Oblation.

The Oblation is a concrete statue by Filipino artist Guillermo E. Tolentino which serves as the iconic symbol of the University of the Philippines. It depicts a man facing upward with arms outstretched, symbolizing selfless offering of oneself to his country. The concrete sculpture, painted to look like bronze, measures 3.5 meters in height, symbolizing the 350 years of Spanish rule in the Philippines. The sculpture is replete with references of selfless dedication and service to the nation, and as Tolentino himself describes it: "The completely nude figure of a young man with outstretched arms and open hands, with tilted head, closed eyes and parted lips murmuring a prayer, with breast forward in the act of offering himself, is my interpretation of that sublime stanza. It symbolizes all the unknown heroes who fell during the night. The statue stands on a rustic base, a stylized rugged shape of the Philippine archipelago, lined with big and small hard rocks, each of which represents an island. The "katakataka" (wonder plant) whose roots are tightly implanted on Philippine soil, is the link that binds the symbolized figure to the allegorical Philippine Group. "Katakataka" is really a wonder plant. It is called siempre vivo (always alive) in Spanish. A leaf or a piece of it thrown anywhere will sprout into a young plant. Hence, it symbolizes the deep-rooted patriotism in the heart of our heroes. Such patriotism continually and forever grows anywhere in the Philippines. Today, that sculpture is only a bronze replica (which was recast from the original in Italy in 1950, under the supervision of Tolentino himself) dedicated on U.P.'s Golden Jubilee on November 29, 1958. The original sculpture is being kept at the Main Library (Gonzalez Hall), the former site of the U.P. College of Fine Arts.

After our return to the hotel Monica had tea with me in the café there, and later we had dinner at a nearby place (I had salad and rice). We had tried to use the internet but it was far too slow to get on line.

Next morning I ventured back to the nearby shopping arcade and managed to get some more cash from a hole in the wall machine. I had a further wander round the hotel grounds taking more photos. I met Monica and Agnes for lunch in a restaurant. Before parting I was most touched by Agnes giving me a friendship bracelet. I now consider Agnes a friend in the same way as I do all my internet friends I have met. I gave her a kiss on her cheek to show her my appreciation. This was the last I saw of Agnes, sadly, but we are now in touch via Facebook and emails. After lunch I was taken by taxi to Dee's apartment in another part of Quezon City. It was nice to see Dee again. Her flat was small and barely adequate, but livable in. We talked a lot, and I read her some of my poems (I suppose I must have got them off my website (www.philatelic.org.uk) because I don't think I had carried them around with me!) Then we went to a mall and had a good dinner in a restaurant, that managed to make me up a vegan dinner. Dee very kindly came with me in the return taxi, to make sure the taxi driver didn't take advantage of a foreign visitor! Obviously I paid for her return trip. Before departing Dee told me she saw me as a kind of father figure. We gave each other nice hugs. Another internet friend I would love to meet again one day.

Before I went to meet Dee that afternoon, Monica told me that her mother had been very sorry not to have been able to meet me, as she had hoped; I was sorry about that too, but she had very kindly arranged for her driver to take me to the airport next morning, and it was an early start, 6 am. Monica had dragged herself up early to be there to see me off. It had been lovely seeing this young lady after having known her in Yahoo groups (Stamp Addicts & Mystical Dreamland) for several years. She has a lovely personality, and is intelligent, and I was so pleased to have had this chance of meeting her. We parted after good hugs. She's another young person I would really love to meet again.

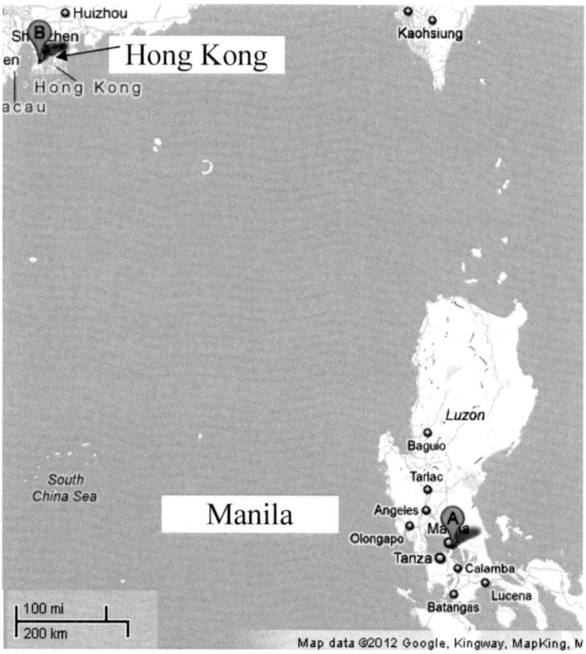

I was now off to a 'country' that was for 100 years a British colony, and is now back in its (to my mind) rightful place, in one of the largest countries in the world, certainly in population, CHINA! And strangely enough I had been here before, only 5 days ago for 8 hours over night. Hong Kong here I return!

Chapter 37
HONG KONG - Centre of the World of Zorpia.

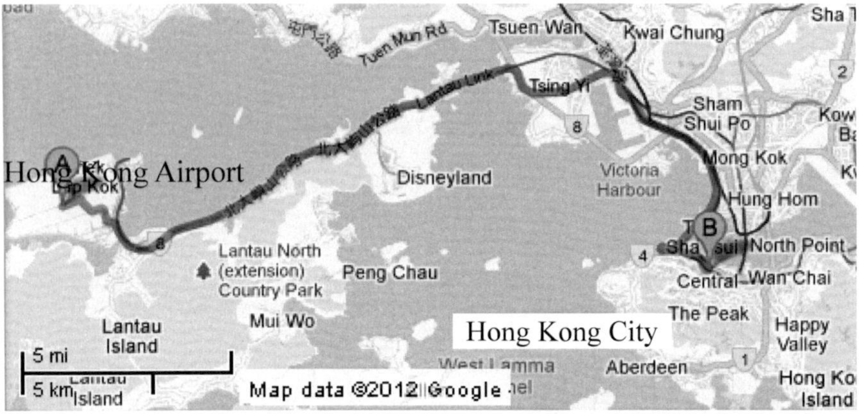

{Jeffrey, Calvin}

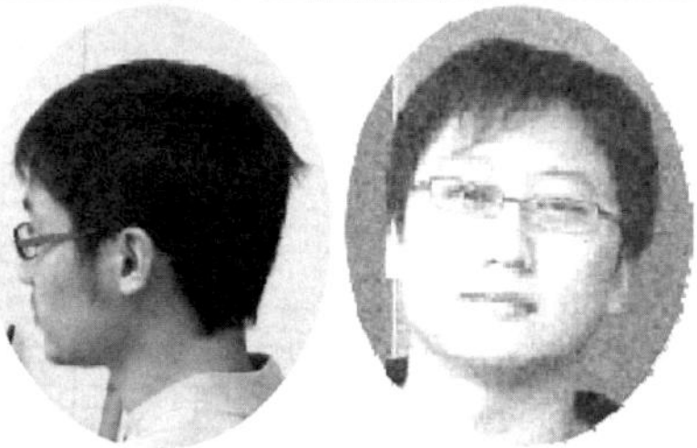

On my second arrival at Hong Kong airport, it had taken 2 hours in actual journey time, but the time it appeared to take was about 1 hour! Even on this short trip they provided a decent vegan sandwich and drinks. Once through all the customs and security etc., I phoned Jeffrey. We arranged to meet not very far from the place where I was to stay in a snug little flat.

Here I must explain a little.

When I originally arranged my trip I was going to stay with Maggie, my half New Zealand half Chinese (Hong Kong) stamp collecting friend. But after I had left UK and was part of the way round the world, she explained that she had suddenly moved to Canada! (After I had left there, unfortunately.) She has since returned to Hong Kong. What a pity, because I had been so looking forward to meeting Maggie. That left me with 5 nights for which to find accommodation. Emailing Jeffrey, I asked him if he could suggest somewhere to stay. He did better than that - he found me a place, not far from the Head Office of Zorpia, which was a small flat owned by a friend of his father's. Jeff kindly took me to the place and I met the owner, who could not speak any English, and I could not speak any Chinese, which of course Jeff could, and it was all settled. There was a kind of shared office room, in which there was a computer I could use, so long as I didn't use it TOO much! I dumped almost all my stuff in my tiny room and Jeff took me to the Zorpia office, which was about 5 minutes' walk away, but there were the added vertical distances to reach the correct floor levels. In Hong Kong buildings are NEVER short! If a building is less than 20 floors high it is not in Hong Kong!

In the Zorpia Office, which was tucked away in a small room behind Jeff's father's Jewellery shop, many floors up (27?), I was introduced to all who worked there. Jeff's parents (who ran the shop), Jeff himself who owned and ran the whole of the great world of Zorpia from this small office, in which he and Calvin and Jackson worked full time. Zorpia was one example of how in the modern day and age a system was virtually controlled from a small room, where millions of people from all over the world could communicate and get to know each other, even though they had little chance of ever meeting. I was so pleased to be given this chance to be at the very centre of the world I had gradually joined over the past year, the world of Zorpia, run by a young man in his mid 20's who had the knowledge and desire to let people with a love of photography and writing join together in a virtual world and make real friendships. Jeff's original desire had only been to allow photography lovers exchange pictures etc, but this social network soon grew far beyond that. It was mainly in Hong Kong at first, then it spread to other S.E. Asian countries, and gradually over most of the world. It was this widening of hori-

Buildings in Hong Kong are TALL

Signs as seen in Victoria Park (It was the time of bird flu)

My room

Hong Kong from Victoria Park

zons far greater than Yahoo and MS that was, to me, so appealing. In the world of Yahoo most members were from the USA, Canada, UK, Australia, and New Zealand it seemed. There were members from countries in Europe, South America, India, and South Africa, but not many. In Zorpia the WHOLE world was there with strong contingents in those countries that I had met in Yahoo, but also, in particular, from The Philippines, China, Malaysia, Singapore, Indonesia, Thailand, India, Pakistan, Palestine, Egypt, Myanmar, Romania, Spain, France, Norway, Mexico, Brazil, Argentina, and many others. Zorpia really was a world within a world.

And here was I, a mere 67 year youngster in the centre of it all. The place which made the world tick. Jeff has several others working for him in other countries as well. I really never in my imagination expected to meet the owner of such a world, and to be entertained. After I spent some time in the office, exchanging photos with Jeff's Dad (on the computer), Jeff and his parents very kindly took me to a nearby restaurant which served vegetarian meals, and was able to do vegan as well. (Sadly this restaurant has now closed). I really felt honoured that night. I never expected that the owner/founder of a social Network would take me out to dinner. This to me proves that Jeff is one great young guy, and that Zorpia really is a REALLY good friendly run social network for the people of the world to enjoy, and not just a big money earner for those running it. Jeff is a really friendly and caring chap.

It was after goodnights and being left on my own to return to my flat that I had a kind of scare. A scare that lasted at least 30 minutes, though it felt a lot longer! Remember I was in a foreign country where the predominant language was Chinese! Well I had no trouble in finding the right building, and the right lift, but for the life of me I could not at first find the right floor! I spent a lot of time going up and down in the lifts. (There were two on at each end of the floor levels.) I walked along many floors trying to find a recognisable door! I had a Key! But naturally I did not want to keep trying keys in other people's flats, LATE AT NIGHT ! After a few tries I decided to try each floor going up one each time, and still not remembering which door number it was! Well it was not funny at the time. EVENTUALLY I looked in my pocket wallet and found the piece of paper with the address on it! Everything had happened in a blur, and I had completely forgotten I had this in my pocket all the time! So eventually I found the correct door, and it was one of those I thought it might be! So my first bed-night on the island of Hong Kong was a welcome place, and I slept well. I was now in China, well, a territory owned by China. Another long day of travelling was over! And what a day it had been. I was thankful for so much to people I had known only over the Internet, and their parents!

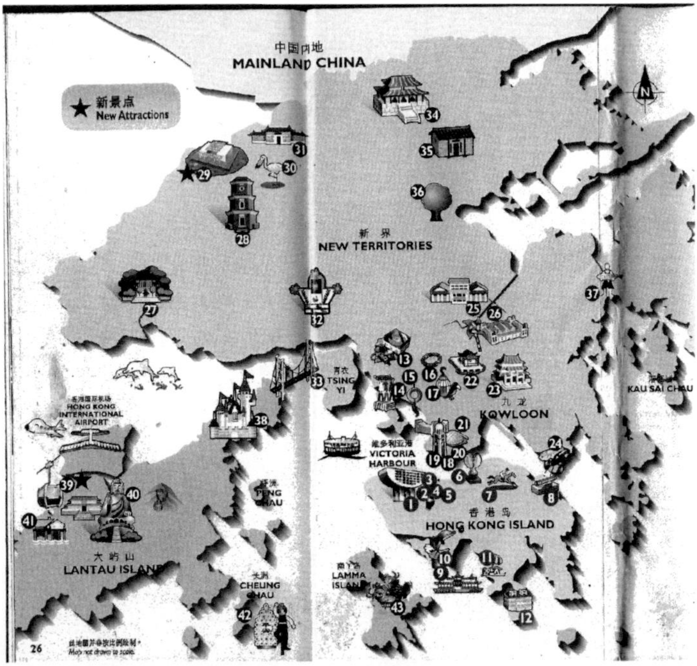

Chapter 38
Hong Kong - The Island of People and Skyscrapers!

{Chris B.}

Hong Kong is not just an Island. The largest part of the territory in land area is the "New Territories" on the mainland of Asia where it has borders with China proper. There I would have needed a visa, but Hong Kong seemed to be the International part of China. Hong Kong is amazing. There seems to be constant movement of people and vehicles. I now had a day and a half to explore part of it on my own.

The first thing I needed was to get some food. After waking up fairly early, but late for me, I needed to go shopping for some breakfast. I took my shoulder bag and luckily my umbrella, because it was raining. I emerged from my building and made sure I had the flat key and address with me! (No more scares like last night!) A hole in the wall cash dispenser was found and out poured Hong Kong money. With currency rates so variable from country to country I was never quite sure how much I needed, and here I took out far too little at first! So I recalculated and drew out extra. Now I could shop! But in the nearby supermarket I could buy with my credit card. I got in a supply of fruit and bought a phone card. I was now ready to face the world. Returned to my flat - no problems! Prepared some fruit and went on line at the computer. OH! NO! Everything on the screen was in Chinese! EVERYTHING! I had no knowledge whatsoever of Chinese! Eventually by guess work remembering the positions of certain key clicking places and the www. addresses of a few places, up came familiar pages in ENGLISH! I spent a while catching up.

My first day in Hong Kong was quite a lazy day. I just drifted around seeing the sights of my part of

Hong Kong City, and its shops. As it seemed to be raining most of the day, I spent most time inside buildings rather than outside. I took photos, found book shops, and bought the next Dan Brown book "Digital Fortress". I managed to phone my other friend I was due to meet in Hong Kong, Chris Bowen, another Hong Kong Stamp collector, who turned out to be Vegetarian; I arranged to meet her the next day. Unfortunately her husband was not free at any of the time I was in Hong Kong.

My lazy day went something like this

Sleeping
Waking
Washing
Dressing
Shopping
Eating
Internet
Wandering
Shopping
Reading "Angels & Demons"
Internet
Eating
Phoning
Reading
Sleeping
Walking
Reading
Internet
Eating
Reading
Internet
Slept.

So ended another, but more restful day!

The next day started more or less the same. I finished "Angels & Demons" and started "Digital Fortress". Looking at a map, I saw I was close to a park,

Victoria Park, and after breakfast I ventured out. The rain had ceased, and I found the Park (*even though it had not been lost!*) and discovered that it was a kind of haven from the hustle and bustle of the city. There was some wild life, with many notices warning not to touch birds. It was the time of the "bird flu" scare. There were many areas where I saw people individually doing Tai Chi and jogging. They even had a designated jogging track. Walking and other activities were banned from this track, except at designated crossing points, rather like level crossings for rail! Otherwise only joggers and runners were allowed. It was here too that I saw (to my punning mind) a weird notice: "FARMERS FLEA MARKET". I snapped a picture for posterity and wondered why farmers wanted to buy and sell fleas! It really was an interesting park, obviously well used, well kept and maintained, and the wild life in it included many sleeping cats!

I returned to my flat and had lunch and a nap before catching a bus to take me to Chris's flat in another part of Hong Kong City. Chris lived in a tower block on the 27th floor. I found my way there without any trouble; her directions had been perfect. The lift was excellent and soon had me at the 27th floor and the flat. She was the third and last Stamp Addicts (Yahoo Group) member I was to meet; it would have been five, but two others, Dave in Canada and Maggie from Hong Kong (who moved to Canada whilst I was away), I missed. I was greeted by Chris at the door and was introduced to her mum and her twin daughters who were only a few months old. Her mum comes to help her take care of the twins. Chris spends most of her time on them and her music. She is locally a well known singer in an all 'girl' group called Sisters of Sharon.
[http://www.sistersofsharon.com.hk/] There are 5 members and Chris is one of the three singers and

Part of the longest escalator in the world

Scaffolding really is made of Bamboo, so much lighter than steel

also plays guitar. She very kindly gave me one of their CDs, called “Underground Recipes”.

With two babies there is little time to do much! So after an hour or two I said my goodbyes and took her advice to visit the famous “Longest” escalator in the world, an outdoor one (though covered) which took one down (in my case) or up the steep slopes of this hillside urban part of the city. About half way down there was the Vegetarian restaurant **Life Organic Health Cafe (Vegetarian Restaurant)** that Chris told me about. I really enjoyed my Salad there, all so fresh and satisfying.

So ended another day in my trip. I had only two more new Internet friends to meet, but that adventure comes in the next Island city in a few days. I still had two more days of fascinating journeys here in Hong Kong. One natural, the other mystical. One low lying, the other high up, and neither on the same island within Hong Kong.

Hong Kong’s Veggie Restaurant

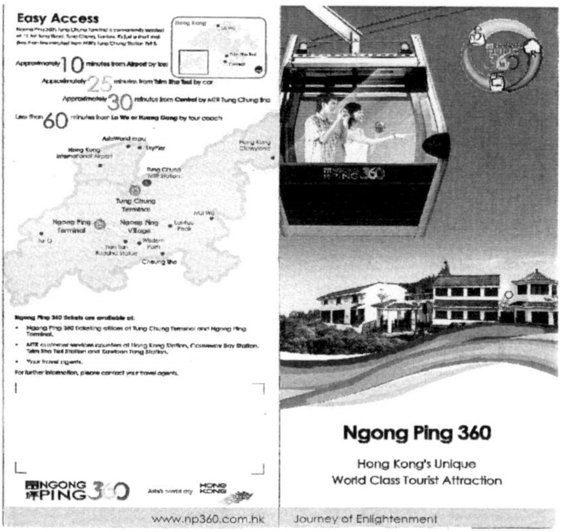

Chapter 39
Hong Kong - Low & Wet, High & Misty

The next two days were days of contrasts. On Friday 19th January I decided to visit the recently opened **Hong Kong Wetlands Park**, a conservation region. This was on the mainland of Asia, but still in Hong Kong, and not the country of China. This was the nearest that I got to the border - in fact I could see China across the wide estuary. This park was part of Hong

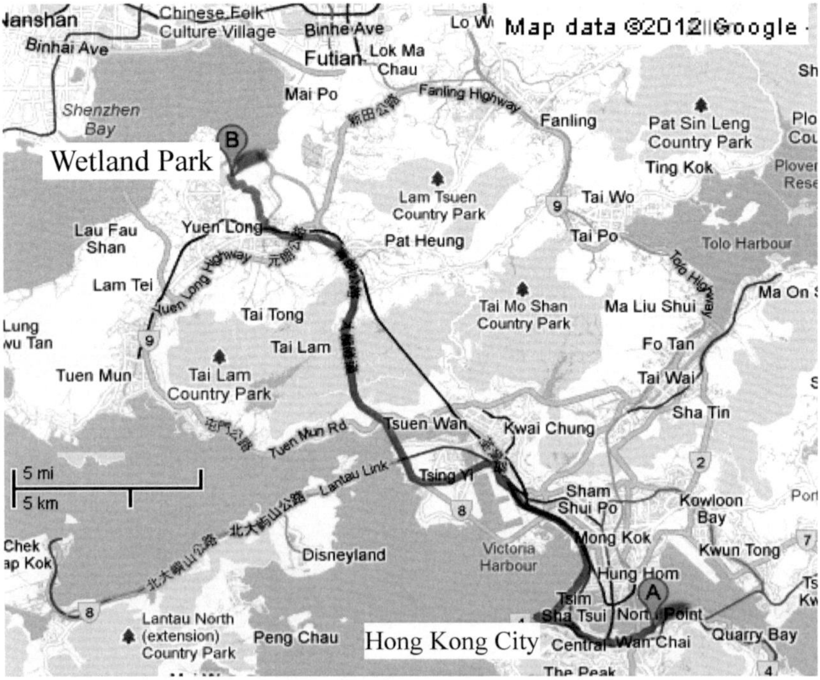

Kong's conservation policy to try to preserve the natural wild life of the region, and at the same time to make it interesting to tourists. The whole area was well laid out, with model streams and waterfalls and wetland type flora, which explained the natural water systems, and without destroying the nearby real wetlands, but from hides, with telescopic, binocular and camera aids, we could view the real nature of wading, sea and wetland birds. Quite a wide range was found here with the changing landscape. I took many pictures; some came out very well considering the all pervasive man-made smog, that seemed to hang around the whole of the Hong Kong region. I was most impressed by this area, and it was not only good for the environment, but good for the education of people who lived and visited, teaching us the importance of preservation of such regions. There was also a very informative museum. Anyone visiting Hong Kong should visit here.

To get here I had to travel by train for most of the journey and then by bus locally.

On my return to Hong Kong city I revisited the Zorpia Office and took a few photos of the office and Jeff and the others. And after that I ate at the Veggie Thai Restaurant, that Jeff had taken me to on my first day.

My next and last full day in Hong Kong was my all day visit to the famous Buddha Statue which is reputed to be the largest bronze statue in the world, and sits on top of the mountain on a small island off the main Island of Hong Kong.

I reached this extraordinary place by train and then the recently opened aerial cable car, which gave us spectacular views crossing the bay on a steep gradient taking us high up to cross the mountains. We looked down upon the international airport. The journey was 25 minutes and deposited us in the town, which was laid out with attractions and shops and restaurants. Here I saw two shows. The first was "Walking in Buddha's footsteps." I was most impressed by this. It told the basic story of Buddha

Ngong Ping Cable Car

is a 5.7 km long bi-cable gondola lift system linking between Tung Chung (where it connects the MTR Tung Chung station) and Ngong Ping (where the Po Lin Monastery and Tian Tan Buddha are located). Between the two terminals at Tung Chung and Ngong Ping, the lift system runs across the southern shore of the Hong Kong International Airport island and Nei Lak Shan, with eight towers including the stations.

It was opened on 18 September 2006. .

The cable car journey offers a 25 minute aerial alternative to the current one-hour journey by Tung Chung Road.

The cableway starts at the Tung Chung Terminal, runs across Tung Chung Bay to an angle station on Airport Island, where it turns through about 60 degrees before returning across Tung Chung Bay. It then runs up the Lantau North Country Park to another angle station near Nei Lak Shan, before finally descending to the Ngong Ping Terminal.

During the 25 minute journey, travellers can see panoramic views over the North Lantau Country Park, the South China Sea, Hong Kong International Airport, the Tung Chung valley, Ngong Ping Plateau and surrounding terrain and waterways. As visitors approach Ngong Ping, they can see The Big Buddha and the Po Lin Monastery.

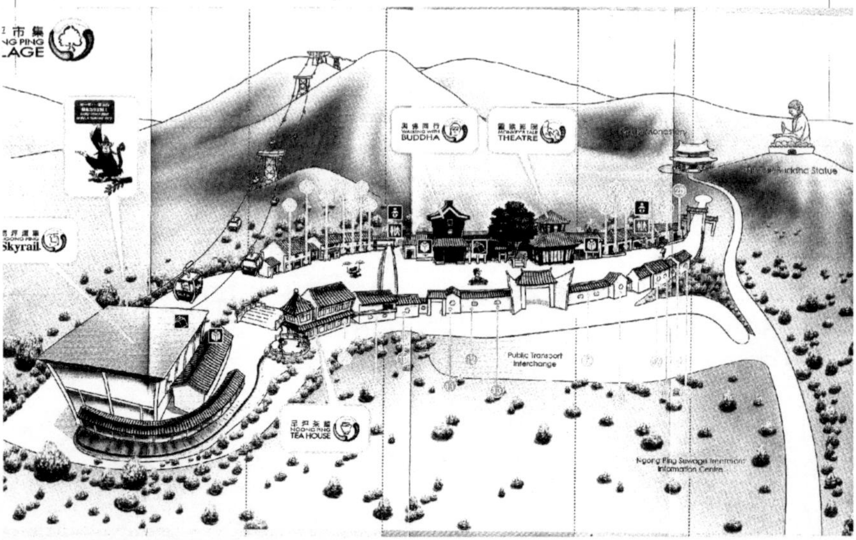

Tian Tan Buddha ; 天壇大佛; also known as the Big Buddha, *is a large bronze statue of the Buddha, completed in 1993, and located at Ngong Ping, Lantau Island, in Hong Kong. The statue is located near Po Lin Monastery and symbolises the harmonious relationship between man and nature, people and religion. It is a major centre of Buddhism in Hong Kong, and is also a popular tourist attraction*

The statue is named Tian Tan Buddha because its base is a model of the Altar of Heaven or Earthly Mount of Tian Tan, the Temple of Heaven in Beijing. It is surrounded by six smaller bronze statues representing gods or immortals. The Tian Tan Buddha is an image of Amitabha Buddha.

The Buddha is 34 metres (110 ft) tall, weighs 250 metric tons and was the world's tallest outdoor bronze seated Buddha prior to 2007 . Visitors have to climb 268 steps in order to reach the Buddha. The Tian Tan Buddha appears serene and dignified. His right hand is raised, representing the removal of affliction. His left hand rests on his lap in a gesture of giving dhana. The Buddha faces north, which is unique among the great Buddha statues, as all others face south.

In addition, there are 3 floors beneath the Buddha statue: The Hall of Universe, The Hall of Benevolent Merit, and The Hall of Remembrance. One of the most renowned features inside is a relic of Gautama Buddha, consisting of some of his alleged cremated remains. There is a huge carved bell inscribed with images of Buddhas in the show room. It was designed to ring every seven minutes, 108 times a day, symbolising the release of 108 kinds of human vexations.

and how he came to formulate his great ideas that are followed by millions all over the world. In many ways I found it very Quakerly. It also made me wonder if Jesus had heard of, or come across, Buddha's teachings, for I believe many are very similar. I also saw the "Monkeys Tale", a more comic cartoon type film, with a Buddhist theme. I walked around the tourist village, then went on to the Buddhist Monks' village. Here all the eating places are strictly Vegetarian. I ate in one of them, having no trouble in obtaining a vegan meal. Very basic, but also filling and remarkably cheap considering it was waiter service. Eating in one of the

Some pictures taken at the Hong Kong Wetlands park

vegetarian restaurants gave you a ticket which gave you an advantage, in busy crowded times, in having priority to go inside the Buddha statue museum and story. That was after one had climbed the "million" steps to reach it. There were certainly a lot of steps. Not only was the statue of great interest, but the views from the top were excellent, spoilt only by the Hong Kong haze! After reaching the main ground level I then went on the Ngong nature trail, wisdom path. Not so many people went here, so it was more peaceful.

Ngong Ping Fun Walk

About half way down the path that leads from Wisdom Path, you find the Tea Garden. At the end of the Tea Garden a side path forks out to the left. That is the starting point of Ngong Ping Fun Walk. It takes only 45 minutes to complete. Although merely 1.5 km in length, it offers six attractions: Misty Lantau, Ancient Gateway, Tree Walk Exploration, Sunrise on Lantau, Scenery of Lakes and Tea Walk.

This was one that I found interesting.

After a wonderful experience such as this it was quite sad to have to return to my flat in the centre of bustle and hustle. The return was by cable and train.

One of my lasting impressions of the Hong Kong bustle was watching incredulously the pedestrian crossings in the day time. Whilst the traffic was constantly flowing you could see the pedestrians gradually build up on both sides. Then suddenly the traffic flow stopped and on the first beep of green light for pedestrians masses of people started to cross in both directions and then they met in the middle! It was like a scrum in rugby only 100 times the number of players! Incredibly both sides reached their destinations before the beeping stopped and the traffic could once

For the site giving all the attractions here
http://www.np360.com.hk/html/eng/np360_exp/village_index.html

Views from Cable car and at the Buddha Village

My Veggie meal at the Veggie Life Organic Health Cafe

again pollute the atmosphere ! I saw many people wearing face masks in the Hong Kong streets.

That evening I went on the internet, phoned Dilys and packed for my last part of my journey, the following day, to another quite different island nation, Singapore.

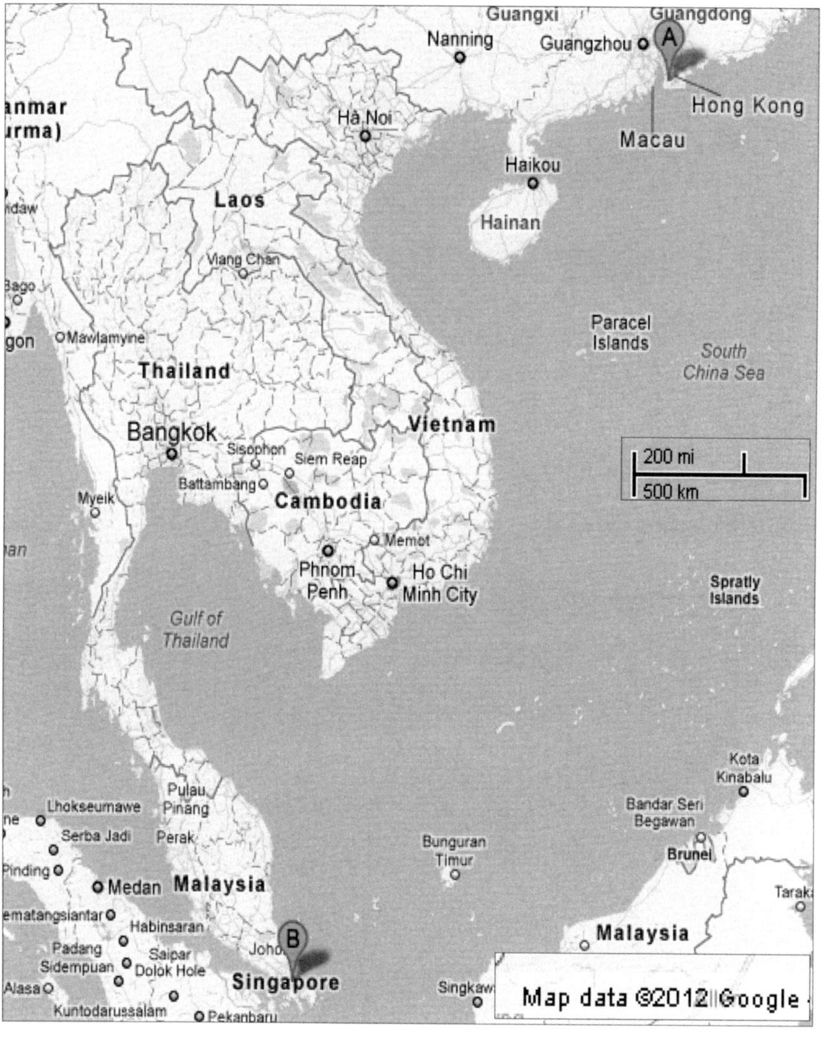

Sign seen on MOST buses in Hong Kong

Please excuse us for not letting
you board the bus yet as
we would like to keep the
engine off until the next departure.
Your support and understanding
will give us a better air quality.

Clock in Victoria Park, Hong Kong

Chapter 40
SINGAPORE - The Island Country, Just North of the Equator.

Republic of Singapore	
Population:	*4.5 million (UN, 2008)*
Area:	*660 sq km (255 sq miles)*
Major languages:	*English, Malay, Mandarin, Tamil*
Religions:	*Taoism, Buddhism, Islam, Christianity, & Hinduism*
Life expectancy:	*78 years (men), 82 years (women)*
Monetary unit:	*1 Singapore dollar = 100 cents*

{Aidan & Nani}

I left my flat at 8 am to be in time to catch the flight, 11.35 am, to leave one crowded island to arrive in another crowded island. It was only a four hour flight.

I was met by two of my most recent internet friends, both Zorpians. I had only known them for just about a year. It was lovely to be met at the airport on arrival by two such delightful young ladies, Nani and Aidan. They had been at school together and had stayed close friends to adulthood. Aidan was married with two young children, but Nani was still single. They were so helpful and friendly, and had it all organised what to do. On arrival there were hugs of greeting, and then they took me to my hotel, Keong Saik, in the China town area. After a bit of unpacking etc., they then whisked me off to the Botanical gardens by MRT, their underground rail system, which seemed very efficient. The temperature was hot, but unlike Hong Kong the atmosphere seemed clean and clear of the constant smog. We took photos of each

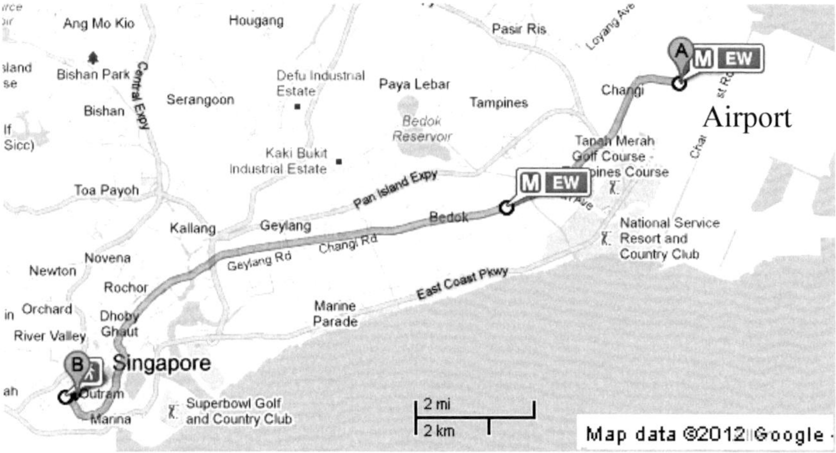

other in the Botanical gardens, and for a short while I was so glad that I had brought my umbrella with me! The rain burst was heavy and warm, but only lasted a short time. We then made our way to the Indian sector, which was so crowded with Indian young men that it was difficult to move! Apparently migrant workers, from India, all seem to fill the streets and restaurants every Sunday. Nani and Aidan took me here to a vegetarian Indian restaurant, I think having forgotten that Sunday was so overcrowded! Here we picked the veggies etc that we wanted and they then cooked it for you as you watched! Later they kindly returned me to my hotel. I arranged to meet up with Nani in two days' time.

The next day I went on my own to the famous Jurong Bird Park, by train. I spent a wonderful day there, seeing and taking many pictures of beautiful birds; a lot of them one could see in natural looking enclosures, and in one there were hundreds of Lories.

I soon found that I was filling up my camera card, and bought myself another one with 2Gb of space. This really was an amazing place, and anyone visiting Singapore should include this on their agenda. Another very beautiful part was the highest man made

The Jurong BirdPark

is a world-famous bird zoo wherein there are specimens of magnificent bird life from around the world, including a flock of one thousand and one flamingos. It is currently the world's largest bird park in terms of number of birds: there are over 8,000 birds of 600 species. Of those, 29 are of endangered species.

waterfall, so natural looking. Look out for the African Waterfall Aviary, and the dark house, for seeing night time birds. Here they more or less reverse the light/day for the birds,

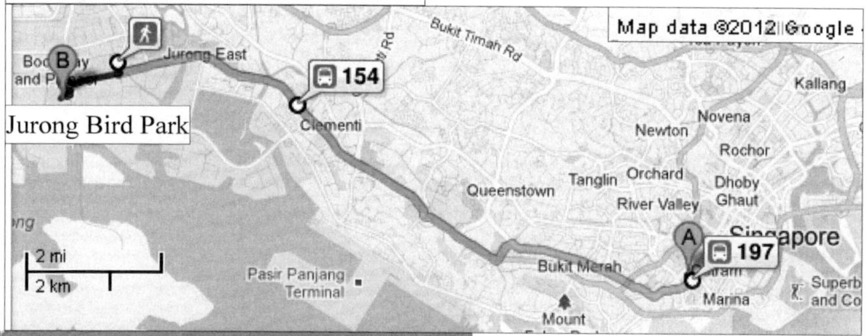

so that when visitors are there it is night for the birds and at night it is "day" light. There was so much to see here that it was not possible to see all in one day. This was indeed a wonderful place.

Both before and after my visit to the bird zoo, I made use of the computer to check emails and messages in Zorpia and Yahoo. I also phoned Dilys, and Nani (to arrange to meet again the next

The Ravishing Birds I met in Jurong Bird Park

Perhaps no other exhibit in the park and many parts of the world can match the breathtaking display of suspended bridges, rich red, yellow, green and blue feathered Lories feeding against the vast skies above. The Lory Loft is the Bird Park's fourth walk-in flight aviary and the world's largest Lory Flight Aviary.
Lories are found in Australia, Indonesia and Papua New Guinea.
The sprawling 3,000 square metres land area and about 9-storey high loft also allow visitors a 360 degrees elevated view of the environs. At the two-tiered central feeding tower, visitors have the opportunity to feed the birds by hand with a special nectar mixture. The amazing experience heightens as throngs of lories gather, chattering gregariously and filling the air with colours of the rainbow.
Colourful, noisy and exceptionally bold—Lories and Lorikeets are great fun to watch.

day.) I bought myself some extra camera attachments, a wide angle lens, lens tube and UV filter, from a camera shop where the owner seemed to know his stuff.

Tuesday 23rd January, my 126th day, was spent mainly with Nani. She is really an amazing young lady, and I felt at ease in her company, so much so that I thought of her as being a kind of sister. During this afternoon, though, I had one of the most unexpected moments of my life, something that the very thought brings shudders of horror!

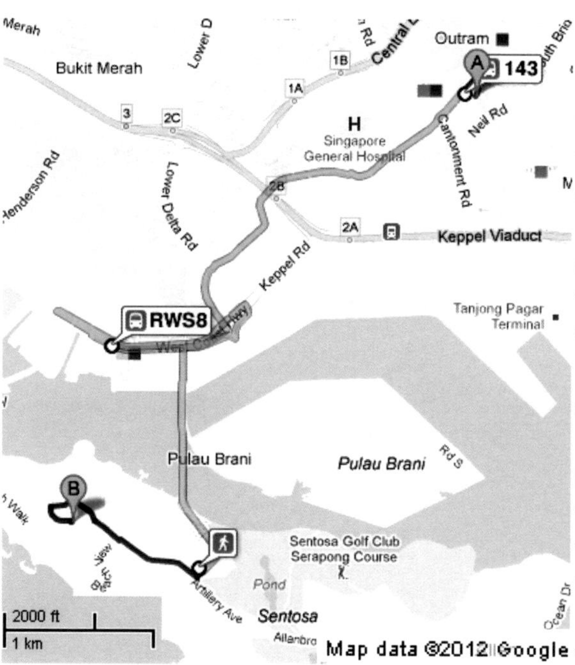

I met up with Nani at a station that took us to the terminus of the new Sentosa monorail, which

Jurong Waterfall

Some wild life in Singapore

Street decorations for Chinese New Year

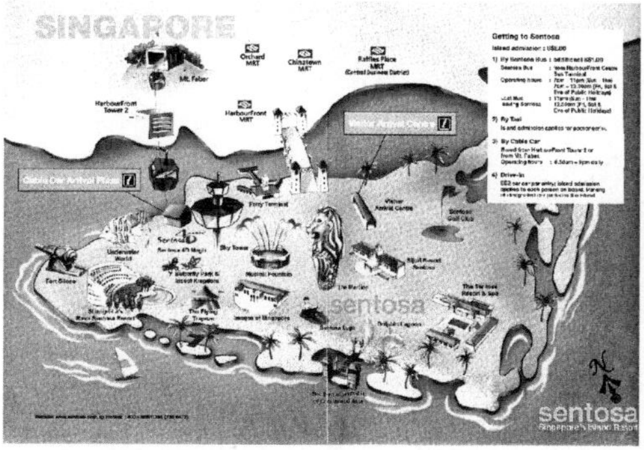

took us over the sea to the Island of Sentosa. We could have gone by aerial cable or ferry. This new train was rather like the London (UK) Docklands railway, fully automatic. This whole day turned out to be such a wonderful and diverse experience. The main attraction on Sentosa was the **Butterfly and Insect Park**. I also spent time in the Merlion statue and saw the most wonderful water display that I had come across, all with my beautiful new "sister" Nani. Of course I took masses more photos and videos. We had lunch, and I had a nice salad sandwich, and then went into the insect park. The collection of butterflies in well arranged and landscaped "gardens" was a delight, and most stayed still long

enough to be photographed. Inside the Merlion tower statue was where the most unexpected occurrence took place. Here were housed many non butterfly creatures. On one floor level we came across a man who was offering to put live Scorpions on one. We watched a few people have this experience, and I challenged Nani, and guided her thoughts to accepting it! Provided we each took photos of each other! It was really eerie have these large 8 legged most ancient of fear filling creatures walking on one's bare arm, knowing they had one of the nastiest stinging tails. These are in fact not insects, but relatives of the spiders, and a very ancient species, pre-Dinosaur period. Anyway Nani happily took a few pictures of me with my bare arms bearing the creepy scorpions crawling slowly. Then it was Nani's turn! Poor girl, she wished she had not agreed I think, but she made one condition: that they were put on her jeans covered legs and not her bare arms! She DID IT, brave lass, and we have the photos to prove it. I might add that the man in charge did show us that they would not sting us by having one on his palm and putting his other hand over it and pressing down on it! He assured us that they only sting humans in self defence, and that was what gave me the "courage".

That done, I next experienced a bright green snake crawling on my hand. I had stroked snakes before, but this was so different, it was like touching smooth soft velvet. We saw a short video explaining the History of the Merlion and Singapore. There was also a scented herb garden to wander around. In the afternoon we were delighted to see the fountains in action, reacting to the music; though this was wonderful, it was nothing compared to the night time display that we watched later. Then they used lighting effects which really brought them to life, and to me the most unusual was using the mist produced by the fountains to project movies onto. But even more clever was how they had the compère, live, apparently interacting with the characters in the movie on the mist. It was VERY cleverly done, and the whole evening was quite spectacular. We need one of these for Scarborough! There was a decent restaurant there where I could get nice salad sandwiches (mid day) and a salad in the evening. What a wonderful experience this day was. Thank you, Nani, for sharing it with me It is always so much nicer having company when visiting such splendid places. I shall remember this day for ever.

That evening before falling asleep I finished reading "Digital Fortress" (Dan Brown).

The next day was again QUITE different. I had the whole day to myself. I decided to take a walkabout taking pictures of the Singapore buildings in the morning. Unfortunately I got lost, and, silly me, had forgotten to take a map; well, I thought I was only going to be close to the hotel. But somehow I found myself miles away from where I thought I was. Apparently familiar landmarks were not familiar after all, and eventually I found myself out of the city. I decided the best thing was to wait at a bus stop for a bus and ask the way to the nearest Metro (Underground railway). A bus eventually arrived and took me to the nearest station, and I found I was miles away in the wrong direction!

I got back safely, and had some lunch (mainly fruit). I spent some time on the internet catching up, and went to the strange looking new Theatre complex, The Esplanade. I booked a ticket for that evening's performance of a new locally written play, "Everything But The Brain" written by Jean Tay. It was the winner of the 2006 Life Theatre Award for best Original Script. It was a witty and heartbreaking play about a young physics teacher who tries to turn back time to save her father who has suffered a stroke. We experienced much emotion but filled with fun and unexpected combinations of experiences, mixing boisterous bears, a handsome doctor, and the Theory of Relativity. The daughter rediscovers her own dad and this leads us on to a magical path to an oasis of love and compassion. If anyone has the chance to see this play I can rec-

Merlion

Butterflies

Scorpions going for a walk

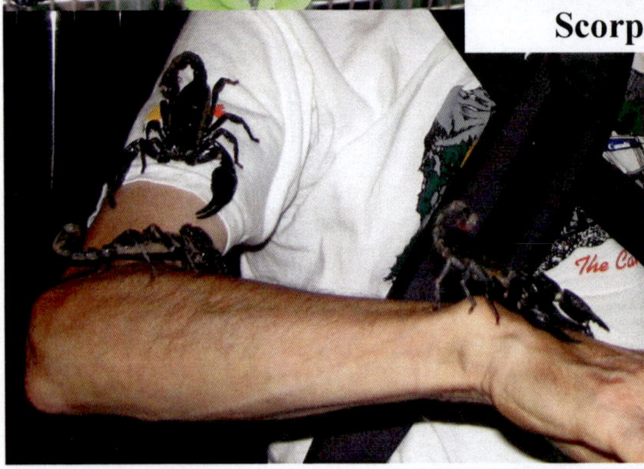

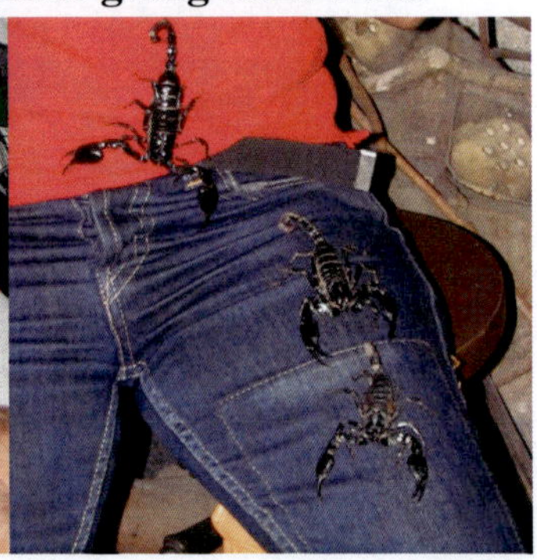

ommend it highly.

I must add that the main part of the building, which houses many theatres and places of various entertainment, was in the shape of the well known Durian fruit. Inside were notices telling us things not allowed inside, which included Durians! In case anyone is in any doubt as to why this should be the case, I must explain that this fruit though, apparently, delicious to EAT, has the most awful smell! So ended my last full day in Singapore and my last full day in a foreign country. The plane was due to take off at 23.59 on Thursday 25th January!

I made the most of my last day. My last day in Singapore and my last day of my round the world trip. Memorable for more than just being the last day - it was just like no other day. For a start it was raining! After breakfast and most of the packing done, I went for a walk in the rain (with umbrella) and took a few more pictures. I then booked out of the hotel at about 10.30 am, and went by Metro to the airport for early check in of my luggage; then I went by metro to the end of the East-West line to Pasir Ris. Here I toured the Mall and spent 2 hours on the net in the Library.

Then I went back one station to Tampines and looked around their Mall. A very English-like stall caught my eye, a street hot chestnut stall. I just had to have some! When I first saw it, they were not yet ready to sell, but I returned later and sampled them. I had previously arranged to meet Nani at the interchange on the E/W metro, which I did, and spent the rest of my Singapore time with my “Sister” Nani. We travelled to the airport and found a place to eat; well, I found TWO places to eat! Not because I was greedy or extra hungry, but I wanted a decent vegan meal! At one restaurant I had salad, and from a neighbouring one had some rice to go with the salad. There were several food shops around a common seating plan,

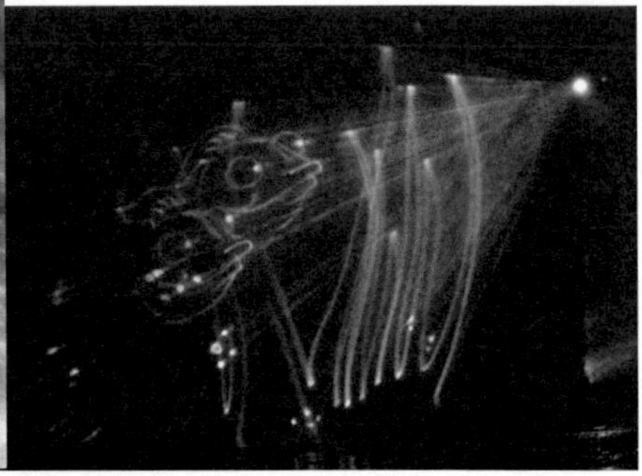

Incredible fountains of Sentosa

so this was quite easy to arrange. Nani also had a meal with me, and after a while of chatting about all sorts of things, Aidan arrived with her son (aged 6). We talked some more and at booking in time I said my sad farewells. Sad because I was saying goodbye to two dear ladies, who had gone to a lot of time and trouble to welcome and make me at home. We parted after some big hugs. I was touched by Aidan giving me a surprise painting from her. I just wished I had seen more of her. I sincerely hope to meet them again in the UK. These two ladies really made my last day, and I was so grateful to them for their kindness. So with a kind of empty feeling of this being the end of a wonderful experience, I boarded the 11.59 pm flight to London Heathrow - but due to an hour's delay I was still in Singapore on Friday 26th of January. Now I was having mixed thoughts of the wonderful trip and being back home and being with Dilys again after 128 minus 1 days!

The flight home was LONG, much longer than the timetable suggested, as we had to cross several time zones, crossing over Malaysia and many other countries in the dark, following the flight path on the video monitors, and sleeping and eating and exercises going to the toilets, on a regular basis. I think I slept for about 3 hours. The journey was in fact 14 hours 21 minutes, yet we arrived at 6.20 am in London. On the flight I was given a nice vegan meal of black-eyed beans, and they even made sure there was vegan marg for my bread. Breakfast was at 3 am (UK TIME!) and was very substantial. Cooked vegetable tart, a roll, bran and fruit cereal + soya milk fruit and orange juice. The tart had much onion in, but I survived.

Surprise surprise, having left an hour late we arrived on time! The winds must have been with us! The only thing apart from the length of the flight that spoilt this journey was the fact I was sitting next to a newly married couple, whose husband appeared to find everything wrong, and made many complaints. He appeared to be the controlling type.... I pity his poor young wife. Sadly she seemed to put up with it and was always "admitting" she was wrong! He gained "free" drinks (from the stewards) to calm him down. The arrival was made more exciting for me by the fact

that I was still in my summer shorts from tropical Singapore, and I had planned to change in the airport toilets (which I did), BUT I had not expected the airport's connecting tunnel to malfunction. We all had to go down the steps to ground level, out into the English winter cold, before quickly entering the airport building and its warmth! Then it took AGES, over an hour, for my luggage to arrive on the carousel. Eventually I got everything together and made my way to Kings Cross station via the underground from Heathrow, experiencing UK prices once again. I could have flown on to Manchester instead for no extra charge, but

Buildings of Singapore

My Hotel

Dilys didn't want me flying any more and had bought me a rail ticket, and arranged with Edwin to bring it to me at Kings Cross, which he did, and I caught the 11.00 am train to York and changed to the Scarborough train, and was met with BIG hugs by Dilys. Though I had enjoyed my trip so much, I was still glad to get back home. For a while things were so different. Though a little tired by that last flight, I suffered no real jet lag problems.

Now I had to settle in back to everyday living and all the Scarborough organisations that I had neglected for 4 months!

BUT WHAT AN ADVENTURE I had had. Now, thanks to my collection of souvenirs and photos and my daily diary, not to mention all my friends who checked my draft and made additions and corrections, at last it is all written down.

Amazing scene on fountains in Sentosa

Chapter 41
THANK YOU

There are so many people I must say thank you to, for making this whole trip feasible and possible.

1) Dilys. My lovely and supportive wife who put up with my being away for 4 months, and proof read (quickly) this book (although in some cases I took responsibility for leaving it unchanged!)
2) The People who actually invited me to their homes and put me up for a night or two or more.

Geeta & Gordon (Manchester UK)
Kim & James (Nova Scotia, Canada)
Geeta's sister Vandana & husband (Toronto, Canada)
Sharon & Sharleen (Vancouver, Canada)
Wendy and her family for the Thanksgiving meal (Whitehorse, Canada)
Maggie (Seattle, USA)
Teri (Shelton USA)
Jeanne & her family for lovely Vegan meal (Chicago, USA)
Mary (Bay City, USA)
Reggie for taking me to Oklahoma University
Ruth & Dennis (Tulsa, USA)
Kami & Jimmy (Stockton USA)
Melisa and her family (Buenos Aires, Argentina)
Rhiannon & her Mum, Joanne (Palmerston North, New Zealand)
Arun & Jayshree especially for making me feel at home for about a week (Sydney Australia)
Mike Dodd for taking care of me for a few hours at his ranch (Near Sydney, NSW)
Sandra (Avoca Beech, Australia)
Chris & Audrey (Canberra, Australia)
Mellissa & Josh for giving me such a Different, up-side down HOT Christmas (Toowoomba, Australia)

3) The kind friends who met me and showed me

around their areas for an hour, or several hours or days.

Erica, Pat Nelson, Maud, Chris & Eileen, Carrie & Jim and Jade, in Canada

Sandra, Jeanne & Fred, Suzanne, Reggie & Joey, Jess, SLT (Domitila), (USA)

Shirley (New Zealand)

Mike Enjo, Mike Dodd for taking me around for a day & Danielle, can't forget Danielle (Australia)

Monica and her Mum, Andy & Agnes, and Dee (Philippines)

Jeff, Chris B (Hong Kong)

Nani & Aidan (Singapore)

4) The unknown kind gentleman who helped me out in Nova Scotia and
5) In San Francisco the coach driver who took me in the coach after the end of the official journey, personally to my hotel
6) The various people I met on the long train journeys, in particular Alice for signing my 'Town Like Alice' at Alice Springs

Number of nights spent in various places

Night/country	UK	Canada	USA	Argentina	N.Z.	Australia	Philippines	H.K.	Singapore	Total
Hotels	0	2	16	0	2	16	4	5	4	47
Friends	1	8	12	6	3	14	0	0	0	46
Train	0	4	5	0	0	8	0	0	0	17
Guest house	0	8	0	0	0	0	0	0	0	8
Plane	0	0	1	1	0	0	0	0	1	3
Car	0	1	0	0	1	0	0	0	0	2
Backpacker	0	0	0	0	0	2	0	0	0	2
Airport	0	0	0	0	0	0	0	1	0	1
Open air	0	0	0	0	0	1	0	0	0	1
Day lost at international date line				0	1	0	0	0	0	1
Total	1	23	34	7	7	41	4	6	5	128

Chapter 42

Lists

A) Countries

Country	Pages	Chapters	No of days
UK	10 to 22 & 310	1,2, & 40	1
Canada	13 - 16 & 23 - 70	3 to 7	23
USA	71 to 137	8 to 19	34
Argentina	138 to 154	20 & 21	7
Chile	155	21	11 hours
New Zealand	156 to 170	23 & 24	7
Australia	171 to 263	25 to 35	41
The Philippines	264 to 277	36	4
Hong Kong	278 to 296	37 to 39	6
Singapore	297 to 312	40	5

B) Places to stay

Canada

Les Amis, Vegetarian Guest House
Paul-Antoine & Michelle Buer
31 Granby St., Toronto, Ontario M5B 1H8 Canada. Tel. (416)591-0635 http://www.bbtoronto.com

"Sunrise" B&B 1211 Sable Drive, Burlington, Ontario bbcanada.com/834.html

Australia

Ambassadors Hotel 107 King William St, **Adelaide**, SA 5000, Australia +61 8 8231 4331

ALICE LODGE BACKPACKERS, 4 Mueller Street, Alice Springs NT 0871 Australia. Phone:+61 8 8953 1975 Email: info@alicelodge.com.au

City Palms Motel, *55 Brunswick Street - **Brisbane**, Fortitude Valley, Australia 4006. (0)1800 655 381*
Metro Hotel Sydney Central, Pitt St Haymarket, NSW 2000, Australia +61 2 9281 6999 ww.metrohotels.com.au431
Kings Perth Hotel: 517 Hay Street (corner Pier St) **Perth** Western Australia 6000 http://www.kingshotel.com.au/index.html
New Zealand
Glen Alton Motel, Glen Alton Avenue, Johnsonville, Wellington 04 478 8146
Philippines
The University Hotel, UP Diliman Off Commonwealth Avenue, Diliman, **Quezon City**, Luzon 2004 Philippines Tel: 63 2 920 5301 *http://www.updiliman.com/*
Singapore
The Keong Saik Hotel 69 Keong Saik Road, Singapore 089165 E-mail: keongsaik@pacific.net.sg http://home.pacific.net.sg/~keongsaik/hotelks.htm
C) Places to eat **Canada**
Tall & Small Cafe, 342 Main Street, Antigonish, Canada
ChuChai (Chu Chai) 4088, rue St-Denis corner Duluth E, H2W 2M5 , Montreal Thai Veggie Restaurant
Vegetarian Haven - Vegan Restaurant - 17 Baldwin Street, (near University & Dundas streets) Toronto 416-621-3636
Le Commensal Vegetarian restaurant. 655 Bay St. Toronto, ON M5G 2K4)

USA

YOU PICKED THIS UP AT:
THE HOME OF WORLDS FAMOUS
13 ESPRESSO SHAKE
ESPRESSO EXPRESS COFFEE HOUSE
916 N. WATER ST. BAY CITY MI
HOT DRINKS COOL COMPANY

Spiral Diner & Bakery ***(HIGHLY recommended)***
1314 W Magnolia (at 6th Ave, near downtown)
Fort Worth Texas 76104. 817-332-8834
Also in Dallas, Texas

Vegetarian café (Recommended)
Casa de Sousa Coffee House, Restaurant, Coffee/Tea/Juice, General Store , W-19 Olvera Street
Los Angeles, California 90012. 213-703-2208 **Now closed**

The Cheesecake Factory 189 The Grove Drive K-90, Los Angeles, CA 90036, United States (323) 634-0511

Argentina

Lotus Neo Thai Vegetarian Restaurant
Ortega y Gasset 1782, Las Cañitas, Buenos Aires,
Phone: 11/4771-4449 www.restaurantelotus.com.ar

New Zealand

The Thai Restaurant, 1141 Tutanekai Street, Lake End, ROTORUA, New Zealand. Phone 348—6677

Australia

The Macquarie Street Gourmet **Recommended**
225 Macquarie St Sydney, NSW 2000, Australia
+61 2 9221 5043

Bliss Organic Cafe www.blissorganiccafe.com.au
7 Compton St Adelaide, SA 5000, Australia +61 8 8231 0205 *HIGHLY RECOMMENDED*

Govinda's Restaurant
(Hare Krishna Food for Life) 200 William Street Northbridge, Perth. RESTAURANT TYPE : Indian, Vegetarian
http://www.iskconperth.net/govindas/menu.html

Baked 'N' Buttered
Mandurah, WA 6210 Australia +618 9586 1046

Geláre, Perth
160 Murray Street, Perth CBD, Western Australia Tel 9218 9088
http://www.gelare.com/cafeLocations.aspx

Lotus Vegetarian Restaurant, Perth
Unit 1, 220 James Street (6003) (at next to Russell Square/in Northbridge) 08-9228-2882 Nyonya Malaysian, Chinese, International, Buffet, Kosher-Friendly

Hong Kong

Life Organic Health Cafe (Vegetarian Restaurant)
10 Shelley Street, Hong Kong Island Tel. 852-2810-9777
Type: Vegan-friendly, Organic, International, Western
http://www.lifecafe.com.hk/site/component/option,com_frontpage/Itemid,1/
RECOMMENDED

D) Famous & Interesting places seen

Canada

Cape Breton Highlands National Park, Nova Scotia; Niagara Falls & Yukon

USA

Cantigny House & Gardens 1S151 Winfield Road, Wheaton, IL 60189 630.668.5161
also the Robert R McCormick Museum

The Brown Mansion 2019 South Walnut Coffeyville, Kansas 67337 (800) 626-3357
http://www.kansastravel.org/brownmansion.htm}

Biosphere 2 Centre is located north of Tucson, Arizona at the base of the stunning Santa Catalina Mountains. 32540 S. Biosphere Road Tucson, AZ USA 85623 Telephone: (520) 838-6200

Also Bay City, Oklahoma, Tombstone, LA

Argentina
Parliament Buildings and Tango dancing

New Zealand

Wai-O-Tapu 201 Waiotapu Loop Road, RD 3, Rotorua 3073 New Zealand Tel: (07) 366 6333 . 38°21’21″ 176°22’03″
Museum of New Zealand Te Papa Tongarewa 55 Cable Street, PO Box 467 Wellington 6011, New Zealand Phone: +64 (0)4 381 7000. Email: mail@tepapa.govt.nz

Australia

Uluru (Ayers Rock), http://www.ayersrockresort.com.au/about-uluru-katatjuta/
Adventure Tours (Alice Springs to Uluru) http://www.adventuretours.com.au/red-centre-highlights/
Cleland Wildlife Park www.clelandwildlifepark.sa.gov.au Summit Rd Mt Lofty, SA 5152, Australia +61 8 8339 2444
Rottnest Island & the Quokkas. http://www.rottnestisland.com/

Also Alice Springs, Sydney Harbour Bridge,
Sydney Opera House, Canberra, Adelaide Market Hall,
Scarborough (Brisbane), Perth Bell Tower

Philippines

San Agustin Church, and Museum Intramuros,
General Luna Street, Manila. Email samuseum@nsclub.net
http://goseasia.about.com/od/philippinestopattractions/ss/wtintramuros_5.htm

Manila, Quezon City & its university

Hong Kong

Hong Kong Wetland Park,
Wetland Park Road, Tin Shui Wai, New Territories,

Buddha Statue
Lantau Island Tel: +852 2985 5248 Website: www.plm.org.hk

Singapore

The Jurong Bird Park
2 Jurong Hill, Singapore 628925 Tel: (65) 6265 0022

Durian Shaped Theatre
1 Esplanade Drive, Singapore 038981, Singapore (65) 6828 8377
http://www.esplanade.com

Also Sentosa Island - Merlion, insect park and the musical fountains.

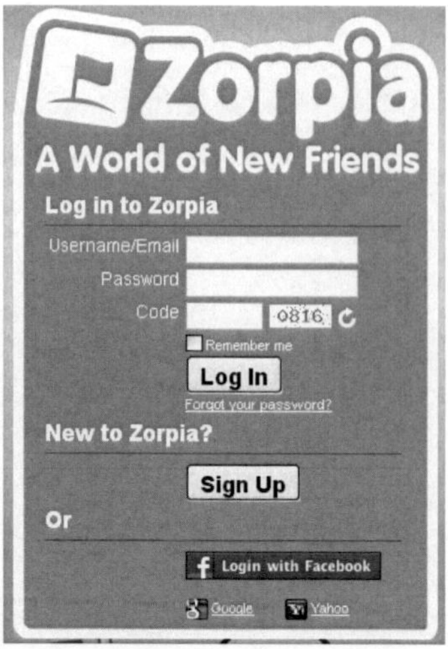

Zorpia is mentioned a lot throughout the book. So if anyone wants to join contact www.Zorpia.com

Lastly a big thank you to my son, Timothy Phillips, for actually getting me into using the WWW. Tim helps run http://www.net-work.net.uk, my ISP company, based in Technology House, Rhewl, Ruthin, North Wales LL15 1TN

E) Planes

UK (Manchester) to Canada (Halifax) Via USA (New York)
Canada, Vancouver - Yukon and back
USA (San Francisco) to Argentina (Buenos Aires) (Overnight)
Argentina (Buenos Aires) to New Zealand (Wellington) (Overnight) via Chile (Santiago) and via (NZ Auckland)
New Zealand (Wellington) to Australia (Sydney)
Australia (Perth) to Philippines (Manila via Hong Kong)
Philippines (Manila) to Hong Kong
Hong Kong to Singapore
Singapore to UK (Heathrow) (Overnight)

F) Long Distance Trains

Canada
1) Truro to Montreal (Overnight)
2) Montreal to Toronto
3) Toronto to Vancouver (3 nights)

USA
1) Seattle to Chicago (2 Nights)
2) Chicago to Flint
3) Flint to Fort Worth (Overnight)
4) Fort Worth to Oklahoma (and return)
5) Oklahoma to Benson (Overnight)
6) Benson to Stockton (Overnight)
7) Stockton to LA
8) LA to San Francisco

Australia
1) Sydney to Adelaide (Overnight)
2) Adelaide to Alice Springs (Overnight)
3) Alice Springs to Adelaide (Overnight)
4) Adelaide to Sydney (Overnight)
5) Sydney to Gosford
6) Gosford to Sydney
7) Sydney to Canberra

8) Canberra to Sydney
9) Sydney to Brisbane (Overnight)
10) Brisbane to Sydney
11) Sydney to Perth (3 Nights)

FOUR SCARBOROUGHS Visited

TORONTO Canada Large Suburb, Population Approx 100,000

SYDNEY, Australia Scarborough Park

BRISBANE, Australia, Region of Redcliffe Bay, Population about 8,000

PERTH, Australia , Coastal Suburb, Population about 14,000

OTHER PLANNED BOOKS by Chris Phillips

(Titles are subject to change)

1) **"Newlands Upbringing"** The story of Chris's young life in Tunbridge Wells. Street games, Olympic Games (1948 - 1951), Stamp Club (Newlands Rd Philatelic Society 1953—1967), and other clubs, firework displays (1954—58), coronation party 1953, Scout Fairs (1951—1953) and other stories.
2) **Miss Chief**
3) **Miss Take**
4) **Miss Hap**

(Three young children's stories written for Timothy.)

5) **Catalogue** of a whole series of Fantasy stamps (1936 to 1972) produced as though King Edward 8th had not been forced to abdicate in 1936
6) **Poems** by Chris (plus, maybe, one or two of his internet friends)
7) Some of my Father's one act Plays